9/00

P9-DCI-569

WITHDRAWN

# THE
# EXTREME
# FUTURE

# THE EXTREME FUTURE

The Top Trends That Will Reshape the World
for the Next 5, 10, and 20 Years

JAMES CANTON, PH.D.

DUTTON

DUTTON
Published by Penguin Group (USA) Inc.
375 Hudson Street, New York, New York 10014, U.S.A.
Penguin Group (Canada), 90 Eglinton Avenue East, Suite 700, Toronto, Ontario M4P 2Y3,
Canada (a division of Pearson Penguin Canada Inc.); Penguin Books Ltd, 80 Strand, London
WC2R 0RL, England; Penguin Ireland, 25 St Stephen's Green, Dublin 2, Ireland (a division of
Penguin Books Ltd); Penguin Group (Australia), 250 Camberwell Road, Camberwell, Victoria
3124, Australia (a division of Pearson Australia Group Pty Ltd); Penguin Books India Pvt Ltd,
11 Community Centre, Panchsheel Park, New Delhi – 110 017, India; Penguin Group (NZ), cnr
Airborne and Rosedale Roads, Albany, Auckland 1310, New Zealand (a division of Pearson
New Zealand Ltd); Penguin Books (South Africa) (Pty) Ltd, 24 Sturdee Avenue, Rosebank,
Johannesburg 2196, South Africa

Penguin Books Ltd, Registered Offices: 80 Strand, London WC2R 0RL, England

Published by Dutton, a member of Penguin Group (USA) Inc.

First printing, September 2006
10  9  8  7  6  5  4  3  2  1

LIBRARY OF CONGRESS CATALOGING-IN-PUBLICATION DATA HAS BEEN APPLIED FOR.

ISBN 0-525-94938-0

Printed in the United States of America
Set in Electra with Univers
Designed by Sabrina Bowers

While the author has made every effort to provide accurate telephone numbers and Internet
addresses at the time of publication, neither the publisher nor the author assumes any responsibility for errors, or for changes that occur after publication. Further, the publisher does not have
any control over and does not assume any responsibility for author or third-party Web sites or
their content.

For Mariah, Sofia, and Trevor,
my three treasures.

# CONTENTS

# The White House

On a warm spring day in June 2002, I approached the White House with a mix of anticipation and curiosity. I had been invited along with a small group of CEOs from IBM, AT&T, and other U.S. corporations to meet with President George W. Bush and his cabinet to discuss one of the central challenges of our time: How should we think differently about the future?

It was a question that had been on the mind of almost every American for the previous nine months. The 9/11 attacks had destroyed more than the lives of those killed by the terrorists. It had drastically altered America's vision of the future by introducing uncertainty and fear into our culture for the first time in generations. The deadly assault on the symbols of American economic and military might exposed our vulnerability and shattered our reality. The almost infinite optimism about the future, so central to the American psyche, was damaged that day along with the World Trade Center towers and the Pentagon. Yet still, here we were.

As I filed past security and entered the back of the Oval Office, I could sense a keen anxiety building in the room. I had been asked ahead of time to prepare a briefing for the president and his advisors, which I had done. So they knew my perspective; now I wanted to hear theirs. I looked around and saw the blue and gold seal of the office of the president, with its bald eagle resting proudly on the podium. The stage was set. As each cabinet member marched in to describe his or her key challenges in such areas as education, energy, security, and health care, the very nature of their comments made it apparent that a transformation was under way. They brought up the inability of computer databases to work together, the lack of trained people to inspect the nation's food supply, the immensity of security issues, and the work yet to be done to protect the nation. The room buzzed with the barely suppressed excitement that comes with the rare experience of hearing straight talk in the halls of power. This was our post-9/11 briefing. We were at the beginning of a sea change. We could all feel it. America's leaders, as well as most Americans themselves, had begun to recognize that nothing would be the same. Everything after 9/11 was a clean slate. There was a new complex future emerging—an Extreme Future of disruptions, risks, threats, and perhaps, new opportunities—that no one, not even our leaders, fully understood.

A door opened suddenly and in walked President Bush. His first words took me by surprise: "We know we do not have all of the answers," he told us. "We need your help in preparing the nation for the future." Few of us in the room were prepared for the president of the United States to address us in such a candid way. In that moment, my realization of the nation's immense challenges that will confront us all in the future inspired me to write this book.

Dr. James Canton
San Francisco
Institute for Global Futures
www.GlobalFuturist.com

# THE
# EXTREME
# FUTURE

# THE TOP TEN TRENDS OF
# THE EXTREME FUTURE

**1. Fueling the Future**—The energy crisis, the post-oil future, and the future of energy alternatives like hydrogen. The critical role that energy will play in every aspect of our lives in the twenty-first century.

**2. The Innovation Economy**—The transformation of the global economy based on the convergence of free trade, technology, and democracy, driving new jobs, new markets, globalization, competition, peace, and security. The Four Power Tools of the emerging Innovation Economy are Nano-Bio-IT-Neuro.

**3. The Next Workforce**—How the workforce of the U.S. is becoming more multicultural, more female, and more Hispanic. Why the future workforce must embrace innovation to become globally competitive.

**4. Longevity Medicine**—The key forces that will radically alter medicine, such as nanotech, neurotech, and genomics, leading to longer and healthier lives.

**5. Weird Science**—How future science will transform every aspect of our lives, culture, and economy—from teleportation to nanobiology to multiple universes.

**6. Securing the Future**—The top threats to our freedom and our lives, from criminals to terrorists to mind control. Defining the risk landscape of the twenty-first century.

**7. The Future of Globalization: Cultures in Collision**—The new realities of global trade and competition; the rise of China and India; the clash of cultures and values; and the ideological battle for the future.

**8. The Future of Climate Change**—How the environment is changing and how we need to prepare for increased global warming, pollution, and threats to health. How we must change.

**9. The Future of the Individual**—Navigating the threats from technology, governments, and ideologies in the struggle for human rights, liberty, and the freedom of the individual in the twenty-first century.

**10. The Future of America and China**—How the destiny of these two great nations—from capitalism to democracy, to innovation and security—will shape the future.

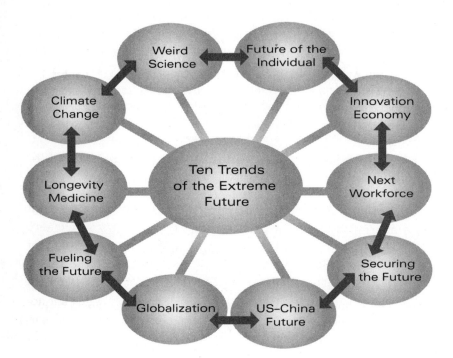

# CHAPTER 1

# Welcome to
# the Extreme Future

Are you interested in the future of your industry? Where your future customers may come from? What about your career—or your next one? Maybe you're interested in your child's future or America's future? Are you interested in identifying the risks that might threaten your life? Do you want to become more aware of what your business competition is thinking? Do you want advance insight into innovations that will shape the future marketplace? Are you interested in how future consumers of your products or services may change? If so, you need this book.

Welcome to the Extreme Future.

I run a San Francisco–based think tank called the Institute for Global Futures. In that role, I advise government leaders and many Fortune 1000 companies about the key trends that will shape the future. Many of these leading companies, such as General Electric, IBM, UPS, Motorola, Fujitsu, Philips, MasterCard, and others have used my firm for two decades to analyze what's coming next. I am a business futurist concerned mostly with my clients' interests in global competition, innovation, people, and profits. At the same time, I have been successful at getting my clients to consider emerging issues such as security, climate, and energy. In many ways, this book has been shaped by my experiences with those clients and their struggles to discover what's next. But this is not only a book for business leaders. Understanding and preparing for the future—and learning to use the tools that make that possible—is a responsibility all of us share, for the sake of our own interests as well as society's.

Everyone needs to think differently about the future, a future that is riddled with change, challenge, and risk. It is a new kind of future, not the steady plodding of progress from one moment to the next, punctuated by brief bursts of innovation, that characterizes much of history. Now we face a post-9/11 future. The future of our lives, of our work, of our businesses—and most of all, the future of our world—depends on us gaining a new understanding of the dizzying changes that lie ahead. I call this future-readiness. This book is an action plan for you to consider how to learn more about the top trends that will drive future change. Radical change is coming. I call this the "Extreme Future." This is a highly dynamic, disruptive, and multidimensional future.

Although the changes wrought by 9/11 and the subsequent focus on global security and terrorism are central to understanding what comes next, they are not the only trends driving the Extreme Future. Events such as the mapping of the human genome, the end of the

## FIVE FACTORS THAT WILL DEFINE THE EXTREME FUTURE

**1. Speed.** The rate of change will be blinding, comprehensive in scope, and will touch every aspect of your life.

**2. Complexity.** A quantum leap in the number of seemingly unrelated forces that will have a direct bearing on everything from lifestyles to work to personal and national security.

**3. Risk.** New risks, higher risks, and more threats from terror to crime to global economic upheaval will alter every aspect of your life.

**4. Change.** Drastic adjustments in your work, community, and relationships will force you to adapt quickly to radical changes.

**5. Surprise.** Sometimes good, sometimes difficult to imagine, surprise will become a daily feature of your life, often challenging sensibility and logic.

Cold War, the rise of China, the Internet, globalization, existing and potential epidemics, and what I call weird science contribute heavily to the need to find new ways to understand the future. These recent events instantly made previous books about the future obsolete. We face a new future in which uncertainty reigns supreme. This book is your briefing on how to understand, adapt, and thrive in the new world taking shape.

## Tracking the Future

I have learned to forecast the future by identifying the tracks and patterns that lead to change. If you've ever walked through a wilderness with an experienced guide, you might have marveled at his or her ability to tell you in advance about unseen risks, such as a nearby mountain lion's den, or opportunities, such as a hidden source of fresh water. Subtle signs, often overlooked by the untrained eye, reveal entire worlds to someone who knows how to read them in context. In many ways, what I do—and what you can learn to do—is not much different. Tracking the future, figuring out what is going to happen when, is as much art as science.

The person who first aligned my perspective about the importance of gaining insights about the future was the author and visionary Alvin Toffler. Toffler is known for his seminal 1970 book, *Future Shock*, which provided a unique perspective on tomorrow. He arrived on the scene with a mission built on a perspective that was powerful yet easy to grasp: As a society, we were becoming inundated with and overwhelmed by technological and social changes, resulting in a stressful and disorienting condition he called future shock. This concept struck a familiar chord with many individuals who indeed were having a difficult time coping with the rapid change that characterizes modern life. Also, he successfully cautioned that, as a society, we were not thinking enough about the future.

This change in mind-sets, to consider the impact of our decisions today and what their impact would be in the future, was important to the art of forecasting. We needed to anticipate our desired futures or we would be dealt futures not by choice, but by happenstance.

I was a graduate student in the mid-1970s. During that time, I worked with Toffler on his various projects, especially the Anticipatory Democracy Network, a U.S. congressional advisory group he founded.

The purpose of the A/D Network, as we called it, was to introduce into the government's decision-making process a foresight capability. Could we embed forecasting into the social policy of the U.S.? This was an early real application of future forecasting in government. This project influenced the thinking and actions of presidents, senators, members of Congress, and other national leaders. It exposed me to a unique perspective that molded my thinking when I became policy advisor to the U.S. government. This set me on my current path.

In the decades since, I have dedicated myself to finding new ways to "see" into the future. T●●is not soothsaying or crystal-ball gazing. I'm talking about taking an educated and informed look ahead at the good and the bad, the scary and the sublime, the beautiful and the terrifying—to identify, sort, and analyze the innovations and trends that will shape the future. I us● variety of tools, from market research and computer models to hum●n intelligence, to map the future. In doing so, I have developed insights into ways to look over the hill to see what may be coming. While others look at today, or perhaps toward next quarter's earnings, or at most ahead to next year, I define time in three categories: Near-term (one to three years); mid-term (three to ten years); and long-term (ten to fifty years).

*The Extreme Future* is actually drawn in part from a long-range strategic forecasting project undertaken by the Institute for Global Futures for a variety of global Fortune 1000 companies and government agencies. The forecasts from this project are used today with clients for strategic planning, investments, product development, risk analysis, business development, and social policy. Those studies, and the key forecasts contained in them, were for the most part accurate, before their time, and missed by others. Yes, I have missed calculations—no one is perfect, especially in forecasting the future. Overall, though, my record has reflected an ability to apply what I call "Future Vision," based not on luck or intuition but on skill and training in the art of identifying logical patterns of events and fitting them together into probable outcomes. What follows are several of my greatest hits, some of which will be chronicled in this book.

Holistic information awareness is the single factor a person can control in making a decision. A more convergent view of different, seemingly unrelated trends like health and security, or economic growth and energy, provides a more accurate path to forecasting the fu-

# SOME PAST FORECASTS

- Information technology, especially the Internet and wireless, will become a strategic competitive weapon in business.

- Energy terrorism will emerge.

- U.S. youth will lack future-readiness to compete in the global economy.

- DNA will be used for predictive health care, longevity, and security.

- There will be a decline in petro-reserves, leading to energy innovations and global conflict.

- China will rise as a competitive global leader hungry for energy, capitalism, and peace.

- There will be a revolution in molecular manufacturing—known as "nanotech."

- Products that think will emerge.

- Human performance enhancement will drive health care's transformation.

- There will be an explosive growth of the personal security market.

- The convergence of nanotechnology, biotechnology, information technology, and neurotechnology will drive innovation in future markets.

- The "Clean Tech" market will emerge, promoting social responsibility and profit.

- Knowledge talent must compete in a global innovation-based economy free from borders.

- Innovation will be a key future driver of prosperity, democracy, and wealth creation.

- Demographic shifts in population will shape the future of health care, security, and commerce.

ture. The question is: What is the right information needed to make an important decision? It's a matter of quality versus quantity. It is vital to recognize that although there are many things a person cannot control—climate, energy, terrorism, bad genetics, etc.—those "X factors" can be more successfully managed in decision-making when individuals cast the widest possible information net.

---

### This book has three objectives:

**1.** To explain the Extreme Future.

**2.** To help you better prepare for the Extreme Future.

**3.** To enable you to adapt, shape opportunity, and avoid risks.

---

## Seeing and Shaping the Future

Most people, though they are largely unaware of it, take stabs at forecasting the future every day. Almost every important action we take or decision we make is linked to our hope or expectation that it will have a positive impact on our lives in the future. Recognizing that this is the first step toward understanding not just the future, but how the future is born, how it emerges, even how it is created, is a way to guide you to improved foresight and decision-making.

As you read on, keep in mind that this book is not just about what the key trends are, but how you can learn to predict trends and distinguish between important and ordinary trends. In other words, this is a blueprint for developing what I call "predictive awareness." Developing a predictive awareness about the future is about knowing where to look, what to see, and how to apply it for benefit.

Some people challenge the viability of forecasting. To them the very idea that someone can predict the future, let alone shape the future, seems absurd. They think the future is a random occurrence of events—unknowable and untouchable until they occur, and only fully understood in hindsight. They are mistaken. If you are someone who accepts this reactive way of thinking, then be prepared to be blindsided by competitors, attacked by invaders, or made to witness changes that are not kind to your denial of reality. A refusal to believe that the future is knowable guarantees the increase of risk. Not only is the future possible to anticipate, but also the way you think about the future—as a sequence of events that can be influenced by personal choice and design—may be one of the most powerful forces in your life.

People who go through life being reactive victims of the future often miss that you can change the future by first changing your perception of it. You can influence your future, but you need

1.  A future vision—clear vision of where you are going.

2.  A sound strategy to get there.

3.  Tools to persuade key people—colleagues, teammates, family members, and so on—to commit to a shared vision and strategy.

4.  Effective execution.

## Future Vision

Two weeks before Nelson Mandela's government took over from the apartheid government of President F. W. de Klerk, I flew to South Africa to talk with leading business and financial executives the first day, and with ministers and advisors to Mandela the next day. This historic moment marked the transition from a failed yet longstanding government based on the institution of racial segregation, to one in which political control would pass to the majority of citizens, the native black South Africans. It was a time of havoc, uncertainty, and excitement.

My meetings with the all-white business leaders and the all-black South African advisors to Mandela centered on one question. How can we work together with the support of the world to build a better future for South Africa? This was the right question at the right time. As we began our conversation, the next question became clear to me: What do you envision to be the future of South Africa in 2020?

It was evident that neither group had considered what the future might look like for their nation by 2020. They did not have a Future Vision. When there is no Future Vision, there is nothing to work toward creating. The lack of a goal to work toward will result in failure. This is a starting point for nations, organizations, and individuals. As Martin

Luther King, Jr., said with certainty, "I have a dream." He knew precisely the future he was pointing toward, working toward, driving toward, and every action he took, every idea he championed, was designed to get there.

What if we ask, "How can the United States vastly improve its public education system over the next decade to ensure that the next workforce, necessary to replace the aging baby boomers (and to finance the future stability of Social Security), will have the skills necessary to compete in the global high-tech marketplace?" Failure to create a Future Vision that will successfully answer this question will lead to more outsourcing, the loss of U.S. jobs, and a reduction in the quality of life. That is not something you can change in ten or twenty years. You have to change it now.

If we do not shape the desired future of a globally competitive workforce, our nation will falter. This is a serious forecast about the future not just of America, but of the economic and security role of America throughout the free world. If America declines in productivity due to the inability of its workforce to be competitive, the engine of prosperity will stall, and the influence America wields on the world stage will be severely diminished. Global security, innovation, and democracy may decline.

We are headed for choppy waters. The chapter on the future workforce will explain these forecasts. Forecasting the future can be dangerous because you are often forced to face realities that can only be dealt with via painful change. You may need to change your ideas about what is possible.

## The World of 2020

I often say to my clients, "What do you envision your company will look like in 2020?" I usually get stares of disbelief. Or, I have asked clients, "Where is the energy industry, given shifting oil reserves, in 2020?" Once the confusion evaporates, clients usually get into the swing of things. "What kinds of products, customers, competition, and markets are you in by 2020, given these trends that we see emerging today? How might changes in economics, technology, climate, or energy shape this future?"

Once we create a clear picture of a company's state by 2020, we can then work backward to organize the plans, scenarios, resources, and strategies to achieve that Future Vision. The directed design of one's future, as an individual, nation, or company, is only possible with a starting point of a clear Future Vision. This end point in some stated future time period five years or twenty-five years hence, is the first step. What does your future look like in 2020?

Most leaders and most individuals have not considered their future as much as they should to effectively create actions today that can forge an optimal desired future. They don't have a clear and concise idea about what they want, making it nearly impossible to achieve future success. My approach to strategic planning offers an alternative to a process that too often bogs down strategy or offers incomplete information, making it difficult to create success.

## The "Kill Your Future" Game

I developed an exercise that I use in this book and I have used with many clients. It is the "Kill Your Future" game. In this game you, the contestant, attempt to kill your future. That is, you envision future scenarios that are conceivable yet so bleak that, if left unchecked, could destroy all that you've created. This approach can be used by business, government, or individuals. I came up with the idea on a project with the leadership of Federal Express. We played Kill Your Future with the executive leadership. I created a scenario in which a competitor stole 50 percent of FedEx's customers with a crafty pricing strategy called shipthis.com. The executives admitted, "This could happen." It led to a new conversation about competition, and a new strategy emerged.

Strategic planning in the global enterprise and in government is flawed. It is not always practiced with an objective approach to having all of the right information to make often critical decisions affecting millions of people's lives and costing billions of dollars. Too much time and too much money is spent looking in the wrong place. By contrast, future planning built on a "Kill Your Future" platform is a fast way of identifying real threats that confront you, your family, your organization, or your nation. That, in turn, can begin to reveal the decisions and actions necessary to minimize or eliminate those threats.

## Lessons from the Future

When I was giving a presentation for Merrill Lynch at the Wharton School's Advanced Management Program in the 1990s, I forecast that the rate of Internet transactions was accelerating at a pace unrecognized by nearly all traditional measures. Consumer adoption was going to be fast and deep in financial services. I forecast a dramatic shift in client assets, involving billions of dollars. Unless companies like Merrill changed the way they did business, they would see customers leaving, actually creating their own competition.

I advised that the loud sucking sound was the future echo of their clients' money leaving for their competitors, but they did not agree. Eventually, though, they came around and made this change. This is not an exercise in self-aggrandizement. I have been insightful about the future, but not because I'm lucky. I work hard to forecast what's coming next. Also, I have an unfair advantage: I spend a lot of time not only advising some of the largest companies in the world, but observing what early stage innovations they are spending billions on. What is in the lab today is in the marketplace tomorrow.

For example, as an advisor today to Motorola, serving on their Research Visionary Board, I have an unfair advantage because I can see the pipeline of future investments in innovations that are coming in pervasive communications. Advising General Electric, I can see the investments in the future of clean energy. Working with Philips, the future of health care. Working with Visa, the future of money. You get the picture. Billions invested in innovation today will likely transform the future.

## Secret Futurists

Though I make my living making forecasts, there are plenty of "futurists-without-portfolio." In fact, futurists are actually all around us. They often go unnoticed, or they themselves don't know exactly what they are doing. They are people who operate with a rare and refined future-instinct. They are intuitive in practice, but futurists nevertheless. While many might seem focused on the present, the most successful leaders—be they business executives or politicians or social leaders—have a keen sense of the future and a sharp ability to see what's next. The top of the hill are those who can enable the future—actually cause the future to happen. We will explore this, too.

# SEEING FUTURE MARKERS— SIGNS THAT POINT TO THE FUTURE

■ What does it mean for the future of entertainment if 80 percent of consumers are on the Internet downloading games, video, music, and information?

■ What does it mean for the future of health care if 90 percent of consumers want tests to reveal their genetic destiny?

■ How will online sales be hurt in the future if identity theft continues and better security doesn't emerge?

■ What does it mean for industry and society if one hundred million consumers control $20 trillion of assets and want to live to age one hundred as healthy and active as they can be?

■ What does it mean to the workforce if we do not attract 20 million immigrants into the U.S. within fifteen years?

■ What does it mean to China if that country continues to grow without becoming a democracy?

■ What does it mean to global peace and security if terrorists, drug dealers, and organized crime link up to attack the world's institutions?

■ What does it mean to Africa and the world if we do not work to cure AIDS and stop emerging pandemics?

■ What does it mean to global growth and productivity if we do not discover new energy sources as oil supplies are dwindling?

■ What is the future of society if global warming and climate change are not resolved by 2050, when there will be close to nine billion people on the planet?

Consider John F. Kennedy's challenge to go to the moon, Ronald Reagan's "tear down this wall" call for an end to a divided Germany, Martin Luther King, Jr.'s dream of racial equality, and Gandhi's nonviolent liberation movement. As different as these men were, as different as their stated goals were, all had one thing in common: A clearly articulated future vision and a sense of the trends of the day that enabled this future to become reality.

In business, the secret futurists are quietly making decisions and strategic moves that define their industries. Though they don't talk much about it unless it serves their strategy, these secret futurists are aware of the strategic trends that will shape the future and are positioning their businesses to take advantage of them. They are predictors and shapers of a desired future—and a profitable future, I might add.

Steve Jobs thinks differently—"outside the computer box"—and has exploded consumer electronics by single-handedly envisioning the future of personal communications with the iPod and the online music store iTunes. Sumner Redstone's investment in MTV ushered in a new global fusion of music, media, and commerce. Barry Diller has been acquiring media and Internet companies to lay claim to the future of interactive commerce. Richard Branson, from his Virgin Atlantic Airways to his Virgin stores, taps customers' needs for style, music, and creative expression.

Each of these secret futurists uses a seemingly uncanny ability to see what's next and to then provide the leadership products and services at the right time to meet the trends and win the day.

## FUTURE FORECASTS

- By 2012, most people will want to use the science of genetics to predict when they will become sick or will have a health problem, so they can prevent illness.

- America's youth will be unprepared in science and math to compete successfully in the global economy by 2010 unless drastic changes to public education are undertaken now.

- There is a strong possibility that terrorists will use IW, information warfare, against the U.S. and its allies before 2010.

- Urban biowarfare will be attempted in the U.S. by terrorists before 2015.

- There will be more jobs than people to fill them by 2015 in the U.S., Europe, and Japan.

Part of the reason I wrote this book was to better share how to predict the future. Too often we focus on one trend area and forget the rest. There is a synergy, an interrelationship I have found in advising leaders worldwide, a fusion of forces that creates the future. It is not just one force, one trend, but the convergence of trends that create the future. This convergent thinking is central to making better forecasts.

## What Da Vinci Knew

Leonardo da Vinci was known for many things, including making predictions of the future through his illustrations of strange flying machines and underwater vehicles. They were visual maps, a type of design forecast that told a story about the future. What Da Vinci knew was a way of thinking strategically about the future. He was the first Future-Mapper. He used visual metaphors to create inventions. He even managed to build a number of his futuristic creations, like his au-

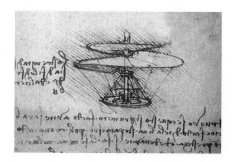

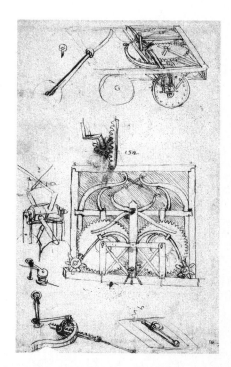

tomobile, which was actually a cart. He was my inspiration for thinking about a new way to conduct forecasts. His insightful process about seeing the future was visual and dynamic. He knew how to transcend time, to fold time, to envision entirely new things. Imagine designing a model for a flying vehicle before there was fuel or materials like plastic. At the time, most of his forecasts were so far-fetched that they were dismissed as ridiculous. But a few people recognized his genius for seeing the future.

Without Da Vinci's patrons in the arts, his immense talent, and the protection he enjoyed from the religious elite, he would have met a burning stake at some point for daring to shatter popular conceptions of reality with his radical visions of the future. His courage to peer into the future, predict the amazing, and report back was a model that should inspire all of us who dare to consider forecasting tomorrow.

## Mapping the Future

Borrowing from Da Vinci's approach of envisioning the future in visual terms, I developed a process called "Mapping the Future." Mapping the Future is a process that can reveal opportunity for an individual, an organization, an industry, a market, a nation, or even a civilization. Future Maps are simple but powerful tools to better visualize trends that may shape the future. Some of these maps are simple designs, while others are Internet, computer-based, or 3-D interactive. They are also useful ways to plot strategy or make decisions and plans about how to prepare for the future. Future Maps capture a view of the convergence of emerging forces that may shape the future state of an industry such as health care, or a marketplace like energy. They identify risks and opportunities that often determine competitive advantage, emerging conflicts, barriers, or ways to navigate change. What follows is a simplified Future Map that illustrates four abilities necessary for successful navigation of the future: Anticipation, Adaptation, Evolution, and Innovation.

As much as Da Vinci influenced me, an equally significant force in the creation of Future Maps is the ancient method of cartography.

For more than two thousand years, humans have been making maps. Even before written language, symbol maps bearing icons of location, geography, and history—pictograms—were drawn on the walls of caves. Icons, or symbols, were used as far back as ancient Egypt and in prehistoric times. The earliest maps were from Asia and Micronesia.

The idea for Mapping the Future came from my interest in old

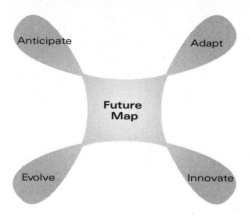

maps, which I have been collecting for many years. Antique maps are fascinating artifacts of time. At any given point in history, a map can be found that tells a unique story about what was known about the physical world, the geography of the era.

Maps are so much more revealing, though, when they're studied closely in the context of when and where they were created. Maps are snapshots of time that chronicle change, the evolution of thinking about navigation, conquest, commerce, threat, and opportunity. They are more than just geography. Maps change when new information is introduced. In the 1500s, maps showed a distortion of the New World, America, because the world was believed to be flat. Asia was believed to

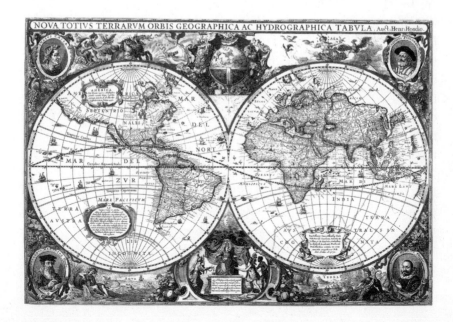

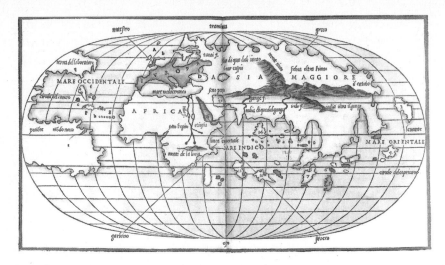

be very close to America's coast. Sea demons were abundant on maps, reflecting the unknown nature of much of the world. Maps made up to the 1700s viewed California as an island.

These strange and often mistaken ideas depicted by maps led me to another interesting idea. Our understanding of the world as it affects our businesses, lives, and futures is only as good as the information we have at a given time. Worldviews change with new and more accurate information that redefines reality. I thought about maps as a metaphor for strategic thinking and concluded that they were a perfect fit for the job. Not because of the inaccurate features of maps, but because of the process of cartography. Just like my forecasts, maps were a product of an ongoing discovery process to navigate not just geography, but change itself.

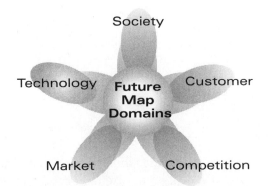

In business as in mapmaking, strategic thinking about the future requires constant redefinition, change, updates and refinement. You are
always dealing with new information and change. You need to constantly change your map—to navigate the waters of change.

Also, since at any given time our worldview is distorted, at best incomplete, the idea of a process to map the future made a lot of sense to
me and, subsequently, to my clients. That's my idea behind Future
Maps. I wanted an effective way to enable my clients to envision their
futures, and I decided that a visual aid was the best way to illustrate the
point. Future Maps give individuals and organizations a way to understand visually what the future may look like and to plot a new course
into the future—the geography of opportunity.

Consider what a Future Map might look like for the future of
health care. Most old-fashioned strategic-planning methods might focus on one or two specific change-drivers, such as technological advances. But that would provide only a one-dimensional picture. What

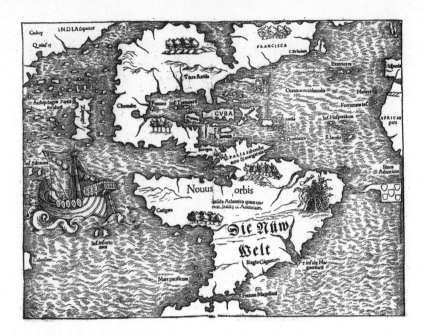

about factors such as the expectations of baby boomers? Or the impact of personal wealth on the provision of health care? A more holistic Future Map of health care might look something like this:

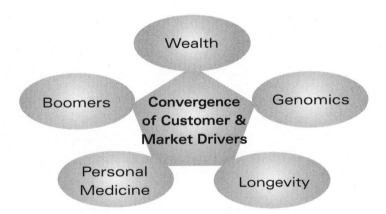

It would certainly be almost impossible to capture all the elements of the future of health care in a single Future Map. But each Future Map—about your life, your company, market, industry, or threat—

may tell a story or a portion of a story that with a visual framework would offer new insights. In various places throughout this book, Future Maps will be offered to help readers better envision the trends and scenarios that will emerge. By better visualizing the future, you can make more informed choices about business or personal strategy toward shaping a preferred future. Consider what the implications are and the impact on you. Future Maps are visual tools that can be used to think strategically about the future, to create better choices about shaping the future, and to make sure you wind up where you want to go. Because as Yogi Berra said, "You've got to be very careful if you don't know where you're going, because you might not get there."

# EXTREME FUTURE INDEX:
## 2025

Percentage of consumers who bought cars using only renewable energy: 80.

Ratio of women to men in the workforce: 2:1.

Percentage of individuals in the workforce that are robots: 60.

Percentage of homes that have robots: 90.

Number of years that consumer terrorism insurance has been offered: 10.

Percentage of Americans who bought or sold DNA over the Internet: 45.

Rank of child enhancements chosen by parents before birth concerning intelligence: 3.

Rank of child enhancements chosen by parents before birth concerning looks: 1.

Percentage of Americans living past the age of 100: 25.

Percentage of Americans living past the age of 100 who are women: 80.

Percentage of Americans who use performance-enhancing drugs: 75.

Percentage of Americans too depressed about their sex life to take drugs to improve conditions: 5.

Rank of plastic surgery as a household expense after food: 2.

Average number of hours daily each American watches TV on the Internet: 10.

# CHAPTER 2

# Fueling the Future

## A New Energy Age

Several years ago, a former Saudi oil minister issued what has since become an oft-quoted prophecy: "The Stone Age did not end for lack of stone, and the Oil Age will end long before the world runs out of oil." It was a lament, an acknowledgment that a day of reckoning was coming that would change the global balance of wealth and power. A fluke of geology had made the vast emptiness of the Saudi desert the number one source of the most important commodity on earth. But the good times would not, and could not, last forever, and he knew it.

If you go back far enough, you can trace the prosperity and security of nations, corporations, and even individuals to energy. And in our petroleum-dependent world, that, for the most

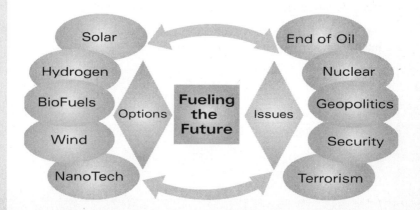

# THE TOP TEN
# EXTREME ENERGY TRENDS

**1.** We are running out of energy. New global demands from every nation will outpace supply within twenty-five years unless plentiful new sources are found. Less energy will be a drag on GDP.

**2.** Democracy is at risk. Energy terrorism will become a future weapon threatening democratic reforms, the rights of the individual, global peace, and security.

**3.** Energy, being linked to all vital services such as health, food, transportation, and commerce, will be a key driver of the future global economy.

**4.** The world's addiction to oil must end. Clean, renewable energy sources such as solar, hydrogen, nuclear fusion, and wind will be essential for future prosperity.

**5.** Foreign oil is politically risky, expensive, and unreliable as a long-term fuel for the future.

**6.** New energy innovations must attract billions in investment. Economic growth and productivity will decline if non-oil energy solutions are not invented fast.

**7.** Pollution from fossil fuels will be linked to a growing number of future public health risks like global warming.

**8.** Energy security will become an explosive battleground in the twenty-first century, ushering in a new era of either global cooperation or conflict.

**9.** Nations will rise and fall based on their access to future energy resources. New economies like China and India will compete with the U.S. and Europe in a new geopolitical power struggle.

**10.** New energy innovations will invigorate global commerce, spawn new industries, and provide new jobs.

part, means oil. Governments rise and fall on it, armies run on it, companies rely on it, and consumers depend on it from the time they wake to their clock radios to the moment they turn off their TVs and fall asleep. For the past century, despite rising prices and occasional "crises"—more often than not manufactured events resulting from political or economic forces—there has always been enough oil available to keep the engines of global growth humming. But that is a luxury of the past; in the Extreme Future, a new and uncertain energy age is emerging.

In 2004, I was having lunch in Paris with a group of clients from around the globe who had gathered to share perspectives, ideas, and solutions on critical future issues. To my right was an executive at the World Health Organization. To my left was a leading Saudi official from Aramco, the government oil company and a member of OPEC, the eleven-member Middle Eastern oil cartel that collectively controls about two-thirds of the world's oil supply.

I had just given a keynote presentation on the future, and I was deep in conversation with my Saudi host, who was the resident forecaster at his company. He quizzed me about my outlook, and I questioned him about his take on future supplies of oil.

"So, how long before we run out of oil? How many years do we have in the ground?" I innocently asked. I expected the stock response that it was impossible to say with precision—a sheikh cannot measure an underground oil field for future production the way, say, a farmer can count hogs to predict his output of pork bellies. At the same time, I anticipated that he would offer reassurance that, although no natural resource would last forever, oil supplies would be plentiful for our lifetimes and beyond.

Instead, between bites of sorbet and melon, he casually answered, "Oh, we think about twenty-five to thirty years before we run out of oil."

I was shocked by his candor. "Really, that's it?"

"Yes," he answered, "about thirty years. Unless, of course, we find more reserves."

"What are the odds we'll find them?" I asked.

"There's always a chance."

Lunch went on. But I couldn't get over his matter-of-fact admission about the end of oil. Blasphemy indeed! My mind was racing, stung by my Saudi friend's perhaps too-honest answer to my question.

The memory of that conversation came rushing back to me in the summer of 2005 when I noticed a daring new advertising campaign from Chevron, in which CEO David O'Reilly wrote an open letter to the world that began with an echo of a warning I've been telling clients for years: "Energy will be one of the defining issues of this century. One thing is for sure: The era of easy oil is over. What we do next will determine how well we meet the energy needs of the entire world in this century and beyond."

This was no longer a Saudi oil minister making a broad analogy about epochal change, or an Aramco forecaster whispering in my ear over lunch in Paris. Now a clear, public warning was being sounded by the head of a major oil company. The question for anyone who cared about the future was no longer whether dependence on cheap oil was coming to an end. Now the question was what to do in the years before the spigot began to run dry.

## FIVE THINGS EVERYONE NEEDS TO KNOW ABOUT ENERGY

- The era of cheap oil is over.
- Alternative energy, though promising, is not ready to produce adequate supply.
- We need to invest quickly in new energy sources.
- We need to learn to conserve energy.
- Energy is a national security issue.

## The Myth of Abundance

Most people in the U.S. are oblivious to our extreme dependence on energy. We expect energy to be there always, everywhere, for every need we have now or in the future. We live an illusion of sorts, perpetuated by the abundance of the moment, far from the reality of the future I am here to predict. Storms of change are brewing, driven by an energy-competitive and energy-restrictive future. Our cheap oil habit and energy abundance, which is so fundamentally linked to everyday existence, is about to end. Unless, that is, there are fundamental changes in energy supply. Even President George Bush admitted, "We are addicted to oil."

First, some perspective. The United States imports about twelve million barrels of oil a day, or about 60 percent of the oil it consumes. In 1970, dependence on imported oil was just 21.5 percent of U.S. consumption, according to the U.S. Department of Energy. The U.S. is the world's number one oil consumer, using more than 26 percent of the world's oil (Japan and China, the next two leading consumers, together account for 13 percent). Roughly 11 percent of global oil production is devoted purely to providing gasoline for cars and trucks on American soil. America spends more than $25 billion a year on Persian Gulf oil. At the same time, the United States possesses only about 3 percent of proven reserves (opening the Arctic National Wildlife Refuge to drilling would increase that by just a fraction of 1 percent). Already, you can see just how close the ties are between oil—especially foreign oil—and what we consider the American way of life.

Looking ahead, world oil consumption is likely to rise by 50 percent by 2020, and the United States is projected to play a leading role in that anticipated increase. If you consider the needs of fast-growing, oil-hungry countries like China and India, as well as the other emerging developing countries in Asia and Latin America, what you have is an unsustainable energy world. China alone is expected to quadruple its oil demands by 2020. Now try adding three billion more people to the planet in the next fifty years. Oh, and did I mention that new global oil discoveries peaked several decades ago?

This all adds up to a picture of tremendous future uncertainty.

As the demand increases for a shrinking resource, so will prices (at least, that is, while there is oil to be bought). The three-dollar-a-gallon prices at gas stations might soon seem like the good ol' days. And as prices increase, so will the paranoia and uncertainty of the market-place, of consumers. Once demand outstrips supply, it would be easy to envision a scenario of financial panic and a global recession, accompanied by political, economic, and social upheaval.

But let's not go there quite yet. There is still time to alter this un-wanted future, as long as leaders—political, corporate, community, and nongovernmental—commit themselves immediately to pursuing alter-natives to oil. Even former oilman George W. Bush has tiptoed toward

# WHY WE NEED TO CUT OUR OIL DEPENDENCE: THE TOP RISK FUTURES

**National Security at Risk**—Oil will become a geopolitical weapon used between the net oil-producing and net oil-consuming nations.

**Global Warming Threat**—Research indicates that the world is undergoing climate change, which will have an adverse impact on the quality of life, food production, economic growth, and financial assets.

**Mideast Conflict Exploding**—Dependence on oil requires Western nations to devote enormous resources in the Persian Gulf region to secure vital energy resources.

**Public Health Risks Escalating**—The linkage between increased public health risks due to global warming and pollution is well documented. Environmental illnesses such as cancer and threats to the food supply are on the rise.

**Increased Costs Inevitable**—Increases in energy demands by nations will drive up the prices of a dwindling oil supply. Other essential oil-dependent products like drugs will cost more as well.

**Unreliable Access at Best**—There is no guarantee that oil resources—at any price—will be able to meet future demands. Oil-producing nations may become radicalized and reserve their oil for preferred customers only.

acknowledging that reality: "We must use our technology to move away from oil if we are to prepare for the future." But is there enough time to change? This will be one of the central challenges in the Extreme Future.

## Postindustrial Dilemma

If civilization's future hinged on one issue—other than a global pandemic or war—that issue would be energy. The lack of energy to fuel transportation, health care, business, communications, or manufacturing would have a devastating effect. The absence of an adequate, cost-effective, abundant supply of energy would doom a society in the developed world for certain. Social stability and growth is linked to a pipeline of abundant energy. It is in the interest of all nations—developed and developing alike—to pursue energy security. Energy for the developing world may be vital to future economic prosperity, poverty reduction, and perhaps, democracy. Energy enables the freedoms and individual self-reliance that is the foundation of a democratic society. Energy fuels democracy.

Ironically, developing nations might at first survive without existing levels of energy resources. But eventually, unless less industrial societies were desirable, they would come to face future challenges along with the rest of the world, just later. The inevitable challenge would be the same—the world needs affordable, abundant, nonpolluting, renewable sources of energy to sustain life, support growth, and maintain or improve quality of life.

As a futurist looking at the total global energy picture, I recognize that there are actually many energy resources yet to be exploited. In the U.S., there are ample stores of natural gas and coal. In North America, there are vast quantities of shale and oil sands, a substance that, with the right extraction technology, may be converted into oil. The shale deposits, if the extraction process is developed fast enough, could produce enough energy to offset the diminishing oil reserves for decades. There is even an argument to return to nuclear power, as the Europeans have. Global gas reserves look promising. But, as we'll see in this chapter, there are even more hopeful technologies that, with enough support financially and politically, might truly be the petroleum substitutes the world will soon need.

There is a timing issue: having the right amount of energy, the supply available when we as a nation and a world need that energy to meet demand. This will be the challenge we will face in the mid-twenty-first century.

## Future Survival

Given current forecasts of gross domestic product, the universal measure of the growth of nations and the global economy, we will be struggling within thirty years to support our energy demands. The U.S. economy's GDP growth is about 4 percent per year. The Eurozone is at 2.5 percent. China alone is growing at almost 10 percent a year. With projected GDP growth in China of as much as 11 percent by 2035, the pressure on the energy marketplace, dominated by petro-sources such as oil, gas, and coal, could accelerate a global competition for energy. That could create a dichotomy of haves and have nots—those who can afford $300 per barrel oil and those who cannot.

# Dead Dinosaurs

None of this is especially important to you if you are living "off the grid," such as those who have not ridden in a car, or seen an escalator, or enjoyed running water, or flipped an electrical switch to turn on a light. But most of the world relies heavily on the benefits, safety, and convenience of having access to multiple energy resources. Much of what we want to accomplish in the future, as nations, corporations, or individuals, revolves around energy access. From growth to poverty, re-duction will depend on energy access.

Enhanced health care, transportation, communications, educa-tion, and commerce require access to affordable and abundant energy. If anything, energy needs will accelerate and increase as nations in the developing world become devel-oped. Strategic actions must be taken now to head off a crisis that will affect every nation and every person on the planet in the twenty-first century if cheap energy is not found.

*HEADLINES FROM THE FUTURE: 2015*

**Oil Hits $300 a Barrel;
World Markets Shudder**

The seeds of this energy-competitive Extreme Future have already been planted. Dead dinosaurs are at the heart of this bizarre global bat-tle. The global competition for natural resources is just starting to heat up. Most governments, individuals, and businesses are beginning to become aware of the brewing twenty-first century battle over energy that is just taking shape today. Some countries and some corporations are ahead of the game. Certain Gulf states and multinational compa-nies like GE and IBM are aware of this growing threat. They are future-ready, plotting for the time when energy independence and sustainability will pay off in growth, security, or quality of life.

Governments in China and elsewhere are today locking up future oil reserves in the ground. The Chinese have contracted with the

South Americans and Africans for future oil supplies reaching deep into the twenty-first century. They are defending against Japanese rights to oil-potential deposits in the seas. They are scouring the planet from Australia to Ecuador for all commodities, especially energy-related ones. The energy wars are here, but not everyone has noticed.

The Chinese recognize that they cannot grow their nation's prosperity, the economic juggernaut that will transform their society from a preindustrial giant to a postindustrial global power, without energy. They rightfully are seeing into the Extreme Future. The Chinese see a global battle for energy resources to fuel their future. Nations that get access to this energy will be the winners. A new global order will emerge, perhaps based on energy. Nations will rise and fall. A massive global power shift is coming based on energy access.

There will be plenty of losers as well, perhaps including the United States, if we don't deal with the energy problem brewing in our midst. In a world of diminishing energy, especially nonrenewables such as oil, there will be a fierce competition among the developed countries of the world for who gets access and who does not. This is truly survival of the energy rich versus the energy poor.

## Fueling a Prosperous World

As an advisor to corporate boards and government leaders for many years, I am used to wrestling with difficult challenges and finding solutions. Forecasting complex, large-systems change is my business. When it comes to energy, the test is daunting, to say the least. But there are solutions.

If we can't fix the coming energy shortage with existing technology and resources, then we need to identify new forms of energy, since no one would seriously suggest that we roll back the advances in society. In fact, quite the opposite.

Developing nations need reliable and cost-effective energy to defeat poverty, install democracy, develop the middle class, and grow commerce. Another forecast is that a battle looms between energy-independent economies and energy-deprived economies. Energy independence may take many forms that are not politically popular or even safe in the short run but essential in the long view. A new global source of tension between nations is being cast today, and energy is at the core of this issue.

The Europeans and the Japanese have invested wisely for energy-independent futures based on nuclear technology and alternative energy like wind. Alternative energy in Germany alone accounts for more than 12 percent of overall energy. By 2020, this approach to diversifying their energy mix with nuclear energy will prove to be strategically smart.

The U.S.—despite having invested heavily in nuclear energy—was never able to deal with negative public perception about it. Nuclear energy accounts for less than 8 percent of all U.S. energy consumption. The Eurozone enjoys more than twice this percentage of consumption from nuclear power. In all fairness, the Three Mile Island accident in 1979, the media, and the nuclear waste problem all contributed to a distorted perception about nuclear energy. There have been many developments in ensuring safety and performance that would make nuclear fast-breed reactors a productive solution for America's future. Also, a futuristic new approach called nuclear fusion, safer yet very costly, could satisfy America's needs.

*HEADLINES FROM THE FUTURE: 2018*

**Energy Thieves Steal Billions Daily**

## End of the Game

The American public, unlike the Europeans, has been spoiled by cheap oil, which has created the illusion of plenty while the reality of diminished reserves has escaped public scrutiny. The Europeans accelerated this public awareness by taxing gas, making it routinely two to three times as expensive as gas in the U.S. More than 85 percent of new auto buyers in Europe are concerned about fuel efficiency. Fewer than 15 percent of Americans care about fuel efficiency, because in a world of cheap oil, they don't have to.

This era is over, and Americans are ill-prepared to meet the challenges of either an energy-restricted future, characterized by slow growth, or one in which expensive energy curbs business productivity and national GDP growth. Everyone will need to face the stark realities of an energy-constricted and costly future. The time to have acted was ten to twenty years ago. Now the world must play catch up, especially America.

# The Path to Self-Reliance

The future-ready strategy effectively used by the Europeans has been a smart way to create a public that is supportive and educated about the high cost of energy. No pain, no gain. This strategy has allowed the Europeans to direct public funds and support toward a lack of dependency on oil at the precise time that actual oil reserves are diminishing. The U.S. has not been as smart, and it will pay later with expensive energy—at least.

European investments in nuclear, which have been put in place over the past decades, will now handsomely pay off as oil prices continue to climb, global energy competition by nations increases, and the geopolitical realities of Middle East oil become fraught with risk. It is a nervous world uncertain about the future. Energy is a key element in this future anxiety, and with good reason. We need to explore new frontiers—and with great speed.

# Future Energy Alternatives

We start this journey of discovery with the U.S. Department of Energy's NanoSummit, held in June 2004 in Washington, D.C. As an early advisor to the U.S. government's nanotechnology efforts, I was gratified to see that nanotech, a powerful new bucket of innovations, was being supported by the DOE. In addition, then-Secretary of Energy Spencer Abraham was giving one of the keynotes along with a colleague of mine, Dr. Richard Smalley, the Nobel Prize–winning chemist from Rice University and a pioneering leader in nanotechnology.

Nanotechnology is the manipulation of matter at the atomic scale to create useful tools and substances. For example, imagine a team of infinitesimally small robots injected into your bloodstream to scrub out the gunk from your clogged arteries. From an energy perspective, nanotechnology is seen as a potential source of devices that could, among other things, generate huge amounts of mechanical and thermal energy and then transfer it into electrical energy.

The Marriott hotel where we were meeting was filled with government lab presentations, each one more interesting than the last. It was an energy-innovation bazaar of sorts, each a unique research-and-development stab at redefining the world's energy future, from solar and wind, to nanotech materials, to lightning and alternative fuels for transportation.

But the real action was taking place inside the closed-door sessions with a rare assembly of experts. I recognized that such a meeting—encapsulating the supply-and-demand dynamics that lie at the heart of the global energy future—was ultimately a window into the Extreme Future. Some 300 of the nation's leading experts—scientists and engineers from universities, industries, and government labs—had been assembled to convey one of the most powerful forecasts I have ever heard in one place at one time. Forecasts usually run the gamut of possibilities: the good, the bad, and the ugly. Then, based on varying data sets, scenarios, and discussions, possible future worldviews emerge. Not here.

## Reality Check

Instead, a forecast emerged that will influence the future of every person on the planet. It can be boiled down to six powerful words: We are running out of energy. Based on current production and consumption technologies and trends, we as a civilization—not just as a nation—do not have the existing or projected energy resources and production means that we will need to sustain growth, security, quality of life, and productivity by 2040—and possibly sooner. This includes all current energy resources and production sources, from oil to solar to nuclear. If the future of democracy, both in the West and in the developing nations of the world, can be linked to energy access, we are in deep trouble.

Talk about a reality check. This was not a politically influenced forecast, but a serious-minded examination of supply and demand. Without discovering significant new sources of energy, we as a civilization may face stagnation. Democracy may be in peril. Capitalism, the engine of global economic growth from China to America, may be hurt. It was agreed that we owe the world our best efforts to solve this energy crisis before it derails progress, growth, and even democracy itself. We are faced with an enormous challenge: How do we not run out of energy? This is what sparks the human spirit.

Although I had been running scenarios for clients on a restricted energy future, and we had come to similar conclusions, this across-the-board consensus, this broad universal honesty, confirmed by the U.S. Secretary of Energy, was unanticipated. I know I was not alone in this conclusion. There was a palpable sense among the attendees that we bore an awesome weight of responsibility to try to avoid a future global energy crisis. But can we? What is to be done now that we know the problem?

The rest of the forecasts, made with plenty of supporting data, led to the inescapable conclusion that even if we were to start feverishly building nuclear reactors, solar and wind farms, hydroelectric plants, and other renewable energy sources, we still would not be able to meet the rapidly expanding energy demands in thirty years. This second forecast, more astounding than the first, was hard to digest, even for those of us who conduct strategic "big picture" thinking.

As the conference continued, I began to focus on the logic pattern that was forming in my mind. Not only are we running out of energy to fuel the world in the future—with obvious critical implications for global security, national security, growth, and prosperity—but even if we start now, building every energy-producing facility from electric to nuclear to solar, we could not meet the growing demand! This was a considerable amount of information to grapple with. I wondered: Where do we go from here?

## Nano-Energy

At this point in the meeting, Dr. Rick Smalley gave his presentation. His eloquence was not limited to the problem—our running out of energy. Nor did he waste time with the notion that we cannot do anything. Instead, Smalley talked about nanotechnology, describing a sweeping vision to transform the energy debate by pursuing an alternative path using nanotech. He proposed a distributed energy plan using leading innovations like nano to provide a new alternative energy network. I recognized his larger point: the need for an innovation revolution in energy sources that we must build toward and invest in today for the sake of our children and the world.

Nanotechnology represents a radical solution, requiring the harnessing of the quantum, the manipulation of atoms. This is fantastic new science that is only hinted at as a remote possibility—it exists today in embryonic form, an innovative theory of the possible. But still, knowing this, our spirits lifted in the room, as though a thousand-pound weight had been removed from each of our chests at once.

It was as though we were all listening to President Kennedy speaking at Rice Stadium in September 1962, when he told the nation and the world that we would send a man to the moon before the end of the decade. The NASA officials listening that day were as shocked as we were while listening to the experts at the beginning of the day proclaim that we were doomed by diminished oil reserves, only to be lifted up by the proclamation that we could meet this challenge.

As Americans, we have always pushed the envelope of the possible in forging new adventures. The quest for nano-energy fit the bill—the transformation of the impossible into the possible. Led by the wisdom of a Nobel Prize winner, it seemed like a good bet. More than that, we wanted—indeed, needed—to believe that nano would work. The prospect of running out of energy is too dire a scenario to consider.

Part of this bold forecast remains highly speculative. Nobody really knows if nanotech can do the job. Nanotech may help to unravel new energy solutions, but nano is only one of a number of solutions to our energy crisis. There is much to do, and we will review this landscape of future opportunities and innovations. Still, despite that disclaimer, I can forecast that nanotech will likely lead to amazing breakthroughs in energy development, storage, and supply—if we invest now.

---

# ENVIRONMENTAL COSTS OF AMERICA'S OIL HABIT

- The U.S. is the world's largest producer of greenhouse gases from fossil fuel use.

- Americans produce, per person, the most $CO_2$ emissions of any citizens in the world—more than 6.8 tons of $CO_2$ per year, twice that of Europeans.

- China produces only 1.1 tons per person per year.

- India produces 0.5 tons per person per year.

- The U.S. is the only major industrial nation that has refused to ratify the Kyoto Accord, which seeks to reduce carbon emissions and limit greenhouse gases.

*CIA, IEEE, 2005*

# The Future of Energy

A variety of energy sources are emerging now that will offer productive choices in the future. Some of these sources have the potential to be significant in becoming viable alternatives to petro-based energy. First, though, it is useful to forecast the preferred ingredients that would drive these trends. The following is a list of six requirements for future energy sources that would make a difference in weaning us off the oil habit and enabling a more sustainable global world. New energy sources must be

- Abundant

- Reliable

- Renewable

- Clean

- Affordable

- Secure

Depending on whom you speak with, there are any many potential sources that might satisfy all those requirements. I'll touch on several, but based on my forecasts, the two that offer the most promise, and therefore deserve the most immediate attention, are hydrogen and nanotech.

# The Hydrogen Future

Are you ready for cars that go 10,000 miles before they need a refill and cost pennies on the dollar? Get ready for hydrogen. It will change everything. Maybe.

On a trip to the East Coast, I interviewed a highly placed executive at Toyota about the future of energy. I suspected that Toyota was ahead of the game in realizing that the end of oil is coming. I was curious about how he saw this emerging trend and how Toyota was positioning the company, or changing the company, to get ready for the future.

He made it very clear that although current hybrids are interesting, they are an interim solution to the auto industry's ability to meet the

# 2030 ENERGY FORECAST

■ The global demand for energy will increase by 70 percent.

■ There will be a 50 percent increase in energy demand from developing nations, especially China and India.

■ Energy access is an essential enabler of higher standards of living in the developing world.

■ Increased energy access in the developed world will be necessary to sustain productivity and growth.

■ Energy has become the leading global and national security issue.

■ China's energy needs will be double those of the U.S. and the EU.

■ Renewable energy will account for more than 35 percent of total global energy needs to offset reduced oil reserves.

■ Innovations like fusion, nanotechnology, and solar will replace oil.

■ Distributed small scale, person-to-person electricity generation will be sustainable.

■ Breakthroughs in hydrogen and renewable energy will provide new energy supplies.

*DOE, CIA, 2005*

real challenge: making hydrogen work. Hydrogen is the future fuel that will define the twenty-first century. Hydrogen represents the most significant challenge that the auto industry has faced since its inception. The death of the combustion engine is upon us, and the death knell will be dealt by the auto industry itself. Key industry leaders understand that they need to make a swift transition from present technology that runs on gas to technology that runs on hydrogen.

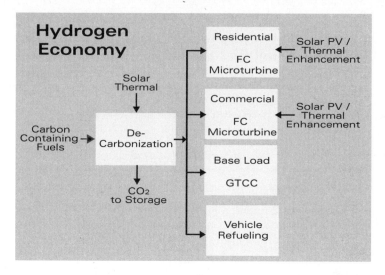

## Splitting Molecules

Hydrogen is the most plentiful gas in the universe. It's also a powerhouse—it has the highest energy content per unit of weight of any known fuel. It's abundant, reliable, renewable, clean (a hydrogen-powered car produces water as its exhaust), and secure (because hydrogen is everywhere, America wouldn't have to rely on foreign suppliers). That leaves just one requirement: affordability. The trick with hydrogen is that it never occurs by itself in nature; it always combines with other elements, such as oxygen or carbon. At the moment, it's quite costly to separate it from those other elements and transfer it into fuel cells, which are the standard storage technology for this form of energy. In fact, the cost of doing so is greater than the current value of the energy created. That's why you don't yet drive a hydrogen-powered car. But that will change.

*HEADLINES FROM THE FUTURE: 2042*

**Hydrogen Energy Trading Exchange Opens for Business**

Hydrogen-powered vehicles are coming in the future. Hydrogen-generating power plants are farther down the road, but they are coming, too. There is one in Iceland, the first of its kind to fuel a city. In fact, the hydrogen economy, a holistic transportation infrastructure, will arrive within thirty-five years.

When you consider how the auto industry started and how the mass market for automobiles evolved, it is not hard to envision the beginning of the hydrogen industry. At the turn of the last century, the idea of personal transportation that people could use to pick a destination and choose whenever they wanted to leave was a revolutionary concept. But it was the relatively inexpensive production of cars that made Henry Ford's breakthrough brilliant. His vision of factory automation enabled the Model T to become a mass-market success.

## Hydro Futures

When hydrogen becomes inexpensive in the coming years, it will follow a similar path into the future. Just as thousands of affordable Model T's came off the assembly line into the marketplace, transforming mobility in America and the world, hydrogen, with a hungry mass market waiting, will find similar success.

To be sure, hydrogen has problems other than high cost. It is unstable and needs to be controlled. The manufacture of hydrogen requires other energy usage, such as nuclear or oil. The technology needed to store and pump hydrogen into vehicles is still primitive and not yet adopted for wide usage. But none of these obstacles is impossible to overcome. Hydrogen will transform the future of energy and ensure a more secure and reliable source of fuel for consumers, business, mass transportation, and even for space travel. Hydrogen is coming fast.

More than $5 billion is being spent around the globe by government and industry for research and development on hydrogen—the United States has already launched a $1.2 billion hydrogen initiative, and auto, utility, oil, and gas companies are falling over each other to rush innovative breakthroughs to market. The largest investments are being made today at General Motors, Shell, Exxon, BP, Toyota, Ford, BMW, and Honda. More than twenty governments are directing their energy investments to hydrogen, sensing that this is the next big thing. Though significant work needs to be done, hydrogen holds the potential for fueling the future, more so than anything else.

The likelihood is that significant innovations in this energy source are coming soon. I forecast that more than $10 billion will be needed and spent on hydrogen research over the next ten to fifteen years worldwide. This will lead to a mass-market set of innovations, similar to the innovations that first launched the modern auto, train, and shipping industries. By 2035, or even sooner, hydrogen will be a viable alternative to oil and gas, meeting as much as 35 percent of our energy needs.

We are at the beginning of the hydrogen economy now. Get ready. It will change everything at a rapid pace never seen before in human history.

---

# TOP FUTURE BENEFITS OF HYDROGEN

- **Reliable Source.** Increased access to a reliable source of energy makes hydrogen worth working toward.

- **Flexible.** Hydrogen can fuel personal and public transportation, and numerous energy-dependent devices, engines, and needs.

- **Self-Reliance.** Not having to count on foreign monopolies and the geopolitics of oil is worth the investment.

- **Environmentally Friendly.** Hydrogen produces water as exhaust, though oil is still necessary to produce hydrogen fuel.

- **Hydrogen Works Today.** We know hydrogen can provide power today—it is just too costly and is not yet ready for mass transportation use.

- **Unlimited Access.** Hydrogen could be an unlimited power source.

- **Ultimately Inexpensive and Cost-Effective.** If the Iraq war costs the U.S. between $500 billion and $1 trillion, and we were to invest half of that in hydrogen, we would see dramatic breakthroughs in energy—fast.

---

## Nano-Forecast

In 2005, my think tank, the Institute for Global Futures, conducted the first forecast and analysis of the exciting new convergence of nanotech and energy. Before describing the results, it is worth taking a moment to explore what, exactly, I mean by "nano-energy."

Nanotechnology is a design science. It is the emerging science of manipulating molecules at the atomic scale. Move a few atoms around and you have wood. Move around a few more, and you have energy like hydrogen or solar. Nanotech, or "nano" for short, may be used to actually design new forms of energy or solve problems that will make other forms of energy productive, available, or useful. Carbon nanotubes have unique properties, such as being a hundred times stronger than steel, yet very thin and light. Nanotubes are also very small, a billionth of a meter. They also have a unique, high conductivity rate for carrying electricity. Today, nano is being investigated with an investment of more than $3 billion by the U.S. government. More than $20 billion will be invested in nano over the next ten years.

Nanotechnology plays a significant role in the coming energy crisis because it represents an emerging strategic platform for fabrication processes not previously available via other means. No one knows for certain if this direction will pay off. It is a gamble. Ultimately, though, nanotechnology may lead to new energy sources not contemplated before. Nanotechnology may express an entirely new paradigm of sustainable energy. This is the goal.

Nano-energy may accelerate the efficiencies of solar, biofuel, geothermal, or hydrogen sources, speeding up access to these renewables. Nano-energy may actually enable the production of more cost-effective sources of energy, possibly including new hybrid energy sources. Also, nano-energy may accelerate the transition toward a clean, sustainable, and renewable energy resource that promotes self-reliance from our current petro-energy dependence.

There are risks associated with the pursuit of nano-energy. We don't know how costly, safe, or difficult this will be, or how long it will take. We are entering new scientific domains. The imagination, innovation, and investment in shaping a new future, however, with the hope of inventing new sources of sustainable energy, looms large. This is one of the great challenges facing humanity today.

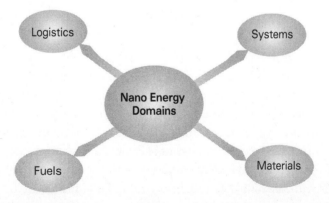

Nano-energy can be divided into four specific domains: logistics, systems, fuels, and materials. This is the current map of nano-energy domains that points to the research-and-development efforts in this new technology. Specifically, however, nanotechnology will have its greatest impact in the areas of fuels and materials. Nanotech might, through the self-assembly of matter, actually *create* a new clean and abundant energy source. Such an energy source would transform the world overnight.

Numerous oil companies, auto companies, and other large corporations are investing billions in research and development on alternative energy, renewable fuels, and vehicles. Nano-energy breakthroughs down the road may be accelerators of hybrid vehicles, fuel cells, and transportation- and energy-system solutions. The U.S. Department of Energy has also taken bold leadership steps to invest in nano-energy, which will help to support private-sector investments. The collaboration of public- and private-sector efforts will be needed on global and national scales to create the breakthroughs needed to transform the energy equation. If nano-energy is to offer new alternative sources of sustainable energy in the future, it will come from collaborations such as these.

There are numerous examples of nano-energy-related research projects that hold potential. Many of these programs are being funded by industry, government and academic institutions. The majority of these projects, however, are still very much in the early stage of development from a commercial perspective. There are still numerous proofs-of-concept yet to be revealed. Companies like DayStar, which is using nano to enable solar, or Nanomix, which has developed a nano-hydrogen storage product, point to a promising future for energy solutions. It is a risk we have to take to prepare for tomorrow.

## Other Alternatives

Although I forecast that hydrogen and nano-energy are the two most promising solutions to the coming energy crisis, they are hardly alone. For instance, there is wind energy, which for the moment is the world's fastest-growing energy technology. One thing that surprises some people is that wind is actually a kind of solar energy—winds are created by the uneven heating of the atmosphere by the sun, as well as by the rotation of the earth and the uneven surface of the planet.

For thousands of years, humans have recognized the power of the wind and have harnessed it to propel ships and provide mechanical power to grind grain, pump water, and perform other tasks. The future of wind energy, though, is in the large-scale production of electricity through wind turbines. Wind turns a turbine's blades, which are connected to a spinning shaft, which in turn is connected to a generator that transforms the mechanical power into electricity. A group of wind turbines could send electricity into a power grid—just like electricity produced by petroleum sources—to serve homes and businesses.

As with any energy source, there are pros and cons. Although wind is clean, renewable, and plentiful, it's also—as anyone who has ever flown a kite knows—intermittent. And for the most part, it cannot be

# WIND ENERGY FUTURES

■ Renewable energy's return on investment is increasing. Renewables can play a larger role in offsetting oil dependence in the future.

■ The U.S. is losing the competition in renewable energy to Europe, which has moved ahead with wind power. Next to invest in wind is China.

■ The U.S. produces less than 1 percent of its energy from wind and solar.

■ Denmark produces more than 20 percent of its energy from wind sources today.

■ By 2025, Denmark expects to produce more than 50 percent of its energy from wind.

■ The U.K. produces more than 3 percent of its energy from wind.

■ The U.K. will produce 10 percent of all energy from renewable sources by 2010, and 15 percent by 2015—wind is the primary source.

■ The future of wind energy lies in offshore wind farms.

■ The U.S. needs to wake up to wind power.

easily stored for times when electricity demand is greatest. An irony of wind power is that the best wind is often found in remote places, far from the cities that need the electricity most. The result is increased transmission costs and a greater initial investment than other energy technologies, though that may change.

Another exciting new energy technology is being developed that may point the way out of our energy-hungry trap. Cadarache, in southern France, will be the location of ITER, a multinational, $12 billion collaboration to build a nuclear-fusion plant. Fusion seeks to harness the physics of the sun. It is safer, cleaner, and yet more powerful than the nuclear-fission technology common today. Nuclear fusion is the exact opposite of fission— it doesn't produce large quantities of radioactive waste and cannot explode, threatening life and the environment. Korea, Russia, the EU, and Japan are partners in this venture.

The fusion reactor would start generating power by 2015 and operate until 2035, producing 10,000 jobs and 500 megawatts of energy. A next-generation fusion reactor called Demo, which is scheduled to go online by 2035, would prove up fusion reactors for full deployment by 2050.

## Toward a Future of Energy Independence

Energy will shape every aspect of the Extreme Future, from security to transportation to health care and growth. We must prepare now by investing in alternative energy sources, some through innovation like nano, and others through hydrogen. We must walk toward a future of energy independence. The future of nations will rise and fall, prosper or decline, based on their access to energy resources. From the vantage point of today, I would forecast that energy expenses for business and consumers will increase significantly—by more than 1,000 percent by 2035—unless innovative and sustainable energy sources are rapidly put in place. Access to energy will define competitive advantage in business.

There is a great danger that our energy needs in the near future— twenty-five years forward—will not be met adequately by current resources. Put another way, energy issues will become central issues to consumers, businesses, and governments as we begin to deplete existing energy sources and place increased demand on energy infrastructures. Energy issues will shape politics, transportation, health care, and security as the cost and availability of energy increases. The threat to national security in a world dominated by foreign oil is a growing risk to the stability of the U.S., the growth of the nation, and the prosperity of the world. We must change this dynamic now.

The good news is that we are on the verge of many exciting new innovations that have the possibility to make much of the world energy independent. This is a promise. New innovations will fuel the future, offering a security and self-reliance about energy we have not had in the past. This new energy access will be an enabler of future prosperity. I would forecast that the future of democracy may also be dependent on the future of energy. Creating this next generation of energy self-reliance will take what Americans are good at—invention, innovation, and marketing. But they are not alone. Many innovators are hard at work around the world in this historic race. An energy-hungry world awaits the new wave of innovations coming in the Extreme Future. Bold new leadership—in industry and government—will be required if we are to fix the energy crisis that is emerging.

# CHAPTER 3

# Finding Prosperity: The Innovation Economy

## Innovation in Overdrive

On a crisp day in spring 2005, I delivered a keynote address about the Extreme Future to a group affiliated with Albany NanoTech, a $3 billion nanotech research-and-development facility, one of the largest in the world. After my speech at a local hotel, I wanted to return to Albany NanoTech's headquarters on the campus of the State University of New York at Albany. Among other interests, I wanted to look around the cutting-edge facility, which includes a 16,000-square-foot clean room used to support partnerships with IBM and other businesses pursuing commercially viable nanotechnology products.

When I walked out of the hotel, I was underwhelmed by the modest car my hosts had sent for me. It was silver and resembled a Honda Civic, a base model with cloth seats and, for all I knew, a scratchy AM radio. It looked like it might belong to a struggling student at the university. Maybe the regular car service had broken down and they had sent an intern to fetch me.

But no, that couldn't be it; my driver was Pradeep Haldar, an award-winning scientist who is director of Albany Nano-Tech's Energy and Environmental Technology Application Center. No, this was no ordinary $12,000 Honda Civic. Not by

# THE TOP TEN TRENDS SHAPING THE INNOVATION ECONOMY

**1.** The Innovation Economy, a new convergence of economics, democracy, trade, and technology, will determine the future leadership of nations, productivity of business, and wealth of individuals.

**2.** The mantra of the Innovation Economy is "free minds, free markets, free enterprise." This offers the greatest prosperity-creating opportunity in the history of civilization.

**3.** The Innovation Economy represents the largest future threat or opportunity for your career or business—depending on whether or not you prepare for it.

**4.** Bits, atoms, neurons, and genes are the new Building Blocks of the Innovation Economy. People and organizations that know how to leverage them will benefit.

**5.** Breakthrough innovations in the Four Power Tools—IT and networks, biotech, nanotech, and neurotech—will create widespread global prosperity.

**6.** Individuals and organizations must quickly develop strategies for the Innovation Economy—before their competition does.

**7.** Now is the time to invest fast in people, technology, ideas, collaborations, products, and services that will build the Innovation Economy.

**8.** The education system is broken and must be reinvented to prepare nations, organizations, and individuals to compete in the emerging Innovation Economy.

**9.** The Innovation Economy will become a potent force for global poverty reduction, borderless commerce, and democratic reforms.

**10.** Knowledge, the power of creative ideas, is the currency of the Innovation Economy.

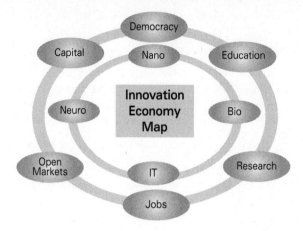

a long shot. In fact, it was worth 100 times that—about $1.2 million. Pradeep had come to give me a ride in one of the world's first hydrogen-powered cars.

We made the twenty-minute drive in almost complete silence. It wasn't that we didn't have a great deal to say to each other; rather, I was nearly dumbstruck by how quiet the car ran. With no combustion engine—just fuel cells that soundlessly generated electric energy and left water behind as the only "waste"—the car seemed like a glider on a highway filled with Boeing 747s. It handled beautifully, accelerated smartly, and rode smoothly. Other than not making noise and belching black, environmentally unfriendly exhaust, it was indistinguishable from the countless utilitarian compacts zipping alongside us.

And that, I learned, was part of the point. The car's designers could have started up their invention in a sleek shell—imagine a silent-running engine with a Maserati body—but instead they wanted to show how normal such a car could be. To borrow from Volkswagen, it was a people's car, one that eventually would make the leap from an incredible, futuristic innovation of today to a mass-produced, hydrogen-car-in-every-garage tomorrow.

## My Time Machine

As we drove toward Albany NanoTech, I was struck by the realization that in some ways I was traveling in a time machine. I was seeing what the world of transportation would be like in the next generation. And as I looked at the modest car, I thought of the powerful gas-powered Fords and other throaty machines that currently rule the road. That thought reminded me that the dinosaurs who once ruled the earth weren't replaced by creatures larger or more fierce. They were succeeded by creatures more nimble, more able to adapt, more capable of evolving—in sum, more innovative—at a time of rapid, radical change.

This story illustrates a future we all face, one in which we will need to evolve, to be nimble and adaptive, or face individual, economic, and even societal extinction. This is not a doomsday scenario; rather, it should be seen as a forecast of economic, social, and political opportunity based on the new economy that is taking root across the globe, an Innovation Economy that will reshape every aspect of human life.

The coming Innovation Economy will herald an age of rapid, dramatic change, one in which ideas that create value, offer solutions, and fulfill needs will thrive, sweeping into the recesses of memory the comparatively primitive ideas, products, services, and processes that came before. Innovation will be the prime source of productivity, prosperity, competition, and potentially even peace. Innovation will be recognized as an empowering force that will drive individual prosperity and global competition.

## What Is an Economy?

An economy is a collective measure of the production, distribution, and commerce in a given area, from a small village to a state to a nation to the entire planet. It is the result of the productivity of workers and organizations. An economy is also about the flow of ideas, capital, markets, talent, and growth.

That textbook definition will be rewritten in the Extreme Future. The new definition will reflect the fact that twenty-first-century economies will survive and prosper only if they embrace innovation. If they do, if the individuals within them understand and capitalize on innovation, they will come to enjoy shares of the greatest prosperity generator the world has ever known.

Already, every economy—local, regional, national, or global—is deeply affected by innovation. Those effects will multiply a thousand-fold over the next fifty years. The Innovation Economy forecasted here is a new direction. No longer based solely on governance, capital, talent, population, and natural resources, the Innovation Economy is based on one thing more—personal access to radical innovation. An avalanche of breakthrough ideas that develop new markets, form new industries, and attract global talent and capital is coming. Without radical innovation, traditional factors that determine the success of an economy—such as productivity, progress, and growth—will not be enough.

You need to get ready to navigate the opportunities of the Innovation Economy. It will change the nature of work, jobs, capital, competitors, markets, customers, and perhaps most important, yourself. The central opportunity that the Innovation Economy offers individuals is wealth creation on a scale never seen before. This chapter will explain what is going to happen, how to prepare, and when and how you can benefit.

---

# TEN EXTREME INNOVATIONS THAT WILL ROCK YOUR WORLD IN 2025

- Teleportation of objects around the planet.
- Specialized DNA for sale online.
- Space tourism to the moon and Mars.
- Manipulating matter to make smart products.
- Four billion people doing Internet commerce.
- Hydrogen engines for transportation.
- Cybernetic health enhancement of humans.
- Downloading memories and drugs.
- Domestic robots.

---

## A New Definition

The Innovation Economy is a new fusion of technology and economics, creating global wealth, prosperity, and power. This emerging trend thrives in democracies where personal liberty is respected by law.

Innovation is defined here as a newly synthesized idea, product, service, or process that has the potential to act as an accelerator of competitive advantage for a nation, a region, an industry, an organization, an individual, or some combination of all of these categories. An innovation creates new value—growth, solutions, profits, increased market share, and return-on-investment. Essentially, every effort within a capitalistic system that creates value that people will pay for qualifies.

An innovation that proves its value is adopted and accepted by the marketplace or society. If a critical mass of customers is willing and able to pay for your innovation, it is a success. Innovation, by this definition, cannot exist in a vacuum. An innovative idea in the lab, or on the envelope scratchings of an inventor, is not enough. As innovative as Leonardo's sketches were, they do not meet this definition because they were too far ahead of their time to be executed successfully and have measurable economic impact. The rigors of capitalism—ideas, products, services, and processes judged by the marketplace—confirm the validity of what is or is not innovative. Put simply, an innovation has value if it is blessed by customers reaching for their wallets en masse.

Having said that, it's worth noting that an innovation that customers are unwilling or unable to pay for today might satisfy the value component of this definition tomorrow. For instance, in the abstract, does the hydrogen car I experienced classify as an innovation? Yes, because it offers a dramatic solution needed today to combat the coming oil shortage discussed in the last chapter. But almost no consumers can afford it at its present price point. It points to the future. The hydrogen car costing $1.2 million today will surely be affordable to the mass market in the future, and only then will it be a contributor to the Innovation Economy. Once that happens, and I'm confident that it will, it will be an innovation with almost unimaginable global impact.

Examples of what I'd call modestly successful economic innovations are already all around us. The overnight-package delivery business exists because there are enough people who want to pay for this innovation. Mini music-storage devices like the iPod that play MP3 songs downloaded from the Internet are an innovation that many consumers are willing to pay for, rewarding Apple and Sony and other companies with the sales of these innovations. Drugs and medical devices prolong health and life, fueling both innovations and new industries like biotech. As successful as these sorts of innovations might seem, they will pale in comparison with what's to come in terms of

# THE WORLD OF 2040

- Ninety percent of nations are democratic and enjoy free trade and open markets.

- Innovation is the key driver of global GDP growth, which tops 7 percent annually.

- Hunger and poverty are virtually eliminated, and innovation has raised the global standard of living through increased trade, better health care, and social services.

- Innovation industries are supported by online quality education that is free to all.

- Innovation has been a key force in establishing global peace and security.

- Innovations in media have enabled more cross-cultural understanding, reducing global tensions and conflict.

- Vibrant global trade enables billions of entrepreneurs to achieve  wealth and self-reliance, and to invest in democratic reforms in their nations.

- Longer life and a marked increase in personal wealth and quality of life are available to all.

- Communications and the Internet are available to all nations and peoples.

products and services, not to mention the changes that will be brought to daily existence.

## Evolutionary Economics

We don't have an economic theory well enough developed to understand and explain the impact of technology and science on the economy. Yet they have always been intimately linked. Think about Thomas Edison. Of his nearly 1,100 patents, we remember him best for his inventions of the incandescent light bulb and the phonograph. He was first a scientist, but his innovations had seismic economic impacts that continue to pay dividends today. Still, a century later, economists and scientists know too little about each other's worlds. This must change if we are to understand the global changes coming in the Innovation Economy of the Extreme Future.

One way to begin is to think about economics in evolutionary terms, like biology: All life adapts to survive. The Innovation Economy is an example of a more evolutionary approach to understanding the changes coming in global business. It is based on the evolution of innovation and how each phase builds on the past. Each innovation drives the next stage of economic growth as it evolves, increasing performance, productivity, and achievement. Already there is evidence of this phenomenon. Microchips—the brains of computers—came first on the evolutionary ladder, enabling the invention of computers. Computers evolved into networks, which evolved to drive biotech, which is driving advances in nanotechnology and which will drive the coming science of neurotechnology, the creation of tools that can beneficially rewire a person's brain and central nervous system. This evolution of innovations will shape the future economy, producing jobs, productivity increases, new organizations, new markets, and new industries.

The seeds of these changes have already been planted. According to the *Digital Planet* report, the total current value of all commerce worldwide is more than $80 trillion in sales. By 2015, that number should be more than $160 trillion, assuming even a modest growth rate. Investments in innovation industries, anticipated to total more than $100 billion between 2000 and 2010, will be the chief accelerator of the Innovation Economy. The increased capacity for innovation and invention—in areas ranging from biotech to nanoscience—will emerge faster than at any time in the past. As dramatic as the industrial revolution seemed at the time, its pace will have been glacial in comparison. Increased computing power, high-speed networks, interactive broadband, distributed genomic discovery, and Internet 2 all are bringing future innovations closer, faster. The Innovation Economy will be the key driver of personal wealth in the twenty-first century. Entirely new innovation markets—from energy to health to wireless entertainment to pollution control—have yet to be started, but they will.

## Democracy Drives Innovation

This is the early stage of the Innovation Economy. Half the world has not made a phone call. When they do, it will be over the Internet.

Health care is not fused with genomics yet; we don't know how disease begins and so how to prevent it. We will. Wireless communication is in its infancy. We don't even understand our own cosmos or have answers to our own existence or nature of reality. This is coming, too. We are still stripping the planet for resources rather than designing matter to create renewable energy. It is still early in the game.

Before much of this can happen, though, there needs to be a continuation and an acceleration of the trend toward democratic governments across the globe. Democracy drives innovation. Innovation drives prosperity. Prosperity enables productive, open societies and is the enemy of terror and war. Freedom drives prosperity and individual freedoms.

In 1974, 59 percent of national governments were considered free or partly free; by 2004, that percentage had risen to 74 percent, according to Freedom House, a nonprofit, nonpartisan supporter of global freedom and democracy. Also worth noting was that in 2004 some 63

## SIGNS OF THE INNOVATION ECONOMY

- One third of U.S. GDP is already based on innovation industries. By 2015, more than two-thirds of U.S. GDP and more than one-third of world GDP will be based on innovation industries.

- Information technology drives more than two-thirds of labor productivity today. By 2015, innovation industries will dominate labor productivity worldwide.

- More than 1 billion people are connected to the Internet today. By 2015, 3 billion people will be online.

- Total information technology and communications spending worldwide is about $2 trillion today. By 2015, it will exceed $5 trillion.

- The nanotech industry generates more than $10 billion today. By 2015, nanotech will generate more than $1 trillion and employ one million workers.

- Where there is a high-tech penetration of computers, wireless, and Internet access, democratic societies thrive and economic productivity is robust.

percent of the world population lived in free or partly free societies; of the remaining 37 percent living under repressive governments, two-thirds were in China. As we'll see later in the chapter, China already stands to play a huge role in the future of the Innovation Economy. A shift in Beijing's political climate toward a more open society would increase economic growth many times over.

## The Personal Wealth Factor

Democracy, capitalism, and innovation are mutually supporting. There is nothing more powerful than an individual living in a free society who has access to the tools to craft his or her own destiny. Only in a democracy can personal wealth creation thrive. If one thing can accelerate prosperity and the shift to democratic societies, enabling individuals to take responsibility for their futures, it is innovation. This is why the new tools of the Innovation Economy will be accelerators of wealth and progress—more people participating faster to improve their lives. Innovation—as a capitalist tool—is a poverty killer. Capitalism, especially free enterprise, is the smartest way for a nation to encourage individual self-reliance, prosperity, and innovation.

It is therefore possible to forecast that by the end of the twenty-first century, repressive regimes that withhold innovation and the resources to exploit innovation, such as education, the Internet, rule of law, free press, or human rights, will die out or be replaced by new democratic leadership. This is the wave of the future, driven by the power of individuals to enhance the progress of their lives.

This is an undeniable evolutionary force that lies at the heart of the Innovation Economy—self-interest in developing one's potential to better one's condition in life, to achieve and to enable fulfillment. This self-interest is incompatible with political tyranny and terrorism. Only democratic values provide people with the incentives and the necessary technological access to create, be productive, and increase prosperity. Innovation tools in the hands of individuals will be the central force to eliminate terrorism and poverty and resist tyranny in the future. The inherent nature of individuals to better themselves, to prosper, to be free to choose, and to create and invent will bring on the Innovation Economy. The Innovation Economy will accelerate the largest personal wealth opportunity in the history of civilization. The deep connection between innovation and liberty will shape the future.

> ## The formula of the Innovation Economy:
> ### I + C + D = P2
> **(Innovation + Capitalism + Democracy = Prosperity and Peace)**

Regardless of whether a person makes his or her home in Calcutta or London or Independence, Missouri—or in a small village in Peru—everyone can be empowered by the Innovation Economy. The Innovation Economy is the next stage of global culture. It is not an ideology. It does not belong to any nation. It is a global revolution in the tools of power. Never before have such powerful tools been available to so many, to change so much, for the better. Cell phones in two villages create a new market in Africa. Factories in China produce fashion for markets in Paris. U.S. drug makers research in India for delivery in Greece. Latin Americans sell over the Internet. In each of these cases the Innovation Economy is emerging and bringing value to individuals in new ways everywhere on the planet.

There is abundant evidence that wherever democracy spreads, improved conditions for both quality of life and free-market economies go hand in hand. Democratic societies enjoy faster, more robust growth. I forecast that innovation will be a chief catalyst for speeding up the establishment of democratic societies over the next twenty-five years. Why?

## Innovation Drives Democracy

- Individual achievement, wealth creation, and self-reliance can only exist in a free society.

- Innovation industries will offer individuals unique opportunities to offer products and services to massive global markets, generating widespread prosperity

- The transparency of a free media meets the demands of free societies for corporate and government accountability.

- An individual's capacity to develop to their full potential and better their lives through education and health thrives only in a democracy.

- Wireless real-time connectivity will open new channels of knowledge, communication, and trade across borders.

- A new global, mobile Internet infrastructure linking business, markets, talent, and capital will accelerate productivity, supply chains and borderless wealth creation.

- Dissent can thrive only in open societies where individual freedoms are protected by a free press, democratic reforms, and the rule of law.

- Free trade opens new growth markets previously unavailable.

- Governments that resist innovation investments that can enable self-reliance and social progress will drive capital and talent to other nations.

- New inventions and intellectual property such as patents can thrive only in a democratic society where individuals are free to invent the new.

## One Billion Millionaires Wanted

In the Innovation Economy, radical innovations and new personal choices will drive prosperity as never before. Personal wealth creation on a new global level, on a scale never before seen, will redefine the global economy, encouraging many more so-called have-nots to participate. Think about Africa, Asia, and South America coming into the global economy, not just as billions of new consumers but billions of new producers, sellers, and entrepreneurs, beyond what even China has accomplished today. Think about an explosive global market of millionaires waiting to emerge, to infuse the global economy with their energy and innovation. If Microsoft created more than 10,000 new millionaires in five years, then the Innovation Economy will make more than one billion millionaires by 2025.

Before demonstrating how this will happen—via the Building Blocks and the Power Tools of the Innovation Economy—it's worthwhile to have some perspective about where it will happen, and where it might not. That is, to look into the future to see which industries have the best possibilities for innovation growth—and which might be eclipsed when innovation rules the economic world.

First, consider some already present trends in the Innovation Economy:

- The U.S. medical-device marketplace in 2005 is estimated at $80.3 billion, with projected growth by 2010 reaching $100 billion.

- The global market for microelectronic medical implants was $11.9 billion in 2004, and is expected to rise at an adjusted annual growth rate of 22.1 percent to $32.3 billion in 2009.

- Renewable energy such as solar, biofuel, and hydrogen is being chased by more than $50 billion in investments by companies seeking to prosper in a new clean-energy marketplace.

- Global retail has been transformed by cheap yet quality producers like China, which manufacture for consumer markets in the Asia, U.S., and Europe.

- The global B2B (business-to-business) e-commerce market in 2005 is estimated at $4.3 trillion. The U.S. B2B e-commerce market in 2003 was $1.6 trillion, while the U.S. B2C business-to-consumer e-commerce market in 2003 was $106 billion. (Source: 2004 U.S. Census.)

- More than $1 billion worth of products contain nanotech today, while the global nanotechnology market was $7.5 billion in 2003 and is expected to reach $28.7 billion by 2008.

With that as the backdrop, the following are industries to watch, to invest in, and to participate in:

# THE TOP TEN INDUSTRIES OF THE INNOVATION ECONOMY: WHO WILL BENEFIT MOST

**1. Pharma/Health.** The extension of human life and health enhancement as a result of major advances in medical, pharmaceutical, and surgical knowledge and treatments.

**2. Energy.** The development of renewable, clean, abundant, and affordable fuels.

**3. Manufacturing.** The development of new processes that will enable the global, fast, inexpensive, and on-demand production and distribution of goods.

**4. Communications.** The creation of new ways to connect information, people, and financial transactions in real time. The software, games, programs, and content.

**5. Transportation.** The discovery of new methods to increase the ability of individuals and companies to be mobile, to ship, and to reach customers.

**6. Security.** The creation of new devices that will both spare lives and increase our ability to protect our society, our allies, and ourselves.

**7. Entertainment Media.** New delivery systems to share ideas, culture, and fun that will make the existing Internet and currently available electronic entertainment devices seem as quaint and outdated as windup toys.

**8. Education and Learning.** The creation of immediate, portable, transferable, on-demand knowledge sources on a scale equivalent to the Library of Congress.

**9. Knowledge Engineering.** The creation of information services that can morph into games, finance, software, programs, and systems to provide value to consumers and business for better customer service, entertainment, marketing, planning, and managing.

**10. Smart Materials.** New nano-bio-neuro materials that are smarter, safer, cleaner, and cheaper to make into any products, on-demand, for any industry.

# Not All Winners

In the emerging global Innovation Economy, there will be winners and losers. It is difficult to pinpoint specific industries and markets that will suffer or dry up completely as a result of innovations elsewhere—as explained above, the market has to accept an innovation for change to occur—and some threatened industries and markets might well adapt and evolve in time.

However, it is possible to forecast that the convergence of new innovation tools and global access to capital and information will cause upheaval in certain industries and markets in the Extreme Future. One way to understand this is to look into the past.

Let's say you were a comfortable homeowner in England in the 1400s and some disgruntled peasant threw a rock through your window. Your only option would be to turn to the powerful Glaziers Guild, which closely guarded the age-old secrets of glassmaking and ensured that the market was controlled by a limited number of skilled craftsmen and their long-suffering apprentices. Remember, glass was a luxury back then, just as it had been since biblical days. So much so that as late as the 1300s, Venetian glassmakers were forbidden from leaving the island of Murano to prevent their trade secrets from becoming common knowledge.

Although glass did become more accessible in the centuries that followed, it was only as a result of a series of dramatic innovations in the nineteenth and twentieth centuries that it became truly an item of affordable, accessible mass consumption, capable of being produced inexpensively anywhere in the world, for use in everything from construction to consumer products such as soda bottles. As a result, when was the last time you heard about the Glaziers Guild?

The coming Innovation Economy will have similar effects, though on a broader scale than ever seen. Commodity-based manufacturing of common, non-niche items such as shoes, clothing, chemicals, and electronics, to name a few, will be radically changed by innovations and the free flow of information and capital across international borders. Current producers of these commodity-based items had better get ready to innovate and adapt, or someone else will do it for them. The same will be true for industries such as consumer electronics, financial services, and hospitality, among others.

# History of the Future

My ideas about what I now call the Innovation Economy began taking shape in 1980 when I joined Apple Computer. At the time, I did not know what I was in for. My interview, which lasted all of ten minutes, was revealing about how little we knew about the role of innovation in 1980.

"I actually don't know much about computers," I admitted to my interviewer. "But I sense they just might change the world."

"OK. You got the job," my interviewer said. "And by the way, no one knows much about computers. You can help us figure that out."

My brief time at Apple was a mind-blowing experience of one-hundred-hour workweeks, intense learning, and superfast innovation. I felt that I was at a global nexus of creativity and talent, where every day was a new discovery. This was the beginning of the computer revolution. I was part of the cabal of early innovators who considered how computing—or more correctly, how personal technology—might change the world. The idea we focused on back then was essentially the same one the world is coming to grips with today: developing personal technology to encourage and empower the individual to be successful, prosperous, or creative.

This was an entirely new paradigm that Steve Jobs understood—then and now—better than anyone on the planet. Digital capitalism was born. The power to inspire the individual to be great and to fully develop his or her potential was as true then as it is today. An individual enabled by the tools of innovation can do great things. This is what is behind the Innovation Economy. Anything is possible.

The world had never witnessed a more vital and enabling tool for transforming the individual. The personal computer, successfully developed for the marketplace by Apple, became the first Power Tool to democratize innovation and enable personal prosperity. The effective term here was personal. The personal computer was the first Power Tool to be put in the hands of the individual—not the state, or the leaders of organizations, or the elite—but the individual. This was an awesome new power.

The pristine energy in the culture at Apple around these fierce global ideas seemed uniquely revolutionary when I was there. It was as though we had all been infected with an enthusiasm and passion for truly changing the world with the tools of innovation. It was never just about the computer; it was all about the power of the individual to use a powerful tool to be creative in a revolutionary way. As extraordinary as that was, it was really about something even bigger, something that took me a while to fully recognize. We were creating engines of creativity and prosperity. This new Power Tool, the computer, was designed to break all the rules. The enhancement of human potential to create, communicate, and invent the impossible was emerging. It was about the beginning of the Innovation Economy.

## Mac and Me

My project at Apple, the Macintosh computer, was being finalized, and we were thinking hard about how this innovation was part of a larger conversation about the future of technology, global commerce, communications, and social progress. I was in charge of global business professions. How might professionals use computers today and in the future? How might doctors, architects, engineers, and scientists use these marvelous new Power Tools to develop their potential?

These were big challenges to consider in 1980. I relished the challenge. We were thinking big thoughts about how we were going to tip the scales of power from nations and corporations toward individuals. And we were right; the personal computer did shift power.

I was a resident futurist; actually in our group, Business Marketing, I was conducting strategic planning, thinking about how artificial intelligence, networks, and computers might transform the future. I was tasked with looking out into the future to consider what was coming next. As I forecasted out into the far future of 2000, then some twenty years away, I used the innovations that we had pioneered at Apple to consider what the rest of the world might find of value.

At Apple Computer in 1980, we had AppleNet, an early corporate-wide e-mail network. I had become aware of the Internet a few years earlier, and we had access to numerous electronic databases. Of course, cumbersome modems were our communication gateways to a world that had not woken up yet. The few electronic databases and Internet meetings were mostly between academics, researchers, and military. Still, as I used AppleNet to communicate with colleagues around Apple, it was possible to imagine how powerful such a tool could be if it were adopted by everyone on the planet with a computer on his or her desk and could be made fast enough to operate in real time, for less than the cost of a phone call. And what if you could reach tens or thousands of people with your message all at once, with the touch of a single button? What an innovation that would be.

Just days before the introduction of the Macintosh computer, I was confronted by a fellow Apple employee, Bill Cleary. He challenged me, "Why aren't you writing books about this future of technology instead of working here?" I told him I needed to better understand how innovation was evolving, and then I would write about it. That was twenty-six years ago; I'm just now getting the hang of it.

## Then Came the Internet

The Internet revolution followed the personal-computer revolution. The Internet was the next logical evolution of innovation change, the next big thing to transform business and society. Just as smarter, faster chips led to computers, faster, smarter, and cheaper computers led to networks.

Innovation, now as the Internet wave, was again the key driver of change, growth, productivity, and prosperity—even wealth. Something vitally important was happening, I thought. Early on, I forecasted the impact of the Internet on business and society as a major new direction that would accelerate individual powers and choices. The Internet, like the computer before it, was digital capitalism at work. This is the perfection of free minds and free markets at play.

Everything was getting clearer—innovation was a chief driver of change. The so-called dot-com bubble, a triumph of the small-minded who missed the big picture of what was truly happening on the global scale, was a brief blip on the map. It was not the bubble that was important; what was important was the invention of global networks that formed into markets, opened up new businesses, and created new jobs and wealth. Some missed this. There was a new conversation happening, and the Internet was a vital part of the story. The Innovation Economy was emerging and it was electrifying every industry—from health care, to manufacturing, to financial services, to life sciences—with change. This was the power of radical ideas challenging the status quo and increasing productivity on a massive scale.

Many folks misunderstood what the Internet was about. Even my friends and clients challenged me that there was nothing new going on, just a new sales channel or a new online catalog. This became clear to me when I was consulting with a major insurance company in 1998.

I was told to downplay the power of the Internet because their industry would never give product information to its clients over the Internet to see and make choices online. Of course I challenged that, and they ended up doing this very thing. In fact, they took my advice to craft a new strategy to outcompete other, slower companies that were out of sync with the realities of the emerging Innovation Economy. Innovation was indeed empowering the individual, creating a competitive advantage.

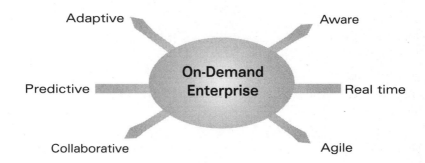

Other than the innovative individuals who were busy making new products, services, and innovations, many people were so happy that the dot-com bubble burst—right up to the moment they lost their jobs. They did not get it. It was never about the illusion of making no profits or the arrogance of never having customers. Yes, there was much hype and many more dreams. It was part of the grand experiment about innovation that was more than just ideas, but an economic force that was truly changing the world by moving cultures, businesses and industries into the future. Entirely new industries were Web-enabled, from genomics to stock trading to online auctions to logistics and supply chains. This was the Innovation Economy at work.

Many clients fought the innovations of the Internet, but eventually ended up deciding to learn to change and leverage its innovations and benefits. Today, 95 percent of all enterprises worldwide use the Internet for conducting at least part of their business. This is just the beginning. Just as it is absurd to consider how resistance was futile to fight the tide of innovation in the past with computers and the Internet, the next innovations will look just as strange. They are likely to meet even more

resistance. Get ready for more radical ideas coming in the Innovation
Economy.

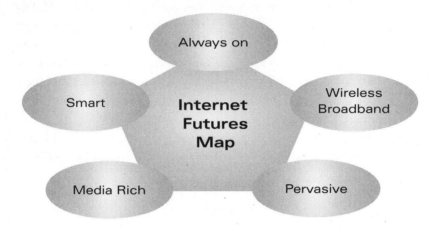

## Mapping the Innovation Future

During the rise of the Internet, there was much talk about the "new
economy." This was actually not new. We had been talking about the
rise of knowledge workers, the shift from the industrial to the information age, for more than thirty years. Something important was happening, something new and different, affecting business and industry. I
sensed it, as did many people working in the computer industry in Silicon Valley in 1980. At Apple, I had already seen business and innovation starting to get acquainted, but it was too early for this convergence.

I remember meeting with officials from the American Medical Association, who listened but could not see the future impact of the computer on health care. It was too early to put it all together. Too few
recognized the vision that we had about innovation becoming the
chief force that would transform society and the economy. In 1980,
there were few personal computers on desks. The idea of digital hospitals using computers, e-mail, or computer-assisted decision-making for
doctors was indeed a strange one.

The computer revolution was just the beginning of a series of innovations that together would come to redefine the economy, business
and society. These innovations, which have now come together as I call
the Innovation Economy, give us a glimpse of our unfolding future.

One more word about the so-called dot-com bubble. In retrospect, many of our forecasts about the impact of the Internet on business, which led to the "overexuberance" in the marketplace, were wrong. Most of our projections about Internet adoption by consumers, Internet shopping and advertising, use of the Internet for creating new businesses and transforming industries, and the Internet's overall impact on the economy, were too low. Yes, that's right. E-commerce sales have actually grown faster and are larger than anyone predicted. The Luddites, those in denial of change, were wrong about the force of innovation to transform the economy.

Imagine what would happen if Western governments placed limits on the Internet, as they do in some Asian and Middle Eastern nations.

---

# TOP FUTURE INTERNET TRENDS: 2020

- The Net will be wireless and pervasive, with access anytime, anywhere.

- Every manufactured product, object, and material will be online.

- The telephone and TV will be fully integrated into the Internet.

- The Internet will develop a type of "personal awareness" of itself.

- Real-time access to 80 percent of all information in the world will be provided free.

- All e-mail will be multimedia, audio- and video-streaming-enabled.

- Real-time videoconferencing will be widely available.

- "Telepresence": The Net will be an immersive experience.

- All merchants, banks, and consumers will be linked.

- The Net will be a vibrant trading market of more than three billion people.

- Collaboration will drive trade, and entrepreneurship will drive demand.

- Personal privacy will be recognized as a major national-security issue.

You would have rioting in the streets. Companies like Wal-Mart, GE, IBM and most others would cease to function. Could anyone have considered the power of this innovation to change so much, so fast, so radically?

It was an authentic transformation of the economy, just in the early stage. We needed to have a longer view. This was the second stage of the Innovation Economy. Computers, to networks, to biotech, to nanotech, to neurotech—the Innovation Economy was evolving. These are the ingredients of the future Innovation Economy, still unfolding today.

We underestimated the fast adoption by the consumer and business. In fact, the reason the U.S. economy has done so well in tough times, still maintaining GDP growth at 4 percent, is due to the productivity increases brought by computers and, indeed, the Internet. This will continue. The Internet is a tremendous success today as an enabler of commerce, productivity, and invention. The optimism about the Internet in the past has been fully justified. This is important to note because what's coming, the Innovation Economy, will make the Internet revolution seem insignificant.

## Moore's Law Revisited: Cheaper, Faster, Smarter Tools

Moore's Law, created by Gordon Moore, a founder of Intel, says that computing power doubles every year. Moore's second law says that in this same period of time, a year, the cost of computing power falls by half. So you get twice the power for half the price—a concept that is central to the Innovation Economy. This is why when I worked at Apple, a computer that sold in 1981 for $2,500 had only a tiny fraction of the power housed in a computer that costs $2,500 today. As I often say in my presentations, "What's on your desktop today, you will wear tomorrow."

Keep in mind that computer chips, the original power tool, have completely transformed the economy by becoming features in every auto, home consumer device, medical device, and piece of manufacturing equipment. Every aspect of every product and service in every industry is now smarter, faster, and more productive because of the proliferation of computer chips—the silicon brains of the economy. Every cell phone, Internet network, DNA sequencer, and business supply chain has been made smarter and faster, more productive and connected. Silicon brains and human brains have much in common.

The point here is that Moore's laws, which have proved to be accurate measures of progress in technology's growing power, are also predictive for making forecasts about most new innovations in the future and their impact on the global economy. So if every product and service in the global economy has been made faster, smarter, and more connected, and if this power is increasing exponentially—doubling each year while costs plummet—what does that mean for the Innovation Economy? Cheap, fast, connected intelligence is coming. Powerful new innovation tools for creating trade, inventing new products and services, and turning knowledge into commerce are coming. Super-accelerated innovation is coming that will bridge the gap between the haves and have nots in society.

By 2025, cheap personal computing power will exceed the power of the supercomputers sold today to governments and large corporations. When that occurs, our ability to invent the impossible, to solve any problem or puzzle, to create new products will be at hand.

This means that vastly powerful and inexpensive tools are emerging that will enable commerce, trade, health care, and communications on a scale that has been unknown—real-time access to all information, resources, solutions, collaborations, and opportunities on a global scale.

Imagine more than eight billion people linked in a vibrant, dynamic Innovation Economy by 2040, all of them buying, selling, inventing, communicating, sharing, educating, and enabling the future through innovations that will still be evolving in power, still becoming cheaper, still enabling the future prosperity of the individual. This is my forecast.

## Enhancing Human Potential

The National Science Foundation, a primary think tank for the U.S. government, acts as a catalyst for planning for the future. Some of the most far-reaching visions for the future are cooked up at NSF. Nanotech, a fantastic new science of fresh possibilities, was originally championed at NSF. I was appointed in 1998 as the first private-sector advisor on nanotechnology to the National Science and Advisory Board. This later became the National Nanotechnology Initiative, the first and largest investment in nanotechnology by any government in the world.

Several years ago, I was asked to present my forecasts about nanotechnology to a group of agency heads and policy advisors to the

White House from NASA and the departments of Defense, Energy, Health and Human Services, and others. Most of the thinking about nanotech at the time was about the implications for science. My presentation looked at the trends and future scenarios that would affect the U.S. economy, jobs, education, and investments—the need to prepare the nation for what could be an important, historic, and even disruptive economic shift.

What happens if nanotech creates new energy sources and we stop using oil? Let's consider the impact on the economy, global security, and jobs, I urged. What about the effect of products that last a lifetime, such as autos? What would that do to the economy? When oil was cheap, we didn't care. Before 9/11, the world was different. I think I changed some minds that day.

One person who took me seriously was Mike Roco, a scientist, engineer, and the director of the interagency group on Nanoscience and Nanoengineering at the National Science Foundation. Mike was and still is a true visionary who pioneered the NSF's support for nanoscience. He had been my host. I had a sense that I had been set up, in a good way, to make the case that we needed to understand the impact of innovation, changes in innovation on the economy for the future. I stood my ground and made my case for nanotech being a disruptive economic threat unless we invested in jobs, education, training, and science research to adequately prepare us for the future. Unless we prepared now, I said, we risk being disrupted by innovations like nano in the future. I suggested we needed a new long-range forecasting capacity for leaders to think about the impact of nano.

## An Intimate Connection

This was an important event because it coalesced my thinking about the role that innovation itself—as a capacity of nations, individuals, and organizations—will play in shaping the future global economy. Innovation will be critical to leadership. Two big ideas emerged. The first was that the intimate connection, the new fusion of innovation and economics, was just beginning. As I was discussing the business and economic implications of nanotech, it became clear to me that something grander was afoot. This was not just a technological revolution; an economic revolution was emerging as well. We were beginning to see first light, too early to grasp the full meaning of this new idea.

The second evolution in my thinking about the Innovation Economy came later. Around 2000, I was at a conference sponsored by NSF in Washington, D.C., on the social and economic implications of nanotechnology. We were there to consider the implications of nanotech on society, and it was clear that a larger framework was needed.

My colleagues and I at the conference considered the challenge. What were the top innovations that would enhance human performance and develop human potential? We decided that the paradigm of nanotech alone was not enough. We needed to expand it. There was, we thought, a larger vision emerging that was vitally important for the future of the nation and the world. We brought the idea to NSF's Mike Roco, who agreed. Eventually NSF and the U.S. Department of Commerce supported this inquiry.

# Convergent Tech:
# Stepping into the Future

That day, a new integrative systems approach was born on what we called convergent technologies, or NBIC—nanotech, biotech, infotech, and cognotech (or neurotech). Converging Technologies for Enhancing Human Performance, which grew out of our conversations, has now become a new global perspective on rethinking science. This new interdisciplinary approach has large and important implications for the economy beyond science. The impact of these innovations together signaled an economic transformation that is distinctly different from anything we'd seen before. It began to fit together with

my idea of the Innovation Economy—the converging of tech and economic trends.

There was something dramatic going on that I needed to investigate further. Of course, talking to scientists about economics or business didn't get me very far. And talking to economists about innovation was equally frustrating. So I started constructing new models for better understanding the convergence of innovations and the impact on business and the economy.

## The Building Blocks and Power Tools of the Innovation Economy

We take for granted the speed of innovation that has created the world around us. But the next fifteen years will see an acceleration of innovation, change, and disruptions on a scale no civilization has ever experienced. Why? As seen in Moore's Law, the tools of the twenty-first century are growing exponentially faster and becoming cheaper and more powerful than at any time in our history.

If you consider the accelerated rate of change in innovation over the past forty years, the progress has been astounding. The lightning speed of computing, the decoding of DNA, and the emergence of new industries like nanotech are just some of the indicators of a seismic economic shift.

An entirely new economy is emerging. This new economy will need to accelerate knowledge exchange, networked markets, fast collaborative work, and workforce education. The building blocks of the next economy will be born from innovation. They represent the shift

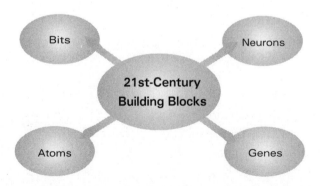

from the steel and oil of the past and point us toward a radical reshaping of the economy and the power of new ideas. The next economy Building Blocks—bits, atoms, genes, and neurons—will be followed by photons and qubits as well. But let's not get ahead of ourselves.

Each of these Building Blocks has a role to play, individually and collectively, but they need to be understood in context, as the raw elements that will be used to drive advances in the Four Power Tools of the Innovation Economy:

- **Nanotechnology.** The manipulation of matter at the atomic scale, producing new drugs, fuels, materials, and machines.

- **Biotechnology.** The unlocking of DNA, life sciences, and the impact of genomics on health care, life extension, and medicine.

- **Information Technologies and Networks.** The impact of computing, microchips, and the Internet on careers, communications, work, creativity, and entertainment.

- **Neurotechnology.** The use of devices, drugs, and materials to heal, manage, and enhance mental performance and functioning.

For example, advances in biotech to build the next generation of drugs—based on genomics and the leveraging of DNA—can only be achieved by computing and Internet innovations. The sequencing of DNA, and the resulting new drugs and personalized medicine, could not be undertaken without fast, powerful computers. Network outsourcing and Internet collaborations are also drivers of nanotech. The building of devices and materials at the nanoscale could not happen without access to smart, cheap, fast computing and cheap bandwidth networking power.

*HEADLINES FROM THE FUTURE: 2020*

**Neurotech Device Cuts Depression by 80 Percent**

Understanding our biology will shape the future of nanotech products that self-assemble and self-heal. Neurotech, or the breakthroughs in the performance of the mind, is due to a convergence of computing, nano, and biotech. Each innovation platform builds on the efficiencies of the previous one—bio builds on computers and networks; nano builds on bio, and so on. These innovations contribute to break-throughs in science but also forge new economics, evolutionary eco-nomics. The economic impact of innovation is obvious: New capital investments, new jobs, new industries, new products, and new services will emerge on a scale that will dwarf the industrial revolution.

As a result, this Future Map is more complete than the one previ-ously shown—which featured only the Building Blocks—because it displays the links to the Power Tools while also showing how, at the very center of the process, lies the goal of Enhanced Human Performance:

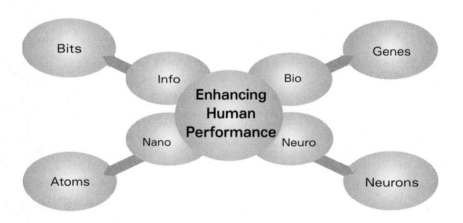

You can already see the marketplace becoming defined by compa-nies that are gaining a competitive advantage through the manipula-tion, production, analysis, and intellectual property associated with these Building Blocks and Power Tools. Work being done in genetic programming at Intel for the next generation of microprocessors, nanoscience-based logic gates created for tomorrow's computers at Hewlett Packard, and IBM's work on nanodrives for data storage are just some examples.

I will delve more deeply into the applications and implications of these innovations in later chapters, notably in Chapter 5, "Outliving the Future." In keeping with this chapter's focus on economics of the Innovation Economy, let's briefly consider the potential future market impacts of these Power Tools.

## Nanotech Market Forecast

Nanoscience represents a radical change in material science, drugs, devices, and manufacturing. Nano-based products could change everything, reducing functions down to 100,000 times smaller than a human hair. Total nanotech investments worldwide were more than $10 billion in 2005. By 2008, the nanomarket may grow to more than $30 billion worldwide. Nanomaterials will drive near-term market growth, while nano-devices will dominate future growth.

For instance, imagine what would happen if developments in nanotechnology reach a critical mass in supplying radically innovative breakthroughs in automated self-assembly. The cost of making computers might be cut in half. Drug manufacturing costs might drop by 70 percent. There would be a dramatic impact on lifestyles, jobs, and economics. Institutions of learning, financial services, and certainly manufacturing will be reshaped.

# TOP NANOTECH FUTURES: 2020

- Hydrogen-nano and solar-energy systems.
- Smart nanomaterials that self-assemble.
- Nanomimetics; products, devices, and materials that mimic nature's abilities.
- Pollution-eating nano agents that clean the environment.
- Nano-manufacturing foundries for rapid, on-demand production.
- Nanobiometrics that provide security scans.
- Military nano weapons.
- Nano-enabled robots.
- Nano-enabled medical diagnostics that probe our genes and bodies.
- Nano-bio devices that heal, prevent illness, and restore capabilities.

## Biotech Market Forecast

The size of the U.S. biotechnology market in 2004 was estimated at $311 billion, divided among 1,473 companies with 198,300 employees. Worldwide it is close to $1 trillion. Biotech is the key driver of health care, a $2 trillion industry in the U.S. and more than $10 trillion worldwide, numbers rivaled only by the defense industry. I forecast that innovations will grow this market to more than $25 trillion by 2030.

## TOP BIOTECH FUTURES: 2020

- Genetic vaccines.
- Gene-replacement therapy.
- Human-enhancement genetic testing.
- Genomic disease prevention.
- Genetic restoration therapy.
- Biocognitive augmentation.
- Bioengineered organs.
- Memory and personality biorestoration.
- Longevity medicine.

## Neurotech Market Forecast

This is the market for drugs, devices, and materials that correct and augment human mental capacities. This market stands at about $100 billion today, and is forecast to grow to more than $180 billion by 2015, according to NeuroInsight's 2005 report on the state of the neurotechnology industry. In a groundbreaking study released in 2005, my Institute sponsored the first *Neurotech Nexus Report,* conducted by NeuroInsights, which identified the leading innovation centers in the world where neurotech research was being conducted. Locations in the U.S., Europe, and Asia made up the top Neurotech Nexus locations.

---

# TOP NEUROTECH FUTURES: 2020

- Stem-cell therapy for restoring memory.
- Brain-machine implants into the cerebral cortex to activate mobility after paralysis.
- Silicon nano-retinas to provide sight—direct sensory awareness into the brain, bypassing the eyes.
- Age reversal on cancerous cells using neuro-pharmacology.
- Genomic neurotherapy to reprogram disease-causing genes.
- Enabling neurons that control robotic arms and legs—human cybernetics.
- Neural engineering to rewire the brain to combat mental illness and depression.

---

## Infotech Market Forecast

This market, the most mature of the four, is comprised of products and services related to computing, telecom, and networks. It stands at more than $2.5 trillion today, and I forecast this to grow to more than $7 trillion by 2020.

# TOP INFOTECH FUTURES: 2025

- The Internet has become the largest global network for ideas, commerce, health care, and education.

- Future chips include nanotech, photonics, quantum, biotech, or DNA.

- More than 100 billion chips will connect every product and most people.

- Future computers have become wearable devices.

- Seamless wireless mobility enables communication with everyone, everywhere on the planet.

- Anywhere and always-on Internet connectivity is free.

## An Innovation Futures Exchange

One example of a scenario of the Innovation Economy that has been mapped by us at the Institute for Global Futures is an Innovation Futures Exchange made up of ideas, intellectual property, inventions, patents, products, and services that companies or individuals want to sell, buy, or collaborate on to maximize value. This future idea marketplace could be an asset to link up ideas with inventors, or patents with companies, to market, trade, and develop ideas into products. Even finished products looking for markets could be offered. The idea exchange, a true innovation futures market, might have a speculative aspect.

We have envisioned an Innovation Futures Exchange, available over electronic resources such as Bloomberg or carried out on existing equity markets like NASDAQ, which would enable virtual financial instruments to be traded just as bonds or future contracts are traded today. This might be a popular investment market based on the supply and demand of certain commodities, branded equities, or even forward contracts to deliver products to certain markets.

Many of the traditional commodity markets today, from coffee to steel to energy and even pollution credits, find an active financial-services marketplace ready to broker buyers and sellers. The financial futures market in many regards fuels the sales of real commodities and has become a vital financial aspect of the life cycle and ecosystem of that industry. An Innovation Futures Exchange would trade in intellectual properties or products of innovation.

It would not be difficult to construct an Innovation Futures Exchange that marketed the intellectual properties, ideas, sales, products, or returns on investment for innovation. Simply put, this future electronic online marketplace could bring together buyers and sellers of innovation products. Numerous licensing and joint ventures could be born.

> **HEADLINES FROM THE FUTURE: 2015**
>
> **Neuromarket Up 200 Percent on Sales of Created Memories**

To give you an example: IBM alone licenses thousands of patents worth millions of dollars every year. NASA and many universities have file cabinets filled with undeveloped patents. This futures market could capture and efficiently bring together buyers and sellers of innovative ideas to make business. Where there are buyers and sellers there will be markets and investment companies interested in brokering the possibility of innovation to create success, profits, and productivity.

An Innovation Futures Exchange is one end of the financial spectrum of fluid capital markets where attractive innovation product offerings worthy of venture capital, debt financing, and public offerings through stock markets would fuel new enterprises. We have seen the early stages of what, even today, is a billion-dollar investment market for nanoscience, biotech, neurotech, and information technology. Ideas and knowledge are the new currency of the Innovation Economy.

## Innovation Supply Chains

Likewise, I forecast an important new emergence of global Innovation Supply Chains that will propel the Innovation Economy. Supply chains are the global distribution systems that facilitate how products get from the creator—the designer, inventor, or developer—to the producer, the distributor, and finally the customer.

Most supply chains are becoming electronically linked by the Internet, integrating finance, distribution, production, and transportation. But with dynamic innovations that are coming, the global supply chain will play an essential role in facilitating the function of creators, manufacturers, distributors, and sellers of innovation products.

Today's logistics companies, running global supply chains, provide more than just the products they distribute for leading brands. They often assemble the products and even produce some parts, providing end-to-end solutions worldwide. This is certainly the trend. But in the future, the Innovation Economy will require the scale of end-to-end global supply chains to be faster, do more, be more intelligent, and become more transparent. Why?

With seven billion people conducting trade by 2030, the immense worldwide population of consumers will place demands on supply chains to serve more, faster, and more effectively. With only six billion people on the planet today, and about one billion on the Internet, the global supply chain is straining to keep up with business and consumer demand. Add another two to three billion consumers and businesses, and you can begin to see the challenges. New innovations, new knowledge, and new markets will emerge at an accelerated speed.

On one hand, I forecast an explosion of dynamic entrepreneurs, fueled by the Innovation Economy. On the other hand, I see huge demand for services that global supply chains, whether they are moving goods or information, assets or products, will not be able to accommodate unless there is a swift and serious transformation.

## The New Knowledge Supply Chains

There are also new Knowledge Supply Chains emerging; the flow of logistics, payments, and transactions would need to meet the enormous trade demands of the Innovation Economy. Many of these Knowledge Supply Chains would be automated and Internet-enabled to capture orders on one end of the world, fulfill orders on the other, and find production somewhere else. These future transactions will be accelerated by Internet visibility, real-time wireless connectivity, and a new global digital cash standard. There is much in place today to begin to see how a future Innovation Economy might perform.

Distribution would be in minutes or real-time and might frustrate tax collection, because where a product was made would change based on where the most tax-advantaged sovereign domain would be. This would open up entirely new opportunities for the developing world.

Today, nations that are often capital-restricted cannot compete in the capital-intensive world of production. But tomorrow they could host vast new Knowledge Supply Chains, both virtual and physical, due to the tremendous cost reduction of a future marketplace of seven billion customers. Just as IT and biotech are driving down prices due to the mass production of products, processes, and services, the global marketplace of tomorrow will become a beneficiary of this change—more customers, more product demand, and more prosperity by a scale of more than 1,000 percent. From new drugs to software or clothing—all market demands will be met.

## Radical Innovations

To companies like Intel, which spends an average of $5 billion per fabrication plant to make silicon chips, the cost reduction due to innovations like nanotech would transform the cost of computing, networking, and information technology overnight.

Whether we're talking about medical devices or transportation systems, this one feature—reducing the cost of silicon by even one-third—would have a radical impact on twenty-plus markets, from autos to computers. This one feature would transform other commodities and finished products, causing drastic cost-reductions and opening up new global markets for growth.

Additionally, the cost of developing one new drug is more than $800 million today. The drug-discovery process could be dramatically more efficient, enabled by innovations in biotech supply chains. The implications of being able to produce new drugs faster, more cost-effectively, and with more accurate precision will transform both medicine and the economics of the bio-pharma industry. Personalized nano-medicine will give us drugs we cannot yet create today—such as a blood substitute or cancer cures. We are headed in this direction now. Radical change is coming, brought on by cheap, fast, and smart innovations destined to meet the needs of explosive new markets in China, India, and the rest of the new global consumer marketplace.

## Engines of Growth

Much of the transformation of supply chains is under way as the Internet and new inexpensive manufacturing capacity has opened up worldwide. It is reasonable to forecast that China and India will play an important role in the emerging Innovation Economy. As two of the largest manufacturing regions and software centers, they will become integral parts of this new future. Stiff competition will define the Innovation Economy. Bars will be raised to new heights. The rush toward outsourcing to India and the manufacturing trade deficits with China point to this future today.

The Innovation Economy may be characterized as being born from the transformation of the existing economy. Just as information technology and biotech have made significant inroads into the global economy—changing supply chains, contributing to the formation of new industries, creating new products, and channeling capital and intellectual property—so too shall the convergence of nano-bio-IT-neurotech play a vital, evolutionary role in the future of the global economy, creating new jobs, companies, and entire industries.

Nano-foundries in Asia receiving orders over the Internet from wireless-broadband-based customers will be codesigning collaboratively virtual in-silico products from DNA object libraries. Models will be designed, programmed for self-assembly, and distributed to waiting markets. Some products, more exquisitely engineered with more features, robustness, or better price, will attract a higher premium. You will still get what you pay for; there may be more choices at lower costs, but with higher prices will come more features.

HEADLINES FROM THE FUTURE: 2028

**New Nanoenergy Devices Can Assemble Themselves and Run on Water**

Some of this convergence is happening organically, as the evolution of interdisciplinary science, a systems approach, and the necessity of sharing tools and knowledge are bringing separate disciplines together. The tyranny of reductionism, too long the unwritten law of modern science, is changing, incorporating a more holistic convergent model.

## Innovation Awareness

In 1999, the Institute for Global Futures deployed a privately funded study to assess the general awareness and readiness of the business community regarding the economic and business impact of nanotechnology. This was the first study of its kind. Interviews were conducted with a broad range of business executives in health care, manufacturing, medicine, real estate, information technology, consumer goods, entertainment, and financial services. The results were disappointing, but not necessarily surprising. The bottom line: Fewer than 5 percent had heard about nanotech. Today, it is unlikely that more than 5 percent of business leaders have not heard about nanotech.

Many innovations that will change the world in the future are not yet on the radar of companies and nations. Leaders often do not know what is next, yet they control the investment dollars that can create or stifle innovations and therefore bring or do not bring new products to market.

How many of you reading this book work at companies that could benefit from quantum technology? How about nanoenergy? Are you investing in biomimetics and/or photonics? Are you prepared for how customers might buy in the future? How about clean tech? Each of the following fundamental new innovations will shape the future of products, services, and industry. **The winners in the future will be those**

# EIGHT FUNDAMENTAL NEW INNOVATIONS THAT WILL SHAPE THE FUTURE

**1. Biomimetics**. Mimicking nature's mechanisms to make new products.

**2. Photonics**. The use of light to create new products.

**3. Nanobiotech**. The combination of nanotech and biology.

**4. Targeted Genomics**. The use of genetic information to make safer drugs, foods, and devices.

**5. Biodetection**. The use of biological information to detect risks.

**6. Neuro-devices**. The creation of micro-machines to enhance or fix brain functions.

**7. Nanoenergy**. The combination of nanotech and energy to create renewable fuels.

**8. Quantum Encryption**. The use of quantum computing to protect networks, products, and people.

leaders who anticipate these trends and prepare their nations and organizations.

# Preparing for the Innovation Economy: Three Futures, Three Outcomes

The following futures are briefly described to generate further exploration and discussion. These futures may be viewed as a catalyst for mapping future impact or avoiding pitfalls in preparing for the Innovation Economy.

Future-Readiness was defined in designing these futures as the awareness and ability to take action. Future-Readiness is viewed as a mission-essential driver of business. Readiness regarding education, capital, talent, coordination, and communications are all integrally part of the same platform.

Preparing for the Innovation Economy may translate into the long-term sustainability of nations, industries and organizations. Readiness, the preparation and planning process, becomes vitally important to define. There will be winners and losers as the Innovation Economy evolves.

### Scenario One: Prosperous Sustainability, 2015

**Economic Environment:** Innovation comprehensively integrated into the economy due to high readiness, effective strategic planning, and widespread investments by business, education, labor, and government. Accelerated national policy and investments produce economic agility and rapid, widespread, large-system change management. A massive change in the education system by 2007 supported by 500 percent investment in science research paved the way for prosperity in 2015.

There is widespread understanding of the benefits from applications of innovation, including its strategic economic value for the nation and its role in maintaining global U.S. leadership. Comprehensive social and industry-wide adoption has led to a positive impact on national productivity and an enhanced quality of life. Hard choices were made and investments in creating the next generation of globally competitive workers paid off just when immigration was slowing along with low labor rates due to falling fertility and an aging society. Innovation investments lead the world.

**Key Characteristics:** Robust GDP growth of more than 5 percent annually; high productivity; global trade leadership; sustainable economic growth; global patent leadership; superior industrial competitiveness; highly skilled education and training resources; accelerated immigration; strong defense; strong investment climate; plentiful capital liquidity; high investment in science R & D; low unemployment; high government and industry collaboration.

**Future Outlook:** Very positive champion of global capitalism and democracy. An ever-escalating predominance in key markets and industries leading to increased investments and innovations. An accelerated, progressive, confident growth prognosis for the economy. An enhanced quality of life for the nation. Global leadership and increasing empowerment of Third World and developing nations. Accelerated investment in R & D and continued coordination with all sectors of society. High global engagement in peace and security. Business and government collaboration has enabled the nation to become Future-Ready.

## *Scenario Two: Playing Catch-Up, 2015*

**Economic Environment:** Innovation partially integrated into the economy due to low readiness and inadequate strategic planning. A sluggish economy playing catch-up. Slow social and industry-wide innovation adoption. Reactive cultural response to investment in accelerated national change management. Only a partial commitment to innovation in national policy. Missed opportunities in stem cells, nanotech, and renewable energy led to a loss of competitive advantage for business and the nation. The demand for skilled workers led to a 300 percent increase in outsourcing. Trade deficit with India now rivals that of China. Dollar in decline.

**Key Characteristics:** Partial loss of leadership in key markets and industries; lack of skilled talent; poor education and training; growing but still low investment in R & D; less active as a global superpower; fragmented

industry support; poor investment climate; insufficient liquidity; fragmented government and industry collaboration; weak defense.

**Future Outlook:** Optimistic, but only if rapid and strategic widespread
large-systems change is undertaken in a concerted effort by business
and government in partnership. Difficult to regain ground in certain
markets, but partial leadership in key markets is a success to be built
on for the future. Limited engagement from world events.

## Scenario Three: Nation in Decline, 2015

**Economic Environment:** Absence of comprehensive innovation plan
and integration, adoption, and readiness, leading to a drastic reduction
in post-industrial growth and poor performance in global competitiveness, with a negative growth impact on the overall economy. Denial of
the strategic value and importance of innovation has led to gridlock.
Politics is a divisive force. Business goes offshore to get talent for workforce. U.S. market in decline. Inability to invest in actions required for
comprehensive large-system change. China refuses to refinance debt,
default a possibility. World Bank steps in.

**Key Characteristics:** Loss of key markets and industries; rising unemployment; chaos in selected sectors; brain drain from talent going
offshore; lack of investment liquidity; low investment in R & D; fragmented business and government collaboration; no longer a catalyst
for democratic reforms; flight capital moving offshore; educational
support low. Weak defense reliant on allies.

**Future Outlook:** Moving into the future, it will be difficult to seize and
maintain market and industry leadership without a significant investment in R & D, education, training, and private/government collaboration. A commanding market share in key industries and global
leadership has been sacrificed. Regaining this ground, not to mention
global leadership, will be a massive undertaking certain to strain capital and human resources. An acceptance of a lower role in global leadership will be the probable outcome. Comparable to when the U.K.
lost its empire. U.S. interests at risk. Questionable role in future global
conflicts. More reactive than proactive in foreign affairs. Domestic
withdrawal and protectionism.

# Killing the Innovation Future

These three scenarios are obviously a form of the Killing the Future game introduced in Chapter 1. The steps taken to prepare for the Innovation Economy in Scenario One are precisely the ones ignored in Scenario Three, with devastating results. The chart below puts the issues into high relief; ignore them only at the risk of your future.

---

## HOW TO KILL THE FUTURE OF YOUR ECONOMY OR COMPANY

**1.** Don't invest in innovation, science, or technology.

**2.** Don't develop, acquire, or protect intellectual property.

**3.** Don't fix the education system.

**4.** Hold back on immigration.

**5.** Stop training workers to invent innovation.

**6.** Restrict investment capital and liquidity.

**7.** Limit personal privacy.

**8.** Allow terrorism and crime to persist.

**9.** Don't protect individual freedoms; no free press, no free trade.

**10.** Create barriers to free enterprise.

---

Conversely, what follows are some ways to capitalize on the coming Innovation Economy.

No one nation owns innovation. But there are some whose success others can emulate. Singapore, Ireland, and Israel stand out as small nations that have successes to invest in innovation.

The Innovation Economy is coming. It will bring a sweeping global change that affects everyone. There will be winners and losers. Economies will rise and fall. Companies, individuals, nations, and industries will compete. Those who embrace innovation and adapt

# HOW TO GROW FUTURE PROSPERITY

**1.** Upgrade advanced science programs in high schools and colleges.

**2.** Create a new incentive program to encourage youth to become scientists, engineers, and tech-savvy entrepreneurs.

**3.** Teach innovation and entrepreneurship to everyone.

**4.** Support free trade, free press, open markets, and free enterprise worldwide.

**5.** Adopt rule of law for intellectual-property protection.

**6.** Seed venture capital investments in new innovations.

**7.** Bring on the Internet and give it to everyone.

**8.** Learn about nano-bio-IT-neuro innovations.

**9.** Support radical ideas that may disrupt the status quo.

**10.** Reward individuals for being innovative.

quickly will win. The Innovation Economy will be the next stage in the evolution of globalization, business, and trade.

Those who will be the most empowered to succeed will be individuals. The Innovation Economy is a revolution in how individuals use ideas, knowledge, and conduct commerce. Great leaps in quality of life, social progress, and even personal wealth will be the outcomes in the near future. Innovation will also be a global force for encouraging self-reliance, democratic reform, individual rights, and free trade. From Africa to the U.S., from India to Europe, empowered individuals with access to innovation tools will become more self-reliant, more productive, and more prosperous than at any time in the history of civilization.

# CHAPTER 4

# Help Wanted:
# The Future of the
# Workforce

## UPS Gets Future-Ready

Ups is an interesting company—a global leader in supply chains, shipping, information, and services. As an advisor to the company in the 1990s, before its global expansion into more than 180 nations, we had a deep concern: The company did not seem to be future-ready to meet the coming challenges of workforce diversity. There were too many whites, not enough women and minorities, and too many sexual harassment and workplace discrimination suits. My data clearly showed that the workforce was changing, and if UPS was going to grow effectively, it had to change, too. The company's leaders took this evidence to heart and committed UPS to becoming more diversity-friendly.

UPS had faced workforce problems

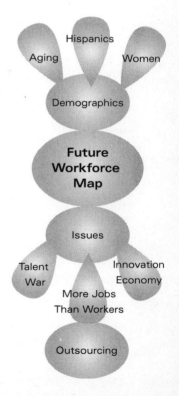

Hispanics

Aging    Women

Demographics

**Future Workforce Map**

Issues

Talent    Innovation
War    Economy

More Jobs
Than Workers

Outsourcing

# THE TOP TEN WORKFORCE TRENDS

**1.** A global war for talent will be the top driver of competitive advantage, pitting nations, individuals, and companies against one another as talent grows scarce.

**2.** The future of the workforce should not be defined by geography, but by talent.

**3.** The aging of the population in America and Europe will have dramatic effects on society and the economy.

**4.** Hispanics and women will dominate the future U.S. workforce.

**5.** Women will comprise a high percentage of new workers and leaders, forever changing the politics of boardrooms and markets.

**6.** Increased immigration will be necessary to enable available talent to keep up with the demands of business and society.

**7.** Finding high-tech skilled employees from a global talent pool will be the greatest challenge for every organization and every nation.

**8.** Innovation will be a key driver of workforce skills, requiring the education system to be completely overhauled.

**9.** The domestic workforce will grow more slowly because of dangerously lower fertility rates.

**10.** Workforce crises that arise in the near future will be traceable to the lack of skilled workers.

before. In the 1960s, the company had more jobs than workers, caused by a lack of skilled labor—not enough drivers. Now it was about understanding women and minorities and a very different workforce than the mostly white, Irish-American ex-Marines who had founded the company.

My firm developed for UPS what became the first and largest Valuing Cultural Diversity program in the world, and the company embraced it to great effect, delivering it to more than 20,000 managers worldwide. Today, African-Americans, Hispanics, Asian-Pacific–Americans and other minorities make up 35 percent of the company's 317,000 employees in the United States. Equally revealing, minorities accounted for half of UPS's new employees in 2003, nearly 30 percent of U.S. managers are minorities, and 27 percent are women.

UPS has further signaled its commitment by publicly declaring that diversity in its workforce, management, suppliers, and customers is "a visible core value that is integral to our business, our community relationships, and The UPS Charter." Fittingly, each year since 1999, UPS has been named one of the "50 Best Companies for Minorities" by *Fortune* magazine, and similar accolades have come from the NAACP, *Hispanic* magazine, the Native American Business Alliance, and the Women's Business Enterprise National Council. UPS saw the future, and it took action.

## The Coming Talent War

Our world is changing fast. Cutting-edge innovations offer information at blazing speed. New threats to security greet us each morning in the headlines. Digital commerce races around the world in nanoseconds. Amid all of this speed, innovation, and change, however, one challenge in particular has the potential to enhance or destroy the future of the U.S. economy: preparing for the next workforce and the coming talent war.

This is a vitally important Extreme Future trend that will affect generations of citizens and corporations, as well as the nation's influence around the world. As a result, it must be addressed soon. America's workforce is changing in fundamental ways. This is an undeniable reality that is unraveling fast all around us. Today there are more than one million high-tech jobs that are not filled. This shortage is not just about people, but a lack of skills. Companies in the Innovation Economy, those on the front lines like Apple, Intel, and Microsoft, have gone off-shore to do research and new product development because they cannot get the same talent here. Talent, skilled human capital, innovative high-tech-savvy people independent of any nation will be the lifeblood of the future organization.

There are clear actions the nation should take, starting today, to offset the coming challenges, such as remedying the massive dysfunction of the U.S. education system. At the same time, some trends are inevitable, such as lower birth rates, and so we will simply have to prepare to confront them in the Extreme Future workforce.

## The Next Workforce

Most organizations and nations are still asleep, unaware that there are problems brewing, convinced that any shortages in talent will be short-lived. Denial runs deep, because no one likes change, especially disruptive change such as the kind described here. The reality is that these are not temporary changes but massive dislocations that will force companies without people resources to move, sell, merge, or go out of business. Entire nations may encounter an inability to build sustainable societies in the future due to a lack of talent, even a lack of population to join the workforce.

The era of abundant supplies of skilled workers is over. The scarcity of employees at a time of increased globalization and competition will be a watershed issue, yet too few organizations are confronting it today to prepare for the future.

Most corporate and political leaders are not ready for these changes, which will be unforgiving, permanent, and sweeping in scope and power. The expectation that there will always be enough employees to fill skilled jobs will end in the near future. The challenges facing every leader, as well as every employee, are monumental. Here is a quick overview of the future of changes coming in the workforce and why we should now prepare for what we can and must change:

**Population Changes:** Changes in population will bring more women into the workforce, along with older workers and more culturally diverse workers. By 2025, one in every three new employees will be female. Also, lower birthrates in the U.S. will mean fewer workers will be available, unless immigration is accelerated. This trend will accelerate outsourcing as talent—independent of geography—will become the most valued asset to corporations.

According to the U.S. Bureau of Labor Statistics, the U.S. workforce will lose the skills and knowledge of forty-six million college-educated baby boomers, who will retire over the next twenty years. They are not being replaced, at least domestically. This will become a crisis, not just in the U.S., but in Europe as well. Unless we drastically open the doors to immigration to offset low fertility and low productivity, quality of life will decline. Although the U.S. labor force has more than doubled in size over the past fifty years, during the next fifty it is projected to grow at only one-third of previous rates. Those new workers are going to be faced with added burdens; in 1950, there were seven working-age people for every elderly person in the United States, but census figures show that by 2030, there will be only three. Population changes will also bring demographic shifts such as those faced by UPS.

The central population dynamic over the next decade will be the aging baby boomers from Western nations and the "youth boomers" in the developing nations of Asia, the Middle East, and Africa. There is a complementary demographic here that might offset the decline of the baby boomers as they retire and the rise of the youth boomers as they enter the workforce: an exchange of almost eighty to one hundred million people from one part of the planet to the other, which might help address the coming talent and skills gap.

**Globalization Changes:** The increased skills of foreign workers, and the stability of their home countries, will be key drivers of U.S. productivity as businesses look to the global workforce for services and solutions they cannot get at home. Outsourcing, which is both cost-effective and holds a competitive advantage, will become a main component of U.S. business. The reduced cost of outsourcing is not the whole story. Increased skills of foreign workers, some with even more advanced skills than those of U.S. workers, will drive this trend in the future. I forecast that although unpopular, outsourcing will continue to be a necessary strategy as companies compete for talent in a hypercompetitive global Innovation Economy.

**Innovation Changes:** Jobs in the future will require even more advanced skills, higher education, and more sophisticated high-tech training. Industries growing from the Four Power Tools cited in the Innovation Economy chapter—nano-bio-IT-neuro—will require advanced skills to manage, develop, and market. But this is just the beginning of the story. There are threats coming that we need to address now.

In every industry, from health care to manufacturing to transportation to financial services to media, innovation will be the key driver of competitive advantage. Having an innovation-savvy workforce will be the central factor that will drive future growth and success in business and society. Yet without significant upgrades to the U.S. education system, our workforce will not be innovation-savvy.

Ninety-seven percent of our youth hope to go to college; 63 percent actually enroll, but only 30 percent actually receive a bachelor's degree, according to the U.S. Department of Labor. More than 75 percent of the workforce must be retrained to keep the jobs they have; 80 percent of all jobs by 2015 will require some sort of postsecondary education, according to the Labor Department. Even worse, employers estimate that 39 percent of their current workforce and 26 percent of new hires will have basic skills deficiencies, according to the Bureau of Labor Statistics.

**Competitiveness Changes:** Compared with education systems in other nations, U.S. schools are not preparing the future workforce adequately to compete in the global economy. The U.S. remains below more than twenty other nations in math and science scores, which points to a dangerous future for the U.S. workforce.

This is one aspect of the trend toward outsourcing. There is a high probability that the U.S. workforce will not be able to compete in the future Innovation Economy without a drastic overhaul of the education system, largely focused on raising the standards of math and science. Consider this: The United States ranked twenty-eighth of forty countries in math and eighteenth in reading, according to the Organisation for Economic Co-operation and Development. With jobs requiring more complex skills like math, science, and technology, Americans may lack the skills necessary to compete in the future global workforce.

# A FUTURE SNAPSHOT OF THE U.S. WORKFORCE

■ Workforce shortages will be highest among managers and skilled employees in tech, science, and other innovation and service jobs.

■ The total projected skilled and unskilled labor shortage may be as high as ten million in 2010.

■ There may be fourteen million more jobs than workers to fill them by 2015.

■ Based on current data, the lack of Future-Readiness of the U.S. workforce due to low high-tech skills will restrict the competitiveness of U.S. corporations in the twenty-first century.

■ America's global leadership will be significantly reduced if workplace needs for skilled talent are not met effectively.

■ The search for innovation-skilled talent will drive global outsourcing—not just costs.

■ New entrants into the workforce will be dominated by women and minorities, especially Hispanic Americans, by 2020.

## The Hunt for Human Resources

As the war for talent heats up, American corporations will be trolling the world for skilled people who can fill the gaps in their organizations. Workers skilled in the challenges and issues of the modern business world who are strong on innovation, multiculturally aware, speak a foreign language, will be highly prized assets in a world of more complexity, chaos, and uncertainty—the Extreme Future.

But learning to deal with the new realities of the workforce will take time. Learning to adapt the culture and strategy of organizations will also take time. A concentrated effort will be needed to reach out to the diverse complexity of Americans and world populations. Some companies like IBM, GE, and Intel are reaching out and have become global talent magnets, recognizing that changes are coming fast. But many other companies, big and small, are not ready; falsely secure in the mistaken belief that little will affect them.

America is headed into a future battle for talent that will define the nation for a hundred years. Will we be ready to make the painful changes in education, population, immigration, and training necessary to prepare for the future? One of the most drastic changes will be an altered attitude about immigrants: In the future, we will desperately need immigrants to come to America. By 2015, we will have more jobs than people—almost ten million jobs will go begging unless we change this situation, fast.

# MEETING THE CHALLENGE: WHAT EVERY EXECUTIVE NEEDS TO ASK NOW

- Where will my company be in 2015?

- Will there be enough skilled workers to grow my company?

- What workforce innovations will drive my company's competitive advantage, or derail it, in 2015?

- Will my organization understand and attract talent from a changing workforce?

- How will marketplace diversity and workforce diversity be similar in 2015?

- How can my organization prepare today to win the talent war?

- What is the fastest way I can upgrade my employees' high-tech skills?

- How must my organization, or myself, change to meet the challenges of the changing workforce?

- How can I make my employees more innovation-ready?

- How can I support national policy changes to increase immigration to provide my company with the talent it needs?

- How can I make my company more attractive to women and minorities?

- What are my competitors doing to leverage offshore resources and talent?

Alan Greenspan, former chairman of the Federal Reserve Board, is hardly a Chicken Little; even if he said the sky was falling, he'd likely say it in such an inscrutable way that his audience might not get his point. But even Greenspan, speaking in 2003 before the U.S. Senate's Special Committee on Aging, sounded the alarm about the aging of the U.S. workforce and the need to take urgent steps in response. One of his main suggestions involved immigrants: "Immigration, if we choose to expand it, could prove an even more potent antidote for slowing growth in the working-age population. As the influx of foreign workers in response to the tight labor markets of the 1990s showed, immigration does respond to labor shortages."

---

**HEADLINES FROM THE FUTURE: 2050**

**Off-World Space Tourism Faces Shortage of Skilled Labor**

---

## Betsy's Job Auction: 2020

For a moment, imagine that you're a corporate manager in 2020, fighting to maintain your organization's competitive advantage by hiring the brightest, most highly motivated, best-skilled employees you can find. Someone, say, like a young woman we'll call Betsy Fong.

Betsy knows she can work anywhere she wants in the world. A first-generation Chinese-American, she graduated at the top of her class at UC–Berkeley and then went to Stanford to pick up an MBA in Knowledge Engineering and Business Analytics. She is part of the new breed of Global NuWorkers who can speak multiple languages and work anywhere for anyone, anytime. She is comfortable in any nation with any customer in any culture.

Not surprisingly, headhunters call or instant-message her every week with offers. Her smart digital assistant, whom she calls Confucius, filters out the offers and replies to most with a simple message: "Thanks, but not interested. Have a wise day." As a marketing manager with expertise in customer data mining, she can find leadership jobs in any city in the world. Her specialty is opening up markets for new product launches. In the past two years, she has successfully marketed wearable GPS watches and Kid-Finders, chips that help parents keep an eye on their children. In the $25 billion intelligent mobility market, she is a well-known player, a star.

But after working in Hong Kong, Shanghai, and Paris, she has decided she wants to be in San Francisco, near her parents' home. In turn, she has created an online talent auction for her services. First, though, she has agreed to a brief videoconference with one of her prospective employers, a company we'll call Digital People, which has been tracking her progress and contributing to her education since she was twelve, when she participated in a company-sponsored innovation fun fair at her middle school.

"As you know, Ms. Fong, we noticed your talent early and invested in your education. Of course, this was a learning grant with no strings attached, as they say," says her interviewer, Hector Rodriguez, a global project manager for Digital People.

"Yes," Betsy answers. "And it was much appreciated, Mr. Ramirez. That's why I have allowed Digital People to participate in the bidding for my contract."

"We are honored," Rodriguez says. "Digital People Corporation has worked hard to earn your trust and the trust of more than 5,000 employees worldwide over the past ten years. Our record of employee loyalty is excellent, I am sure you know."

"Yes, I am aware of your record. Now, to my offer: When the auction begins, it will be open for ten minutes. If you accept my terms, or choose to exceed them, you should be aware that I am using eBay's job

---

**ATTENTION ALL BIDDERS! DR. BETSY FONG'S EMPLOYMENT AUCTION BEGINS NOW!**

*Terms:* Offer Good For Ten Minutes. All Certified Corporations Must Register with Apple-True Identity Plus. Funds to be Deposited in PayPal Account # 450dk

*Salary:* $285,000.

*Bonus:* $70,000 per year with increases based on performance of 50 percent per year.

*Vacation:* Six weeks paid with first-class travel and hotel.

*Required Title:* Knowledge Engineering Global Manager.

*Personal Enhancements Package:* Platinum Full Mental and Physical Cybernetics Policy, twenty-five-year Upgradeable Term, Stem Cell-Enabled.

*Continued Education Credits* toward three PhD programs.

*Closing Bonus:* $50,000.

Sponsorship of Woman in Science Scholarship of $20,000.

*Housing Bonus:* $1.8 million U.S.

*No-Fault Separation Agreement:* Five years bonus paid in full.

Full Health Care and Benefits for Life.

*Life Insurance Coverage:* $2 million.

Accelerated Fertility Adoption Package With Maternity Leave.

search engine. Contract payments will be made to my account on Paypal in Sinodollars, please."

"As you wish," Rodriguez says. "Can we see the offer now, before the real-time auction starts so we can prepare an advance bid that might avoid the necessity of the auction?"

"I'm afraid not. In the interest of fairness, I will be making my offer simultaneously to all the companies I have qualified as bidders. I must go now, so I can begin the auction. Good-bye and good luck, Mr. Rodriguez."

> *HEADLINES FROM THE FUTURE: 2020*
>
> **Women Hold 80 Percent of Management and Professional Jobs**

## America's Youth Looks to the Future

To get an idea of what tomorrow's workforce might look like, my firm conducted a national study in 2002 called America's Youth Looks to the Future. We did this work with Roper ASW, the market research company, under the sponsorship of the Student Loan Financing Corporation, a leader in the education financing industry. Norg Sanderson, CEO of SLFC, was concerned about how prepared America's youth were to face the future. His vision and support for our study were essential.

This was the first study to examine the future of the workforce from the perspective of the individual, the youth of today. America's youth will become America's future workforce. Our polling sought to understand what America's youth thought about the future: their opinions, their dreams, and their concerns.

We also considered whether these young men and women were Future-Ready to meet the challenges and competition of the global economy. So we created a model of Future-Readiness and measured 1,500 sixteen-to-twenty-four-year-olds against it. We examined key areas such as career, finance, technology, family, values, leadership, science, and education. We asked a series of questions to determine which respondents were most prepared to face the future—who is Future-Ready and who is not—based on generally accepted measures of success. We identified five must-have Future-Ready skills factors that we associated with youth being able to achieve future success:

To be certain we were on the right track, we reviewed a strong body of secondary research on America's youth relating to why these readi-

# FUTURE-READY SKILLS

- A positive outlook on the future.

- Family and community involvement; a commitment to values.

- Higher education.

- Acquiring science and tech skills.

- Financial awareness skills and personal money management.

ness factors are valid. We know, for example, that factors such as completing college and having technology skills provide enhanced career choices and a higher earning potential. We know that money-management skills are important to success. As a result, the combination of all five Future-Readiness factors represent a compelling formula for predicting future success.

One of the revealing findings of this survey is that although virtually all young Americans want some measure of success, unless dramatic changes occur a significant number will not fulfill their dreams, largely as a result of a lack of preparation. Some are more Future-Ready than others, and therefore their capacity to achieve their dreams will vary with the degree of preparation they attain. Some key findings provide insight to America's youth.

The implications for the future workforce, markets, global competitiveness, and the economy may prove to be profound. Certainly this is an early warning that we must do more to help enable America's youth to succeed in the future. A central purpose of this study is to raise awareness among all leaders with a call to action.

The good news is that many of these obstacles can be addressed today by providing more access to financial resources for college, increasing financial awareness, developing high-tech skills, and supporting higher education for all. We can change the future by what we do today. We can remedy the issues that our youth are bringing to our attention in this study. We can work toward shaping an optimal future for all Americans.

Even after 9/11, America's young people remain amazingly resilient. They are members of a generation of hope and aspirations for

---

# AMERICA'S YOUTH TRENDS

■ Overall, America's youth is optimistic about its future.

■ Although four out of five youths are optimistic about their future careers, ambitions, and family lives, fewer than half (47 percent) are optimistic about the country's future economy.

■ One in four young people will likely lack the resources, financial savvy, and skills to achieve their college and career goals.

■ One in four will lack the skills needed to achieve success in the future economy.

■ One in five feels strongly that the education system is not preparing them to succeed in the future workforce.

■ African-Americans, Hispanics, and women will make up the majority of those who do not go to college.

---

their future and the future of the nation. But they are not of one voice. This survey identified four distinct segments that make up America's youth. The lines between these segments are drawn based on degree of Future-Readiness, and therefore, likelihood of future success.

The segments range from the Future-Trailblazers, those who are the most prepared, most resilient, and most future-ready, to the Future-Frustrated, those at greatest risk of being left behind. In between are the Future-Traditionalists, who are likely to achieve some measure of success despite lagging behind the Future-Trailblazers segment. The fourth segment, the Future-Activists, is perhaps the most interesting. Collectively, they can either become a force for productive social change or for social unrest.

## Four Future-Readiness Styles

### Future-Trailblazers: The Most Future-Ready

Future-Trailblazers are tomorrow's leaders, innovators, and explorers. They may ultimately guide the way for others, who may emulate their behavior and realization of success. They are the most Future-Ready and resilient. This group is destined to be a productive contributor to society and at the same time achieve individual satisfaction.

Future-Trailblazers are ambitious and have a positive outlook on the future. They are goal-oriented, technology-driven, and highly materialistic. In terms of the conventional measures of societal success, they are the most prepared to meet the challenges of the future. They are most likely to desire wealth as a major goal, and they believe they will have jobs that will pay them a lot of money in the future.

But their careers aren't just about money and success; they are also most likely to believe they will have a job that interests them and that makes a difference in society. They will probably set the national policy agenda in the future via the voting booth or through their involvement with institutions of industry, government, and the professions.

Future-Trailblazers are very positive about technological innovations and are most likely to strongly agree that the development of new technologies is important to America's future success. They want to see continued advances in the development of new drugs to cure diseases and prevent aging. They support investment in space exploration, the development of new food sources, the protection of the environment, the cloning of organs for transplants, the development of drugs to enhance physical and intellectual abilities, the invention of machines that can think for themselves, and the use of personal identification technologies. They are the segment most likely to trust our government on technology issues, as they are most likely to strongly agree that our government leaders are doing a good job on important national issues. They are positive in their view of the nation's ability to meet future challenges.

Education is key to their ambitions. Future-Trailblazers are most likely to have a favorable impression of their own college experience, the college education system, their own K-12 experience, and the public K-12 education system. They are also most likely to believe that they have attained satisfactory computer and technology skills, leadership skills, and money-management skills at school. School is also about networking; they are also most likely to believe that they have met people at school who will help them advance their future careers.

To this segment, education is often about furthering their aggressive and focused career ambitions. They are also most likely to feel that getting trained for a specific job or type of work is important to future success in the workplace, and they consider becoming an expert in a particular field to be a major goal. More than any other segment, they value the development of math and science skills, computer and technology skills, and leadership skills. They are most likely to view job opportunities as a major factor in their selection of schools.

Future-Trailblazers view themselves as financially savvy, which may help them attain their educational goals and future ambitions. They are most likely to be familiar with the different financing sources available for college and most likely to say they know a lot about how to save money. They are the most Future-Ready, based on the scorecard of future readiness factors in our study. Their capacity to be successful is high.

### *Future-Traditionalists*

Future-Traditionalists are less money- and career-focused. They tend to be family-oriented, yet education is a necessary enabler to help them fulfill their goals. They are most likely to consider raising a family to be a major goal and most likely to believe they will have children and be married once. They respect the traditional value of "family first." They are Future-Ready to the extent that they will embrace the skills or education that will enable them to achieve their definition of success. They are positive about their future and the nation.

Future-Traditionalists are not looking to be innovators or leaders in the traditional sense. They are not aggressive achievers in the mold of the Future-Trailblazers. They are least likely to say a major goal is to be famous or creative as an artist or musician. They are least likely to have received an award for achievement or written a song, poem, or story in the past year, served as the captain of a sports team, participated in a theater production, or written an article for a newspaper or magazine.

They don't value networking in school, either. They are least likely to think that knowing people who can help advance their careers is important to their future workplace success. They lack the drive, but they are no less competent or creative than the Trailblazers. Though supportive of technology advances and understanding about the need for financial knowledge, they are not as gung ho as the Future-Trailblazers. They will be satisfied with fewer goals attached to materialism and wealth and will elevate family goals instead.

Future-Traditionalists are the least likely to think they will live past the age of one hundred and are unsure about futuristic innovations. They are the most likely of all segments to be female, who appear more committed than men to higher education, yet are not as aggressive or achievement-oriented as the Trailblazers.

### Future-Frustrated

The Future-Frustrated are uncertain about the future, withdrawn from mainstream activities, and lacking in financial knowledge. They are the least likely to attain higher education. They are the least likely to succeed in life or career. They are the most pessimistic about their personal futures and those of the nation. The future, overall, seems gloomy to them. But unlike the Future-Activists, below, they are not engaged in trying to change the system. They are the least likely to have done volunteer work or community service, least likely to have voted in any election, and least likely to have written or called a politician. They are the least Future-Ready based on the factors identified.

Money is definitely a problem for this group; its absence will hold them back from their educational goals and further dampen their future prospects. They are the least likely to know details about investing money online, investing in the stock market, applying for a car loan, saving for retirement, applying for a student loan, developing a personal financial plan, managing their debt, balancing their checkbook, or opening a checking or savings account. Technology skills as an enabler of future success are not appreciated by this group.

The Future-Frustrated are the least Future-Ready. They are the most likely to be unprepared to effectively cope or succeed in the future. They comprise the "left behind" group of America's youth. A high-proportion of them are African-Americans, Hispanics, and women. Given the resources and skills needed to compete in the workforce, get the job of their choice or achieve personal success or satisfaction, the likelihood is that they will remain frustrated unless they change—on their own or with help.

If you take into consideration other trends in this chapter, it should be clear that this group should be targeted immediately by social, political, educational, corporate, and other leaders for recovery and enablement.

## Future-Activists

Future-activists are contrarians, dissatisfied with the educational system and our national leadership. But they are not standing idle. They are engaged; looking to fix what they think doesn't work. They are highly active politically and in their communities. This group seeks to make a difference in working for a more productive society. Though Future-Activists have the potential to be the "seeds of dissent" and a destabilizing force in society, they also can be a catalyst for constructive social change.

Future Activists are the least likely to believe that our government leaders are doing a good job on important national issues. They are also very disappointed with the education system. They are the least likely to think that our schools are doing a good job preparing our youth for future success.

They are the the least likely to feel the education system has provided them with a good general education or skills to work well with others. They do not believe that schools have taught them how to work hard or to communicate their ideas effectively. They do not believe schools have given them good math, science, computer, or technology skills, taught them how to become leaders, given them specific training for a particular job or field of work, helped them get to know people who will help them advance their careers, or taught them good money-management skills.

Soured on education, they are the least likely to believe that getting a good postsecondary education is very important to their future workplace success, even though many come from educated families. They are the most likely to have a mother with a master's degree and a father with a doctorate degree.

Dissatisfied with our government leadership and education system, Future-Activists take things into their own hands. They are most likely to have done volunteer work or community service, most likely to have voted, and most likely to have made a speech, served as an officer for a club or organization, attended an organized political rally or protest, written an article for a newspaper or magazine, and written or called a politician. They may be positive about technology and will use innovation to further their goals.

Future-Activists are a potential wild card. They may evolve into

Future-Trailblazers or Future-Traditionalists, given their capacity to achieve success in their efforts to remedy society's ills through produc-tive social change. If not, if this group is unsuccessful in achieving constructive social change, or if so-ciety is unable to enable them with the resources necessary to achieve success, the likelihood is that they will join the ranks of the Future-Frustrated or become a destabiliz-ing social element.

HEADLINES FROM THE FUTURE:
2008

**70 Percent of Companies Say
Workforce Not Skilled
For Today's Tech Jobs**

## America's Youth Potential

These four segments provide a mosaic of the future potential of our na-tion. This is not the last word on America's youth and the future. But the survey does give us a valuable glimpse into what youth think about the days and years ahead. A central mission of today's leaders should be to enable America's youth to achieve success, for on the shoulders of their personal success shall ride the success of America. Preparing youth today for the future may be the most strategically vital role for leaders and for us all.

Today's youth are tomorrow's workers, voters, consumers, and teachers. They are the leaders and architects of the next America—hopefully a productive, secure, and strong nation. A Future-Ready na-tion is one prepared to succeed. We had best listen to our youth, helping them not just to dream but enabling them to embrace the suc-cess that this survey reveals they want. Only then will we be building a better nation for today's youth to inhabit in the future.

## Lost Wisdom: The Boomers Retire

More than seventy-six million baby boomers will retire over the next twenty years. They will take with them the collective wisdom of a gen-eration. Can the future survive without the boomers' talent, wisdom, and insight? This is a contributing factor to the crisis awaiting most organizations—the loss of wisdom. Also at risk is the amazing re-siliency that the boomers incubated, shaped, and then brought into the culture. These are largely overlooked future challenges that will have

# WHY EDUCATION MUST CHANGE TO PREPARE THE FUTURE WORKFORCE

**1.** The current education system has failed to complete its most vital and strategic mandate: preparing the workforce for the future.

**2.** Education does not have the leadership, guts, or vision to reinvent itself.

**3.** Most schools, kindergarten through college, are not in sync with changes in the marketplace—more competitive, more complex, more global, more innovation-driven.

**4.** Without educational change, more companies will outsource to find skilled talent offshore, creating unemployment in the U.S.

**5.** Teachers are not the problem. Pay teachers double and retrain them for the Innovation Economy. Measure their performance, hire the best, and fire the slackers.

**6.** Political leaders have lacked the courage to create a Future-Ready national innovation curriculum: more science, more innovation, more high-tech, a more global outlook, more entrepreneurial skills.

**7.** We are teaching kids about the past. We need to teach kids about the future. How to survive in the Extreme Future.

major implications, some quite devastating, for organizations that fail to anticipate them.

Without a serious commitment to using technology and crafting mentor programs to extract and pass along the knowledge of the boomers, significant amounts of critical knowledge may be lost and unrecoverable. We encountered a similar situation around the Y2K computer scare. Though the worst-case scenarios never materialized, it is notable that during the months preceding the end of 1999 it was difficult to find older tech workers who had the specific knowledge necessary to fix the older systems that operated with "lost languages." Many companies struggled to find the right people with the right expertise. In the end, we got off easy; no disaster materialized. That was because we prepared so well. Fear is a beautiful motivator for dealing with change.

This challenge of the changing workforce will not happen by one well-publicized date, so we will not be able to plan with the precision of Y2K. It will simmer, evolve, and then sputter into reality just when we need those people the most. They will not be there. Without advance planning, their absence will restrict our ability to compete for that next contract, meet that next project deadline, provide service to that next customer, or train employees for that next skill.

The loss of the boomers will pose other, more complex challenges. In the decades to come, companies and individuals will be dependent on more elaborate life-sustaining systems that will control

---

*HEADLINES FROM THE FUTURE: 2030*

**Internet Broadcasts Boomer Advice**

---

security, pollution, electricity, transportation, communications, and health care. The designs of those systems will date back to boomer days, and when the boomer engineers retire, they will take that knowledge with them. We are beginning to see the early warnings of this future in which insights about leadership, marketing, and product development, among other business essentials, may be lost as new generations come forward to take their roles as leaders.

We analyzed this trend closely in one company. An inventor had tried to pass along the secrets of the business, in textile research and chemicals, to the next generation. There was too much information to communicate, however, and too little time. This experience will be repeated countless times unless awareness of the issue increases quickly. Presently, necessary proper preparation for transitions in companies, where aging boomers will be required to codify, communicate, and share their wisdom, is just not happening at the rate that is needed to pass the knowledge on to the next generation.

Technology can help to supplement this knowledge-transfer process. The development of a data library where video and multimedia can be used to capture, store, preserve, and then distribute knowledge on-demand has been used effectively. The problem is that most companies are not looking far enough ahead with an eye toward confronting the problem—becoming Future-Ready by capturing knowledge for educating future talent. Too often, the expertise of talented managers is wasted by not being captured.

This aspect of the workforce, though not disappearing, will certainly become a faint memory by 2030. What will become of the boomers' wisdom, wisdom that defined an era, when they are gone? This could be a hidden asset, a secret resource today, if captured and shared. It could be an enabler, a wisdom enabler of the future, for many other workers and organizations alike. Or, if ignored, it could be a future-killer for many businesses.

# TOP JOBS BY 2015

- Neuro-Medical Techs.
- Person Protectors: Personal Security Techs.
- Organ Cloners.
- Biofuture Therapists.
- Quantum Scientists.
- Real-Time Business Executives.
- Online Consumer-Marketing Wizards.
- Health Enhancement Therapists.
- Cancer Enablers.

## Two Workforce Futures

Each of the following scenarios could happen. Significant changes will occur in the decade ahead. There are some constants, though, that will shape the future: population size, fertility levels, geographic location of people, and mobility of talent. Having stated this, there are offsets to these trends that could change the entire equation.

For instance, the mobility of talent will be an important factor to offset the dearth of people being born in Africa or Latin America who can migrate to more economically opportune areas of the world, assuming the immigration doors are open. Some nations might turn them away, while others will welcome them in droves. Japan, for example, is not as open to immigration as the United States. The Japanese, rather than opening their society to foreigners, are heavily investing in high technology and robots for a new cybernetic society. This is why the most innovative research in Japan is about replacing people in the future. With foresight, increased immigration could offset dropping fertility rates in the U.S. and Europe.

The mobility of workers, desperate for a more economically sustainable life, will be a key enabler of economies—and the death of some as well. Nations that restrict immigration will falter, perhaps even die. Those that embrace immigrants and retrain and retool them will fare better in a talent-enabled global information economy of the near future.

Some readers might read the above comments to mean that workers need to be physically located at work, under the corporate umbrella. But they miss the point. Just as the corporation of the future will be more global, it will out of necessity need to be more virtual. The corporation of the future will need to be adaptable, flexible, and agile, given the needs of talented human resources. If a corporation exists to perpetuate self-interest in getting workers to adopt and conform to the physical constraints of the enterprise, workers will flee to more attractive shores.

Here, then, are two futures that tell very different stories about how workforce talent may be treated in the twenty-first century.

### The Talent-Centric Future: 2015

**LGA: A Leadership That is Future-Ready** The Talent-Centric future scenario is based on an organization that seeks to build business around global talent pools that can serve specific markets. Imagine a company called LGA, a $15 billion global corporation that values talent and invests in future opportunities based on talent. LGA's Talent-Centric future strategy says that since talent is scarce, we should build sustainable businesses around specific talent that can develop and manage these opportunities.

This guiding philosophy identifies a lucrative market opportunity, in which demand is high, such as producing biosensors for health-care equipment. For instance, LGA might identify undeveloped patents that could be used to start a line of business. The strategy then locates talent; say, in Asia or the U.S., with expertise in mining these patents. Soon this combination of talent, knowledge, and opportunity gets to work developing a new biosensor, a type of computer chip that monitors the performance of medical equipment.

The company then provides investment capital, buys a license, hires more talent, and invests in this business to bring it to a global market. LGA hunts for talent to develop the business, leveraging the intellectual property, the patents. This is regardless of any prior expertise, interest, or so-called core competency in life sciences. It is about finding the best fit between the value of talent and business.

---

# TOP JOBS BY 2020

- Knowledge Management Advisors.
- Nano-Bio Entrepreneurs.
- Artists, Writers, Poets.
- On-Demand Supply-Chain Designers.
- Global Headhunters.

---

LGA's approach is an agile, fast-to-market, highly entrepreneurial strategy that revolves around acquiring the right talent for the right market and the right industry. In the final analysis, this strategy is all about enabling talent to succeed. This is a talent-centric scenario that is a forward-looking and productive way to plan for and exploit new opportunities in a talent-scarce global labor market. The mining of talent and fitting this talent with market opportunity is a winning future strategy.

You can see companies beginning to leverage talent-centric scenarios today in supply chains. Talent-centric scenarios are based on leveraging specific talent for specific, very lean organizational ventures that have a high probability of success because of the people involved. This lean-driven future will become even more popular, profitable and even required as talent becomes scarcer.

## The Expendable Future: 2015

**DSC: A Leadership in Denial** Now let's consider a company we'll call DSC, a global IT services company that has more than $13 billion in sales across financial services, federal, health-care, and retail industries. Led by a capable group of managers, DSC has one key flaw that will lead to its decline.

Although they are quite competent, DSC's managers treat their people based totally on the bottom line. Senior management is focused on putting numbers first, employees and customers second. Although DSC occasionally issues statements filled with platitudes about considering its associates, suppliers, and customers as "family," its actions tell a different story. There is no evidence that DSC cares to build client relationships, develop workers' skills, or prepare customers and employees for the future. With DSC it is all about the immediate bottom line: How much you are earning right now for the company.

Although the strategy might satisfy Wall Street for the moment, it has worrisome long-term implications in terms of driving away talent and eventually customers. As a result, the forecast for DSC is not promising. Clients have begun to see that the best talent can write its own ticket and does not need to stay at the firm. In fact, one client has happily hired away DSC managers, who were more than willing to go. Competitors in the IT services industry, more committed to Future-Readiness and more willing to experiment with flexible work styles, have already cherry-picked some of the best executives and managers from DSC.

DSC is creating its future today by its managers' actions, investments, and values. Already, the company is struggling to keep up with customer demands. Though outsourcing has taken some pressure off the firm, a continual brain drain makes it vulnerable. In a knowledge-

---

## TOP JOBS BY 2025

- Reality Interactive TV Producers
- Gene Engineers
- Robotic Psychotherapists
- Cyjacks: Antihackers
- Personal Privacy Advisors
- Personal Identity Finders

intensive industry where thought-leaders drive the business, talented people mean everything. Or should. As we move into the future, companies like DSC that do not understand the changing workforce will not make the cut.

You can see this model alive and well in some organizations that believe there will always be someone to fill the boots of those who cannot cut it. This is the attitude of the dinosaur organization. This is a future that is based on a short-term naïveté that there will always be job applicants, that talent is always abundant. This illusion of abundance will lead to the inability of an organization to grow and develop new talent, and it will eventually spell disaster.

## A Self-Fulfilling Destiny

The two scenarios presented here are self-fulfilling destinies for companies that prepare for the emerging changes in the workforce or remain in denial and ignore the future. The changes that I have identified here will require organizations to change strategy in how they attract, retain, and manage their most important resource—people.

Forecasts we have conducted at the Institute for Global Futures point to the disturbing lack of Future-Readiness of many companies in their ability to prepare for the future workforce. They are either too focused on the here and now, the short-term myopia that this entire book is describing and decrying, or they don't have the right visionary leadership in place to effectively prepare for the changes that are coming. The attitude can be summed up: "When it happens, we will deal with it." Or, "Our shareholders need results this quarter, not in two or three years." If leaders don't embrace more future-focused strategies, they will fail to avoid the real risks of the twenty-first-century talent wars. Talented people are the essential force of the successful organization—today and tomorrow. Smart leaders understand this emerging crisis.

Short-term thinking is a typical reaction to change even in the face of mounds of data. Sometimes this is an acceptable reaction. The problem is that the war for talent will be waged at a time when there will be fewer workers to choose from, and that means the challenge will not be successfully met by everyone.

One way or another, the future workforce will be a game-changer for business. This is not just the traditional challenge of having the right talent. With the talent pool shrinking in size and changing in nature, a crisis is brewing that will only worsen over time.

# TOP JOBS BY 2030

- Space Market Planners
- Climate-Change Forecasters
- Solar-Fuel Developers
- Holographic-Game Developers
- Poets
- Customer Knowledge Mining Specialists
- Antiterrorism Techs
- Neuro-Marketing Managers
- Hydrogen Marketing Managers
- Renewable Energy Entrepreneurs
- Real-Time Supply-Chain Designers
- Nano-Manufacturing Agents
- Health Performance Enhancers

## Putting People First

The ability or inability to effectively plan for the future—a future of a changed workforce—will alter the competitive landscape of global business. Those who see this coming today, who are investing in Future-Readiness, will establish a competitive advantage. Those who don't will not build sustainable organizations.

Dealing with these massive workforce changes will be a decisive factor in surviving and prospering in the Extreme Future. Older workers, fewer workers, and more immigrants, women, and ethnic employees will require a different way to think about business. The competition for talent will define the future of nations and organizations. The talent war that is coming—the workforce crisis—will be a disruptive force unless we are well prepared.

The complications of a complex new workforce will determine winners and losers. Preparing for the future workforce and enabling its participants for future success will test the leaders of the twenty-first century. When you think about the changes forecast in this book, it should become immediately apparent that having the right people with the right innovation skills will be a critical survival factor in the Extreme Future. Leaders and organizations that understand this essential trend will best navigate the challenges of the future.

# CHAPTER 5

# Outliving the Future: Longevity Medicine

## Living Longer, Better

If you could live an extra fifty years in near-perfect health, would you want to? Of course, you say. How much would you pay to live an extra twenty-five years with the vitality of a twenty-five-year-old? $25,000? What about $100,000? Are you willing to buy a health-enhancement insurance policy that gives you the right to medically enhance yourself at a certain date? You're intrigued, right? Well, industry is listening, hungry to tap into a market of billions of consumers eager to enhance their health and extend their lives. This is the beginning of Longevity Medicine, and it will change everything.

We will soon be offered vast new choices in health and medicine that we can hardly imagine today. Longevity Medicine will affect who gets the job, who gets the girl, and who gets to live—and for how long. The individual's right to enhancement will become a hotly contested social and ethical issue in the future.

The largest global marketplace in the near future will be shaped by Longevity Medicine, offering a variety of anti-aging and health-enhancement products. Everyone who wants to live longer—and can afford it—will be able to stay healthy. In some nations, the state will pay; in others, consumers will pay.

The ability to extend healthy life will have earthshaking

# THE TOP TEN
# LONGEVITY TRENDS

**1.** Within ten years, humans routinely living beyond one hundred will be an accepted reality.

**2.** Longevity Medicine will postpone aging and promote health, enabling people to be more active, more productive, and enjoy longer lives.

**3.** Health-enhancement rights, fueled by the wealth of aging baby boomers and the fusion of nano, bio, IT, and neuro innovations, will become a fierce social issue.

**4.** Mapping personal DNA profiles, and linking that knowledge to prevent illness, will radically change medicine, making it boldly predictive.

**5.** Health enhancement via biotech, stem cells, and genomic drugs will enhance human intelligence.

**6.** Supercomputers, artificial intelligence, and advanced medical information technology will usher in a new era that will empower doctors to extend the quality of life.

**7.** Personalized DNA diets will greatly enable longevity as people learn which foods enhance their health and prevent illness.

**8.** Life-extension treatments, from genetic vaccines and designer DNA "surgery" to smart drugs and neuro-medical devices, will augment health, improving intelligence, and maximizing beauty.

**9.** Cognitive brain-science breakthroughs will protect the aging mind, refreshing vital memories, improving physical agility, and promoting human performance enhancement.

**10.** The evolutionary transformation of human beings, via emerging breakthroughs in Longevity Medicine, will provide vast new choices of an astounding and alarming nature for individuals and society.

societal, political, financial, environmental, and individual consequences. Destinies and futures will be enhanced and broken. Careers and relationships will be shaped and chosen. Longevity Medicine is not just about the future of health care; it is about a personal and social transformation in culture that will define how individuals will live, work, and interact. Laws may be passed to grant enhancement rights to citizens.

Not all of the choices enabled by Longevity Medicine will seem fair, morally right, or even desirous by all people. There are dangerous decisions ahead that will raise fundamental questions about the nature of humanity and human evolution. Every domain of civilization will be affected, none more than that of the individual.

## The End of Primitive Medicine

There is nothing wrong with medicine today, except that it doesn't have the knowledge and tools to do the job. Medicine as we know it is woefully unprepared to deal with its primary charge of eliminating disease. We bombard cancer, attempting to kill it with radiation. Antibiotics mount the assault on infections. We surgically carve out diseased tissue as a routine practice. An amazing array of drugs have more side effects than the illnesses or problems they were designed to address.

Medicine is only performing at its current level of discovery. The truth is that what we call modern medicine is quite primitive and can accomplish only so much until we invent new tools. This is not a slam on medicine but an observation about where medicine is today, how it will change, and why it must change. Doctors are waiting for the next generation of innovation tools that will enable them to do more to heal, restore, and prevent disease.

Most disease begins at the atomic level, where subtle interactions between DNA, genes, the environment, and other parts of the body and mind interact. We don't yet have the tools in modern medicine to see and understand this atomic level of the human body. By the time disease happens, we are way downstream in the organs and tissues. This is a frustrating fact. By the time you feel a lump in your breast, experience pain, or notice something is wrong, disease has already moved into the organs or tissue. What if we could look into human atoms and DNA to identify the potential triggers that form disease? What if we could turn off those disease-causing triggers? The result, increased health, would save billions of dollars and enhance the quality of human existence. U.S. health care costs $2 trillion. This is larger than the GDP of China. Today's U.S. health care costs too much.

There is a new medicine emerging born of the fusion of biotechnology, information technology, nanotechnology, and cognitive science. Together, these fields—the convergent technologies I review in this book—will provide the tools needed to "see" and heal at the atomic level. That's what's next.

This may sound like a tall order, but we are making tremendous progress in that direction. Remember, we learned to decode the human genome only over the past few years. In a sense, medicine is about to emerge from the equivalent of the Middle Ages into the glory of the Renaissance.

In the Extreme Future, speculation about disease and treatment will give way to a more precise, predictive, and health-enhancing type of medicine: Longevity Medicine. Medicine that has, at its core, an ability to peer into the genomic map of a specific individual, from birth to death. Doctors will have an unparalleled diagnostic tool: a person's own DNA. The next stage will include engineered disease prevention, health promotion, and life extension.

It is entirely possible that most children alive today will live to see the dawn of the twenty-second century. Medicine's mandate is to heal, improve people's health, and yes, extend life. Medicine is primed today for tomorrow's longevity and enhancement. It is inevitable. Modern medicine is only 150 years old. If you look at the time line of medicine, we are only a few inches away from doctors offering patients wooden paddles to bite down on as the only palliative for pain.

# THE DANCE OF THE TELOMERES: AN AGE CLOCK

Might there be a mechanism in the human genome that controls aging? A type of genetic clock that determines how long you live until your body breaks down and you die? Telomeres—specialized nucleoprotein complexes found on the ends of chromosomes—are such a mechanism. If we could better understand them, we might be able to manipulate our aging clock.

# Fountains of Youth

If you take the average life span throughout human history, it would be about eighteen. Socrates was brilliant and dead before thirty-five. Hannibal led armies at twenty-two. Due to immense progress in public health, medicines, and the war on infectious diseases, humans are living longer. Today we are living longer than any humans have lived on the planet, but this life extension is just the beginning. There is no real end in sight.

The dream of longer life is powerfully seductive. From the legendary quest of Gilgamesh, to Ponce de Leon's search for the Fountain of Youth, to our modern-day bio-alchemists tinkering with the human genome and stem cells, the pursuit of immortality is ancient and enduring. The desire for longer life is embedded in the social DNA of humanity and expressed in countless myths and legends. The pantheons of gods and goddesses were immortal beings, and that was the point: Immortality was an attribute of the gods, yearned for yet unattainable by humans. Humans never stopped trying, though, and now medicine is starting to deliver what the storytellers could only dream about.

In the decade to come, medicine will be revolutionized. The convergence of pharma, biotech, and nanotech industries will form the biggest global marketplace with one underlying theme: life extension for sale. Botox today will lead to gene-replacement therapy tomorrow. Face-lifts today, nano-engineering stem cells for babylike, wrinkle-free skin tomorrow. Prosthetic titanium hips today, growing new organs tomorrow. Even memories will be for sale, with superagility and enhanced intelligence thrown in for good measure.

The seeds of this trend are firmly in place today. Longevity scientists that I have met are unlocking the secrets of age embedded in our genes, and as organ-replacement and stem-cell research frontiers are being crossed, I forecast that the era of longer living, beyond one hundred years of age, will become common within ten years and be considered a birthright by 2025, due to Longevity Medicine. The individual's rights to be enhanced—genetically, physically, cognitively—will become a complicated social issue in democratic societies. Success may be determined by enhancement features like beauty, intelligence, or skill.

These breakthroughs will transform markets, lifestyles, and culture.

Are you ready to be enhanced? If not, you may not be able to compete in the future. This is forbidden fruit that is too seductive not to be tasted. The research has already started. Billions are already invested. Breakthroughs are coming in the Extreme Future.

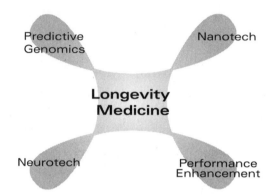

## Medicine 2020

I got my first hint about the future of medicine and health care when I was still a boy, back in 1963. My grandfather, George, handed me a plastic tube made out of white, fine, almost weightless material. Similar tubes had been implanted in his legs by the legendary cardiovascular surgeon, Dr. Michael DeBakey. They were DACRON arteries, one of DeBakey's many innovations, and they were necessary for my grandfather because of the damage he had done to his body from smoking for fifty years. It made an impression; I don't smoke, and I keep a close watch on the latest life-altering medical innovations.

The achievements of DeBakey and other medical pioneers of the past half-century were truly life-altering, but they will pale in comparison with what is to come. What will medicine and health care look like in twenty-five years? The following is a list of key characteristics that will revolutionize this practice, making it unrecognizable to the medicine we know today. Medicine in 2020 will be

- **Predictive**—forecasting future health status, predicting disease.

- **Preventive**—stopping or avoiding illness, dysfunction.

- **Restorative**—bringing back functionality such as sight, or restoring memory, health, or mobility.

- **Regenerative**—restoring bones, muscles, organs, and cells.

- **Life-Extending**—lengthening life while maintaining health and productivity.

- **Performance-Enhancing**—developing an individual's full mental and physical potential for realizing maximum healthy performance.

- **Replacing**—providing viable substitutes for a person's body or mind in order to restore healthy functionality.

- **Augmenting**—enhancing special-purpose mental or physical functions, some may be superhuman.

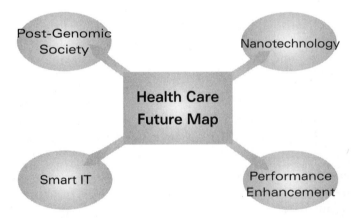

## Be a Tiger

In a culture where we are accustomed to paying to enhance ourselves through science, where we straighten our teeth with braces, fix our eyesight with contacts and glasses, and augment our beauty and features with plastic surgery, would we want to enhance ourselves further by living longer and becoming smarter, stronger, and faster? The answer is that we will, and the baby boomers will lead society down the slippery slope toward human health enhancement. We are already on our way.

Ads show Tiger Woods proudly claim that his eyesight is better than 20/20, due to this company's enhanced eye surgery technique.

The stem-cell and therapeutic-cloning debates are just the beginning of the breakthroughs that are coming. With Alzheimer's striking one in three men over the age of seventy, with cancer and cardiovascular disease cutting people's lives short, why would we not want to enhance ourselves? First we will heal, then we will enhance. Get ready.

# FUTURE LONGEVITY MEDICINE INNOVATIONS TO WATCH FOR

- Personalized DNA tests, which will tell stories about individuals' unique genomic profiles and also reveal future disease risks.

- Nanotechnology, the manipulation of matter at the atomic level, introducing a new generation of very small medical devices, materials, and procedures for prevention and health enhancement.

- Stem cells that can be used for healing disease, growing organs, and rebuilding human beings.

- Genomic foods that consider the unique DNA of an individual and what is best for that person to eat for optimal health.

- Medical devices that have intelligent functions to turn on or off genes related to desired or unwanted behaviors, diseases, or functions.

- Human-enhancement engineering, which will provide surgery to augment intelligence, memory, appearance, or performance.

- Health-enhancement therapies, from gene vaccines and human performance to neuroceutical augmentation.

- Breakthroughs in robotics that will create mobile systems to augment human movement.

- Cognitive replacements for dysfunctional brains.

- Access to vast supercomputers to map the next generation of biotech drugs to unlock complex diseases such as cancer, AIDS, and SARS.

Longevity Medicine will make Botox treatments seem primitive. Rather than face blindness, deafness, or a bedridden lifestyle, who wouldn't choose sight, hearing, or the active freedom of mobility? A multibillion-dollar market will emerge.

Before we move forward, though, it is essential to recognize that personal choice, freedom of expression, and individual rights should be considered important features in this emerging future forecast. We should tread carefully toward this future, a future in which ethical concerns, values, and laws may be cast aside too quickly. We must be aware of the choices, but also be careful to do no harm—as Hippocrates, the father of medicine, instructed us. Governments may seek to control individual's rights to enhance themselves, to better their future. We should carefully guard against any use of medicine to restrict personal liberty.

## Life Extension

I charted the future of Longevity Medicine, where the promise of life extension has slowly become an undercurrent of national health policy. The stem-cell referendum passed in California for $7 billion was one piece of evidence; other, larger investments from biotech to nanotech are charting the future of life extension.

Just as the seventy-six million baby boomers, those born between 1946 and 1964, have redefined every aspect of culture, from media to technology to sports, so too will the boomers redefine health care, making it about life extension and human enhancement so they can extend their power, influence, and themselves into the future by living longer and healthier. This is a critical motivation for the most affluent demographic group on the planet. What appears at first to be a narcissistic desire for survival will actually set into motion a (mostly) constructive future.

If you consider this life extension trend in context with the need for society to keep the highly skilled boomers employed in the future workforce longer, you begin to see the larger social issues at play. Longevity medicine will lead not just to longer lives, but to longer, more productive workers. In a future at risk of depopulation due to lower birth rates, longevity medicine, I forecast, will become a much-needed social entitlement.

I have looked out into the near future of anti-aging and human performance enhancement with leading scientists, physicists, physicians, engineers, and policy analysts. I realized that the convergence of population changes—the aging baby boomers combined with innovations in life science—will completely transform medicine in the near future.

This represents the most far-reaching forecast on the planet about the future of humanity, not just the future of health care. This is certainly an Extreme Future, but one that is plausible, even desirable to many. The conditions are in place today for a radical change in the way we think about health. The longevity lifestyle marketplace, and its impact on society, will define the Extreme Future.

As we move forward, I will explore the three trends in human performance enhancement—Therapeutic, Augmentation, and Designed Evolution.

## Therapeutic Enhancement Trend: Fixing What's Broken

Therapeutic refers to the enhancement of human performance to restore normal human capabilities to the disabled or dysfunctional. Conditions resulting from disease, birth defects, or accidents would fall into this category. This domain has already emerged and will be accelerated by the coming nano-bio-IT-neurotech convergence. Examples of therapeutic enhancements include

- Restoring Sight
- Restoring Hearing
- Prosthetics for Limbs
- Genetic Vaccines
- Depression Management
- Personalized Medicine
- Organ Cloning
- Memory Restoration
- Mobility Restoration

# Augmentation Trend:
# Expanding Possibilities

Augmentation refers to the development of human performance to enhanced levels. Anyone who is a candidate for therapeutic human performance enhancement will want augmentation as well. Augmentation will begin to appear in the next five to eight years. The augmentation of cognitive, physical, and other capabilities could have a broad degree of customization based on career, age, and interests. Examples, and their potential target consumers/patients, include

- Enhanced memory; total recall (everyone).
- Infrared night vision (security workers).
- Wide-spectrum hearing (musicians).
- Long-range vision (soldiers).
- Specialized tool augmentation and cybernetics (doctors, engineers, and artists).
- Embedded wireless communications (knowledge workers).
- High-velocity robotic limbs (athletes).
- On-demand strength augmentation (construction workers).
- Cognitive multitasking (project managers).
- Personal genomic-optimized analysis (medical techs).
- Multimedia cognitive high-capacity storage (poets, inventors).
- Real-time visual and voice-data mining, search, and discovery (media, game designers).

# Designed Evolution Trend:
# Radical Change

Designed Evolution refers to human enhancements involving the human genome that we might choose to make prior to conception, in vitro, or after birth. This could include in vitro enhancement of memory, intelligence, speed, agility, and certain behavioral and physical attributes. The largest area of Designed Evolution will be the in vitro identification of undesired genes that might be precursors for dysfunction or disease, such as cancer or alcoholism. They could be altered, or even eliminated. Of course, choosing more attractive physical attributes, such as beauty, or enhancing the "intelligence gene," might be desirable as well. Although this domain of human enhancement is eight to fifteen years away, decisions and choices will be made in the near future that will set the stage for its acceptance or rejection. Tough choices will drive social debate surrounding the issues.

Different cultures will choose different paths, some in direct conflict with their citizens and other cultures. Ideology, politics, and religion will collide with science as experiments driven by the brazen and bold, unfettered by social responsibilities and ethics, will create radical geopolitical risks. Examples include

- Longevity enhancement.

- Optimized immuno-defense.

- Coevolutionary man/machine cyborgs.

- Organ engineering.

- Stem-cell, total-body, and mind rejuvenation.

- Anti-atrophy muscles that resist degeneration.

- Bones that replenish through self-assembly.

- Super agility and speed.

- Intracellular disease scavengers that search and destroy on demand.

- Elimination of unwanted genes that trigger undesirable behavior.

# Social Implications:
# Rights and Revolutions

As people live not just longer, but with new replenished capacities and even higher performance, the world we live in will change in dramatic ways. Think about this for a moment. How different would your life be if you believed you had not just sixty or seventy years to live with diminishing capacity in old age, but 125 years, with the vitality of a much younger person along with the wisdom of experience? This is just one way to think about the how Longevity Medicine might affect you.

Perhaps you will be enhanced, or choose enhancements that will make you more robust, more beautiful, more intelligent, more physically agile later in life than you were when you were younger. How different your life will be! How about five careers? Maybe you can live multiple lives with more risk and adventure. Who wouldn't want to live many lifetimes in one? You might have enough time to contribute new solutions to overcome the planet's woes. There are fundamental changes coming in the Extreme Future, and they start with extending our lives. I forecast that enhancement rights will become a political agenda as common as the rights to education, work, or freedom.

Now, not everyone will choose to live longer or be able to afford every health enhancement that the Longevity Medicine marketplace will offer. Some people will never give up their disease-creating lifestyles and will demand to be restored later in life. It's like flossing your teeth. Everyone knows it helps keep teeth in good health later in

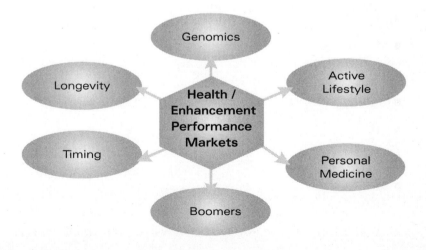

life, but relatively few individuals are willing to make the commitment today. The lazy consumer will fuel future innovations that will restore or replace healthy organs or functions like memory and mobility. Just as Prozac reframes anxiety and Viagra alters sexual relationships, there are new "solutions" coming. The bio-pharma industry will come running to our rescue with products, soon—for a price, of course. Or will employers and governments pay to enhance health and human performance as it serves their interests? Might advertisers pay to enhance consumers to live longer and, of course, buy more? Yes.

## The Ethics of Life Extension

I'm not endorsing this market, any more than I'm advocating other disruptive trends that await in the Extreme Future. My job is to inform, provoke, and stimulate your thinking about what trends are coming fast and how they may influence you and our world. Life extension is one example of a mixed bag of sorts that will challenge traditional values and introduce some new ones into society.

Just as human cloning has been rejected in many countries, there should be debates on what life extension means and what will and will not be made available. There are vital ethical concerns that many will and should debate. We must above all protect the integrity of the humanity from forces that might seek to destabilize it. We must protect individual rights and liberties from governments that may seek to use future medicine to further social repression. We want to tread carefully, with ethical science, global stewardship, and social welfare in mind as we navigate the new domains that life extension may bring. Radical opportunities and risks will emerge.

There are trends emerging in the current debate about stem-cell usage and therapeutic cloning that are instructive. Outside the United States, stem-cell research is proceeding unfettered. But for the first time in U.S. history, a fundamentally new technology with clear value for human health and medicine has been bushwhacked by politics. In light of the globalization of science, the proliferation of Power Tools such as nano-bio-IT-neuro, no technology can be restricted for very long if there are clear and certain benefits for enhancing human health and if a market exists for its products. Stem cells are an indication of consumer demand for human enhancement that will play an important role in the emergence of a new global market that no government will be able to fully control.

The easy passage of California's $7 billion stem-cell bond was a direct response to the federal government placing restrictions on stem-cell funding. Prepare for more of this type of reaction from consumers/voters who want to live longer, healthier lives in the twenty-first century.

By the same token, therapeutic cloning for organ replacement will become a reality in the United States, even if you're forced to acquire your organ offshore. Certainly, you will not allow your wife, son, or father to die because you cannot get the organ you need in the U.S. when it is available in Europe or Asia. More than 60,000 Americans will die this year from not having the organ they need. That will not happen in the Extreme Future.

# SEVEN REASONS LONGEVITY MEDICINE WILL TRANSFORM HUMANITY

**1. Personal Liberty.** Predictive forecasts will provide individuals with customized health plans so they can choose health enhancement and a longer life.

**2. Desire.** People have always wanted to live longer, taking control over their destiny, cheating death if they can.

**3. Money.** A large concentration of baby-boomer wealth will be invested in what most boomers want: to live longer, healthier, and more active lives.

**4. Productivity.** As birth rates drop, nations and employers will come to support longevity of their citizens and workers to preserve a productive population.

**5. Social Investment.** Health-care costs for healthy people are lower than they are for the sick, reducing the burden on government and individuals.

**6. Genomics.** The science of the human genome will make it possible to understand the genetic origin of disease and to take action to extend life.

**7. Healing Tech.** A host of new restoration therapies, using stem cells, genetic vaccines, nanotechnology, and advanced medical devices will be deployed to extend life.

As Longevity Medicine and human enhancement become reality, there will be an emergence of new ethical codes and models, not to mention a new sense of entitlement to the wonders that await. Consider, for instance, what might be contained in a "Global Human Rights to Enhancement Creed":

- We strive to enhance our quality of life.

- We believe in the rights of the individual to freely choose enhancement.

- We believe in the democracy of science.

- We desire to enhance our physical performance.

- We desire to enhance our intelligence.

- We desire to extend our healthy life to the maximum years possible.

- We seek to develop our full human potential.

- We desire to positively contribute to society.

- We desire to eliminate disease.

- We choose to coevolve with innovation.

## Inventors of Tomorrow

The inventors of tomorrow will redefine human existence. With access to vast new Power Tools they can, for the first time, ask questions that would have seemed absurd a few years ago. Their tool chest is growing by the minute, including

- **Stem cells.** Universal cells that can be turned into organs and muscles, and cure disease.

- **In-silico DNA computer models.** Programs that design potential drugs, devices, or solutions.

- **Supercomputers.** Powerful devices that map hidden proteins and DNA interactions at almost-human brain speed.

- **AFM** (Atomic Force Microscopy). Microscopes that can peer into the nanoscale to better understand DNA and the human body.

- **Nanowires.** Nano materials that can be programmed to self-assemble.

- **Internet 2.** The next Net for research and health-care collaboration.

## You Are What You Eat: Nutra Genomics

Are there foods that could promote your health, even protect you from disease? Perhaps. A new innovative science of nutra genomics is being researched with much early-stage potential. The matching of our personal DNA with diet will play an important role in enhancing health and longevity. Even now, studies have shown that certain men in Greece, who were unable to lose weight after all types of diets, enjoyed immediate results after doctors came to understand their DNA profiles.

Can it be as simple as the replacement of certain food groups and the elimination of others to achieve a desired health outcome? The Greek study showed that the men, when introduced to more potatoes and onions, lost weight. Not because this is a new diet rage, but because the diet was customized based on their DNA profiles. It is possible that we could understand diet differently, as food is medicine and medicine is changing to extend life. This may alter worldwide food production and marketing overnight, as people want to know how their biochemical individuality may require them to partake in some foods, and avoid others, to be healthy.

Though early research on red wine, for example, shows promise for extending life, we don't actually understand this yet. In the near future, genomic matching to determine our diet might point the way to living a longer life. Certainly this relationship is not new, but a new understanding of specific foods, genomic foods that fit our biochemical individuality, could open up a new era in health. This development will play an important role in the future of Longevity Medicine.

## Stem-Cell Boogie

In a fundamental way, stem cells are the master builder cells that can fix you when you are broken. At least that is the potential. More so than many of the innovations reported in this book, stem cells may hold the most promise to heal. Stem cells will protect life, accelerate healing, and extend life for individuals like your wife, mother, or yourself. Stem-cell research is progressing, but so far has more potential than a real tool kit. This will change very soon.

Stem cells have been used to date to grow new bone and tissue, and to heal certain types of cancer. If you are interested in life extension, then you should be interested in stem cells. I estimate a market of about two billion consumers. We will look back from 2020 and wonder why we did not invest in this fantastic new science sooner, I forecast.

## The Race for the Future

There is a stem-cell race going on—mostly offshore in places like China, Singapore, and Europe—that indicates the commitment of nations, corporations, and universities that are investing billions to beat the Americans. What is the race? It is the race to introduce the first organs, tissues, and bones made from stem cells to a hungry global market—a $5 trillion opportunity.

There are numerous multibillion-dollar efforts being spent on inventing the future of Longevity Medicine. Taiwan has invested in more than a hundred companies doing work in nano-bio-IT. Singapore's $5 billion is only the beginning in stem-cell research. Even Canada, seeing America drop the ball by restricting government-funded stem-cell research, is moving fast to outcompete the Yanks.

Stem cells represent a fascinating look at billions being invested for the first time—mostly offshore, but not in the U.S. There is a new innovation economy brewing. Up until the California stem-cell referendum passed, the U.S. had its first-ever brain drain. That's where talented, even genius-level scientists were leaving the U.S. for locations in Canada, Europe, and Asia to conduct stem-cell research. This was the first time the U.S. had ever suffered from being anti-innovation in its refusal to fund a fundamental new scientific endeavor. The U.S. cannot be competitive in the future without reinvesting in basic science innovations like stem cells today.

## U.S. Falling Behind

With most Ph.D.'s getting educated here in the sciences and then moving offshore to work, the stem-cell fiasco, if repeated in other areas of innovation, will cripple the competitive advantage of the U.S. Americans cannot afford for this to happen. Not now, not ever. This is not the way to protect national security or a strong economy. When it comes to the market for health-enhancement products and services, there is little doubt that it will cater to a global consumer. The products based on stem cells are close but not 100 percent here. As billions of dollars more are invested worldwide, products will get closer to market.

Need that new kidney by Christmas? How about those memory cells? Don't replace the hip, grow a new one. Stem cell–enabled products will heal faster, prevent longer, and extend the health and life of millions once innovations move out of the labs. Nothing drives innovation more than the market economy of billions of consumers. Even if you have to fly to Rio or Hong Kong for that stem-cell treatment, it may be worth it to those who want to live free of pain, or walk again, or see their cancer retreat.

A quiet collection of patients are sharing information and contacts

---

# DISEASES STEM CELLS COULD BENEFIT BY 2010

- Heart disease, to restore hearts.
- Nerve disease, to grow new nerves.
- Cancer, to restore healthy cell growth.
- Immunity diseases, to provide protections against disease.

about offshore stem-cell treatment centers in China, Brazil, and Thailand. Some of the treatments for increasing mobility and restoring nerve cells are dramatic in their outcomes. Reports we have followed indicate the fast growth of foreign stem-cell centers, where U.S. patients who have not gained access in the U.S. are being treated.

In one closely watched court case, a man sued BlueCross BlueShield and won. His award was treatment by stem cells for his leukemia. He is alive and well today.

## Health History on a Chip

Even before some of the most dramatic advances of Longevity Medicine, consumers/patients will soon enjoy numerous innovations that will enhance their health. For instance, critical lifesaving information delivered when we need it and where we need it, will soon be common with small, robust storage devices—the next generation of the "health chip." Each of us will soon carry a personal health record "smart card" that contains the relevant data about our health history on a tiny chip. These cards will include our entire health record, including the drugs we've taken, operations we've had, medicines we're allergic to, and diseases or conditions we've suffered. The next stage of health chips may be embedded in our skin. Upgrades via the wireless web will keep our personal health history current.

---

# WHAT STEM-CELL TREATMENTS MAY OFFER BY 2030

- New organs, including hearts and lungs.
- New bone growth for legs, arms, and backs.
- New sensory functions and optic nerves to restore eyesight.
- New cancer treatments.
- New nerves to heal muscles and to restore movement.
- New cells to offset the aging brain.

Such advances in medical information, facilitated by the convergence of health care, computers, and networks, will have a comprehensive impact on consumer health. They may prevent the more than 100,000 mistakes leading to deaths that the U.S. health-care system makes each year. This is a serious step in the right direction, one in which all of your personal health info would be available on demand, anywhere you go.

Looking a bit farther down the road, our genomic profiles will eventually be catalogued on our digital file. This information, critically important to our health, may be even more essential over time as new drugs and interventions born from unlocking the human genome will steadily become available after 2015. These smart cards, hooked into the Net, can quickly alert us to new research on a mutant genetic trait we've inherited, or to a new "smart drug" that can help cure memory lapses we've recorded.

Our health card (eventually even a chip embedded in our bodies), acts as a tiny computer, another gateway to the Net, searching out information for our specific needs, and alerting the hospital or specialist when we need their services. It watches our health statistics and knows what we need, and when. Our health chip might one day save our life.

In the new era of Longevity Medicine, information access—both personal and updates on the latest discoveries—will be essential to living longer and healthier. Longevity Medicine will continually be upgraded, refined, personalized, and improved with time. Consider how we will be able to deliver individual health-care solutions anywhere, at any time of day, when all physicians, hospitals, HMOs, and clinics are connected to the same online network. We'll call it the "Global Health-Net." Savvy companies will anticipate that and get ahead of the competition by matching specific patient needs with information resources available via the Net.

Much of the job of extending life and enhancing health will be about getting the right information to the right people in the right time frame to create a result.

## Future Longevity Devices

The makers of medical devices are also gearing up for the future markets of the twenty-first century, with products to help people cope with disease and dysfunction. New surgically implanted devices, similar to the way a pacemaker works to keep the heart beating normally, are being developed to remedy the symptoms of epilepsy, Parkinson's, tremors, chronic pain, incontinence, and sleep apnea. Memory enhancement is next.

But medical devices that are implants may be where the action is in the future. Devices, injected microprocessors, bio-implants made from organic materials, and even DNA implants will be a thriving industry. Neuro implants will be used to enhance memory for Alzheimer's patients, replace limbs, retrofit nerves, and replace organs such as kidneys or eyes. Implants will also be used to enhance human performance. Neuro devices to enhance life will be quickly adopted, even faster than pharmaceuticals.

## Robo-Surgery, Anyone?

High-speed network communications will allow physicians around the world to do more than consult routinely with each other. Surgeons

# FUTURE LONGEVITY MED-DEVICE APPLICATIONS

- Brain devices for enhancing memory and intelligence— including new languages and skills.

- Devices to enhance, regulate, and augment heart functions.

- Titanium and ceramic devices for legs and arms to strengthen them or make them adaptable.

- Stem-cell devices that rebuild and restore organs on demand.

- Bio-devices for replacing eyes, ears, or noses, or enhancing sight, sound, smell, or taste.

- Devices that "watch" for cancer.

- Injectable DNA genetic devices that will automatically scout and neutralize disease-producing agents.

- Nano devices—100,000 times smaller than the head of a match—that will deliver drugs for procedures on demand from inside patients.

could use robotic techniques to operate on patients remotely. One possible scenario has the surgeon remotely guiding a robotic arm in real time, with the device filtering out any of the surgeon's minor hand tremors.

The benefit of such surgery is twofold: The best surgeons will perform the operations they do best with the assistance of remote robots, and unique and "perfect" operations could be viewed by medical students in different locations as part of their training.

Robotic and robotically assisted surgeries can, in fact, be highly effective, because they can be programmed. Imagine a surgeon at Massachusetts General Hospital's telemedicine center using a virtual-reality environment to "walk through" a complicated organ transplant procedure that will take place the following day in Los Angeles. The surgeon can program his robotic assistant in Los Angeles to carry out the step-by-step operation while he watches in real time on his video monitor.

His colleagues at the University of Southern California are also monitoring the program and are ready to step in physically, if need be, should a problem arise. Bringing in doctors from Harvard and Tokyo University via teleconferencing could add new insight, as needed, for a delicate experimental procedure. Voxel Digital Holography routinely uses data collected by Computed Tomography (CT) and Magnetic Resonance (MR) scanners to produce true three-dimensional images. The life-size, transparent holograms, called Voxgrams, literally extend out in space. Voxgrams enable a physician to interact in, around, and through an image as though it were a real specimen of anatomy, making the programming of an operation a feasible goal.

---

**FUTURE ALERT: 2025**

**Nano-Robo Devices Search
Bloodstream for Cancer Cells**

---

By using such tools, we will also move toward less invasive surgery. Laser Industries, Ltd., and Biosense, Inc., for example, are jointly developing a system for using a catheter-based navigation system to guide laser beams to heart muscles for the relief of angina and coronary artery disease. The system (www.sharplan.com) allows for the delivery of energy to selected sites on the inner side of the heart wall and may do away with the need for 300,000 coronary artery bypasses each year.

Patients will benefit handsomely when telemedicine solutions involving robots, virtual reality, and computer-generated doctors reach the mainstream.

## Cyberdocs

In the United States, medicine over the Net will be pervasive by 2015, and virtual "face-to-face" doctor-patient relationships will exist without the barrier of time and space. Sometimes, however, the doctor may be a computer, or cyberdoc.

Just as we have accepted other human-machine influences, from voice mail to computers, we will come not just to accept, but also to demand and trust, cyberdocs. It is likely that consumers may get more help from an interactive, intelligent computer than a stressed-out human physician. This makes sense especially if there is a life-threatening illness and there is no room for human error.

Humans may no longer monopolize medicine after we develop robotic surgeons that are more precise than their human creators, and cyberdocs that perform routine diagnostics with predictable precision. This will lead to cheaper care available to vastly more people in need. In fact, insurance companies may come to require that robodocs and cyberdocs be used because their precision and reliability are higher than that of humans. The use of robotics or cyberdocs will be a shock to many at first, but so was voice mail and shopping on the Net.

> *HEADLINES FROM THE FUTURE: 2020*
>
> **New Poll Shows**
> **People Prefer Cyberdocs**

## Longevity Empowerment

In the decades ahead, we will demand that our cyberdocs, robodocs, and real docs support a mass-consumer emphasis on preventive medicine—a program of taking care of ourselves through lifestyle management to prevent illness and preserve life. It will spawn the creation of hundreds of new companies in the twenty-first century.

Fitness will continue to grow as a subsegment of the emerging health-enhancement marketplace. One new service that health clubs of the future might offer is "Virtual Health Adventures," which add excitement to exercise. Through a blending of virtual reality, holography, and interactive multimedia, we could be transported to exotic places or adventurous liaisons. One offering could be a realistic dinosaur hunt where we would burn calories and get our heart rate up to a healthy pace in a dramatic escape from a tromping tyrannosaur. A real-time calorie-burning chart could show our progress.

Health insurers will offer virtual cash and prizes for people to slim down, stop smoking, or reduce stress. There will be a variety of incentives for us to stay healthy. If dinosaur hunts are too dusty, we could sign up for a virtual white-water raft trip down the treacherous Bolo, or a climb to the top of Mt. Everest. For something tamer and in the confines of our own homes, there's always software that can bring us tennis lessons in our bedroom with Wimbledon champion Andre Agassi, or a weight-lifting workout with Arnold Schwarzenegger. The possibilities are endless. We'll have to pay to play, but the results will be worth it.

Net companies could match these adventure firms—or other types of service providers—with "bundled" packages for customers who are likely to buy and use these products to take more responsibility for their health. Predictive programs containing advanced artificial-intelligence agents will be a key part of prevention programs. For example, with permission, they will analyze a patient's DNA and accurately compute the probability of a cardiac condition.

## Smart Drugs

If you're still asking for more evidence to convince you that Americans are enhancement-friendly, you don't need to look far.

More than one half of all Americans today are on some type of medication, according to a 2005 study. The Philips Health Index, which my firm, the Institute for Global Futures, worked on with Philips, gave us a deep insight into the health behaviors of Americans. Over a third of those on medication are altering their moods or taking drugs for psychological reasons—stress, anxiety, or depression. We are already enhancing ourselves with drugs. We are a medicated society familiar with using drugs to alter our mental state of being, to help us better cope with life. This data suggests we should take a hard look at what kind of society we are creating.

Over the next ten years, "smart drugs" will include a new class of neuroceuticals, which are mixtures of nutrients, vitamins, and synthesized chemicals. These techno-cocktails will enhance productivity, memory, physical performance, and even entertainment and pleasure. Their growing acceptance may even eliminate street drugs, replacing them with legal pharmaceuticals. This, too, has disturbing consequences. Smart drugs today represent an emerging billion-dollar market, mostly in Europe, and increasingly in Asia and the U.S. The potential of the industry is unlimited, as biotech discovers and creates potent new energy and brain boosters. Once these hybrid drugs are accepted, much as coffee is accepted as a stimulant today, they will shape the way we work, live, and play. Many of the emerging drugs that will be used to fight diseases of aging will also be used to enhance neuro abilities, from smarter minds to sharper memory. Some of us will depend on these drugs to compete in the future workforce.

Part of this trend will inevitably include ways to package pleasure. Antianxiety and antidepressant drugs are just the beginning. The idea of packaged pleasure in a pill will challenge the assumptions we have about leisure, work, and entertainment. Pharma magic in the twenty-first century will necessitate a brand-new look at the influence of drugs on society. Will we need smart drugs to cope, manage, or even understand the future we are creating? Perhaps we have already answered this question.

## Medicating Performance

A notable percentage of people using Prozac—an estimated fifteen to twenty-five percent—do so to enhance their performance. They use it as a smart drug. Wouldn't we all like to eliminate anxiety, work smarter, be more productive, and be more successful? The pharmaceutical companies hear us loud and clear. Better performance through biochemistry will be a multibillion-dollar industry in the stressful, competitive, and chaotic world of tomorrow.

The highly educated and intelligent CEO of a billion-dollar company admitted to me that his choice of recreational drug was Cialis. This sexual enhancement drug works for thirty-six hours and guarantees performance. The CEO is married and his use of Cialis is a personal choice, not a medical response to erectile dysfunction. His decision is a canary in the coal mine of legitimate pleasure pills becoming part of the enhancement culture of America. Professors and researchers I know use drugs prescribed for ADD to create more focus and alertness so they can keep up with their students.

Chemically improving ourselves will become the rage as twenty-first-century smart drugs help to realize new human potential. Slow performance will become abnormal and déclassé. Future techno-brews will do the job more predictably with DNA precision. A recent discovery offers an excellent scenario for illustrating how to market such smart drugs. Supposedly, a component of green tea called ECGC may stop cancer by interfering with the way the disease invades cells and breaks down healthy tissue. An entrepreneur could buy a supply of green tea, isolate the ECGC, and then combine it with other known anticancer substances. The new tablet could be made chewable and marketed as "Cancer Fighter," via the Internet, where it would be targeted to disease-specific groups and potentially avoid regulatory oversight.

Who wouldn't want to take this anticancer cocktail to ward off disease? The $10 billion-a-year vitamin market, fueled by more than one hundred million Americans alone, is a strong indication of the power of this movement. I forecast more than a billion smart-drug devotees ingesting more than $2 trillion of instant health and performance products by 2015.

# FOUR "SMART DRUGS" THAT MIGHT BE IN PHARMACIES BY 2020

**1. Refresh.** A drug to refresh your brain from fatigue with a biotech brew that stimulates and enhances alertness.

**2. Speed-Up.** A drug that enhances thinking, productivity, and creativity.

**3. Xtasy.** A short-term pleasure drug that enhances touch, emotion, and awareness while slowing down the perception of time.

**4. Recall.** A drug that gives you total recall and photographic memory perception, allowing you to learn a language in an hour.

# Future Longevity Medicine Trends

The following trends will transform the health-care system of the future. They represent the next generation of breakthroughs that will offer bold new choices for people interested in life extension and health enhancement.

- **Holographic projection.** The use of life-size, transparent holographic images of a patient's DNA or body projected into a room or onto a virtual space online for physicians to interact with, and to collaborate with other physicians to diagnose or intervene.

- **Assisted reality.** Supplementing the real world by adding virtual objects so that goggle-wearing surgeons, for example, can "see through" a human body as they perform surgery or genetic enhancement.

- **Robotic surgeons.** Performing operations in which their movements are controlled by a specialist at a remote site or preprogrammed for a specific task and monitored by a physician.

- **Wetware devices.** Neuro-enhancements allow direct brain access to extend intelligence, skills, and memory. Embedded intelligence becomes as natural as breast implants.

- **Stem-cell synthetic tissue and organ growth.** The growing of tissues and organs for human transplantation.

- **Neurogeneration.** The repair and growth of spinal cords, nerves, and brain cells.

- **Therapeutic-cloning banks.** Repositories of an individual's cells that can be grown into organs on demand to replace diseased body parts and prolong life.

- **Longevity tourism.** Vacations where people can medically enhance their appearance, health, performance, fitness, or mental well-being.

- **Designer gene banks.** Where consumers can choose genetic health enhancements.

- Wireless real-time patient-information systems.

- **Decision-support smart agents.** An interface between agents, doctors, researchers, clinicians, and patients.

- **Online distributed intelligence.** All current updated medical information, procedures, and drugs to support both patients and doctors.

# Scenarios from the Future of Medicine

## THE LONGEVITY LIFESTYLE: YEAR 2018

Frank is a thirty-five-year-old designer living in New York City who is concerned about his weight. He needs to lose twenty-five pounds, exercise, and get healthier. He knows his genomic history is not a healthy one. His father died of a heart attack at forty-five, and his mother is overweight and diabetic. Frank's DNA health-profile scan shows that his health-hazard appraisal gives him five years before he is at risk for a heart attack. Frank has decided to take action now.

Using his wireless videophone, he calls his Internet agent, Nanette, a Digitized Engineered Personality (DEP), who is bright, alert, and a bit pushy—characteristics chosen by Frank. He has committed to himself and his family not to die from denial about his medical history. He wants to deal with it.

He asks Nanette to assemble a customized weight-reduction package that takes into account his rigorous business schedule. He also asks her to scan the Net for available data related to his personal health records and to check for any bonus premiums of cybercash credits offered by his employer, HMO, government, or insurance company. Nanette is configured for Max Intelligence Level 517. She also serves with a passion. She gains upgrade credits that she can use for wanted improvements to her neural net brain. She is self-aware enough to desire.

Within three minutes, Nanette compiles a complete report, which she downloads to Frank's wireless wearable cell phone as an interactive holograph with music, graphics, and charts. It is also delivered in text to his smart-card fax.

Among her findings is a cybercash credit program offered by McDonald's-Wal-Mart Health Solutions. She registers him and will help him stay on track with a customized health-enhancement program of diet, exercise, and med-device monitors. As a true DEP, Nanette is able to self-evolve, learn, and adapt based on the moods, behaviors, and actions of her creator. For example, she knows Frank's limitations—such as being in denial about the reasons for his weight—and is able to integrate his responses to her in order to come up with solutions for achieving her prime directive, helping Frank trim down: "Twenty minutes on the treadmill will lose you twenty pounds, which gets you twenty years of extended life."

Toward this end, Nanette will navigate through all parts of Frank's life, and will, for example, actually lock the refrigerator after 5:00 P.M. if necessary. "I'm sorry, Frank, snacking is not approved on your diet."

Food not on Frank's diet is no longer approved for purchase at the supermarket checkout. Unapproved items will not clear the cash register. Ditto with cigarettes, which Frank has vowed to quit as part of his new lifestyle. Nanette sends him this message each day: Veggies okay. Easy on meat and dairy. Low- and no-fat is the ticket. Exercise is key. In addition, Nanette offers encouraging reinforcement by hunting down discounts at Frank's favorite Italian clothing stores. She also builds a network of support with Frank's friends and relatives by letting them know his progress and how they can help him achieve the end goal. Nanette advises Marcia, Frank's mother, not to drop off any more of those chocolate-chip cookies. She arranges regular tennis, running, and exercise partners and coaches to fit in with Frank's schedule.

Frank made it clear that Nanette should be relentless in helping him fight the battle of the bulge. Frank's contract for these health changes cannot be canceled for six months, and he has to live with the consequences of Nanette's zealousness.

The kicker comes when Nanette, unsatisfied with Frank's initial progress—his weight is still high, as is his cholesterol—puts together a holographic "This is Your Life" health magazine that depicts his family history of weight-related health problems and early deaths. A lifeline for Frank shows that unless he sticks to the program, he's due to keel over at age forty-five. Even the funeral is depicted in this multimedia show. Shocked by such in-your-face data, Frank joins the gym recommended by Nanette and quits avoiding the prescribed medications. He stops sneaking snacks and swears off nicotine.

Before the six months are up, Frank has reached his goal,

dropped his weight, and has to spend a bundle on slimmer, more fashionable clothes. He's also got another problem—a sudden flock of admirers.

# LONGEVITY NET-MED TRAINING 101: YEAR 2019

The famous heart surgeon Dr. Robin Karinchy in her operating room at Stanford University Medical Center, is guiding an intricate triple-bypass operation thousands of miles away in a Singapore hospital. She is training a new generation of doctors in Longevity Medicine—experts in every procedure to prolong life. Medical students from fifty medical schools around the world are watching the procedure via videoconference over the Net as part of their resident training.

"Now with this technique, which I am still perfecting, I have found a way to make more refined incisions by using a fiber-optic-tipped scalpel that is a stem cell–enabled nano-bio device," Dr. Karinchy describes. "Now I can gently insert the nano-probes so they will form a gateway around the heart, monitoring the heart's performance and augmenting it if needed with a nano-bio stem-cell device."

"Does that mean that this process is more precise?" asks one of her students, Sanji Patel, who is beamed in from India.

"Hi, Sanji, good to have you here today. Greater precision is one part of this new procedure, but speed is also a result of the smart-targeting of the nano-bio probes, so we can extend the patient's capacity to live longer. The insertion of the stem cells directly into the heart will enhance the therapeutic impact as well."

More than thirty different languages and cultures are represented with simultaneous real-time translation of the exchange between Dr. Karinchy and her team. After an intense one-hour operation, Dr. Karinchy answers questions from the local and remote locations. Her answers and the questions are captured and shared over superfast networks and e-mailed to all present.

"Remember that this course is worth six credits if you download the homework and e-mail it back before April 3. Visual simulations are required, so please don't submit your work without them. Dr. Karinchy offline."

Some of the residents later download the operation over the Net and simulate the teacher's actions to learn her technique. Other students interact with other teachers and students over a groupware

Net link where they can make notes and diagrams while they play back the operation in slow motion.

The patient's vital signs, displayed as information streaming across their wearable net screens, allows them to monitor the operation's progress. All of this information and the procedure can be redesigned, simulated differently, or stored for playing out different scenarios. The visualization of the surgical procedures enables the students to learn a new type of medicine—Longevity Medicine.

# ON-DEMAND LONGEVITY MEDICINE: YEAR 2015

Larry has had a long day. He feels tired despite having taken an anti-fatigue pill called "Aware" to get through the last Internet videoconference on the company's newest product. A happy hour beer-fest at the ZLounge is tempting, but just after leaving the building; a sharp chest pain stops him cold. The pain finally subsides, and he quickly speaks to his cell phone, activating his Personal Health Record by uttering the word, "Emergency."

Immediately, Larry is routed via the Internet to his health plan's Clinical Emergency Center for a diagnosis. This involves answering a series of yes-or-no questions about the symptoms and vital signs asked by a MedTech on-duty computer. Larry places a finger on the screen where his biosignature converts his BioScan signals and sends them instantly to the Emerg-Med Team via a virtual Net center many time zones away.

The GE cyberdoc decides that Larry's condition may be acute cardiac ischemia and dispatches a Clinic-Mobile to his exact location. En route to the nearest emergency-care unit, a battery of tests, including another BioScan, are performed and transmitted via a wireless device to a lab for interpretation.

By the time the local emergency team reaches Larry, the doctor on duty has the results, along with a second opinion by a cardiac specialist on duty in Bangalore, India. Larry's Personal Health Card has also provided his medical history and genetic predisposition to the on-duty doctor.

The doctor has authorized several categories of treatment for the condition—a partially clogged artery. The receptionist takes Larry to a voicenet monitor, where he can see and talk to both physicians who have studied his condition. On the split screen, the duty doctor shows Larry holographic 3-D color images of the vessel blockage via a microscopic camera inserted into his bloodstream.

The doctor recommends injecting an army of nanoscrubbers

to clean out the arteries. Larry is asked to rest while the physician takes a virtual tour of his bloodstream to code in the correct markers for making the noninvasive procedure a success. Once deployed and completed with their mission, the nanoscrubbers dissolve harmlessly.

The actual operation takes only eight minutes, and Larry is discharged shortly afterward. Before leaving, he's given a customized holographic health disk with an analysis of what dietary or lifestyle changes are needed for him to avoid another such episode. All info is uploaded to his virtual agent and his home doctors.

An always-on, wireless, Internet accessible wristband will unobtrusively monitor Larry's condition for the next couple of days, but he feels fine as he strolls out of the neighborhood care unit. In fact, he still has time to make happy hour. He just has to watch what he orders. His updated personal health record may warn him from ordering beverages that are not on his diet. Larry may hear this message: "Light Nutri-beer suggested—and only two servings."

# THE NEW ELIXIR—STEM CELLS: YEAR 2018

The black market for stem cells emerged in the latter part of 2009, when the health value of stem cells became more fully understood and exploitable. The issue was no longer *if* stem cells could heal cancer, reverse heart disease, or grow new bone or organs. The only issues were where could you get them, and at what price? Access became the challenge, and in the supply-and-demand market for medical longevity, stem cells were king.

Overnight, there was a surge, first in the stem-cell black market and next in the legitimate medical tourism industry. You got what you paid for, but then the Chinese got into the market with very inexpensive stem-cell products. China woke up after the trade wars of 2010 when the trade imbalance with the U.S. and Europe became a political concern.

Stem cells put the sizzle back in the marketplace for new customers, new products, and new markets. Off-the-grid locations in Thailand and Rio, which had been havens for cheap plastic surgery, were now upgrading to stem-cell treatments marketed to a hungry world of aging baby-boomer affluents looking to live an extra fifteen years. Just as growth hormones have spawned the longevity medical boom, stem cells have become the next youth elixir.

# GET YOUR DNA ON EBAY: YEAR 2025

When Sylvie discovered that she had a rare DNA strain that could be synthesized and used by others, she was suspicious. She didn't understand it. How could this DNA strand be used to prevent breast cancer? But that's what the GeneTechs told her after her test was done.

"You mean I have special DNA?"

"Very special. In fact, rare," Phil the GeneTech told her. "And we might be interested in buying some, you know, for research."

The first time Sylvie put her DNA for sale on eBay's bioMart she got three offers in the first five minutes that were 100 percent over her asking price. She was astounded. At $25,000 a DNA slice, she thought it was a high price to begin with.

The Longevity Medical Market is open for business.

# THE DEADLIEST DISEASES BY 2020

Most diseases operate like the living beings they attack. Diseases function like living entities with purpose, adaptive skills, and the capacity to fight for survival. In many ways, diseases affecting humans share many of the aspects of their victims. For example, the virus is a marvel of nature, a bio-engine that is self-reliant and persistent. By 2020, we will have learned to eliminate many diseases, but others, still dangerous killers, will defy a cure. This will frustrate medicine, making health care challenging in the future.

Given what we know about existing diseases, it is not hard to imagine what the future might have in store:

**1. RetroAIDS Virus.** The new retro strain is deadly, fast-adaptive, and resistant to drugs. RetroAIDS keeps mutating its DNA, even after 1,000 generations, and is always adapting to new survival threats.

**2. ALZ.** This is a complicated killer, similar to Alzheimer's but a hundred times worse. Not one disease but a combination of interwoven diseases that come together to attack the nerve cells. ALZ is lethal, inoperable, and fast-acting.

**3. Zimba the Flesh-Eater.** This type of flesh-eating strain will qualify as the fiercest and most deadly disease in 2020. This new strain causes painful death in two hours.

**4. Zengue Fever.** New forms of dengue fever that mutated with the plague after a biowar attack in London are mutating and spreading faster than science can keep up due to poor sanitation conditions in Africa.

**5. NuBola.** A distant relative of Ebola but ten times more deadly.

**6. Avian-X.** A mutated, more powerful form of the avian bird flu.

# Beyond Health

Yes, this all sounds strange, alien, and weird. I admit it. My job as a futurist is to inform you that new and radical choices are coming. Do I think that all human enhancements are positive, ethical, or productive? No, but I do call for an open debate on and recognition that Longevity Medicine, free choice, and democracy are on a collision course in the Extreme Future. As a policy advisor to three White House administrations for more than thirty years, I can forecast that the very concept of health care is being changed now.

The era of Longevity Medicine is upon us. It will offer the ultimate fantasy product to billions of consumers—more time to live. More time to love, to spend, to create, to care, to play. You want it now. We all do. We all want more time to exist in a state of enhanced health.

Emerging innovations, from stem cells to biotech, entice us every day with promises of the next new thing. Clearly, as DNA discoveries merge with medicine, everything from diets to disease will be radically revamped. More than 300 new drugs are in the pipeline waiting for FDA approval over the next two years. Billions in research is targeting the longevity consumer—you. You want to live longer and business wants to charge you for the privilege.

Medicine is in the midst of a revolution in mission and purpose. In the past it was about disease management and healing. In the future it will be about prevention and enhancement. This is the future. It is inevitable and logical given the rate of innovations exploding today. The possibilities for medicine to deliver on health enhancement and prevention are good during our extended lifetimes. As innovations persist, and as the boomers demand to reshape aging, a new era of Longevity Medicine driven by global market demand will emerge. The revolution in longevity is coming faster than you think.

Keep in mind that the drivers of Longevity Medicine may be other trends as well. Lower fertility rates leading to a smaller population—

fewer workers to keep pace with productivity—would be offset, perhaps, by people living longer and healthier. The simple desire of companies to make money by capitalizing on life extension will drive this
market. Along with personal choice to live longer will come governments, even corporations, that will invest heavily in Longevity Medicine with self-preservation in mind. Healthy people, longer-living
people, lead to productive, sustainable nations.

Vast new questions remain unasked, let alone answered. Who gets
to be enhanced? What are the limits to age? Who will pay? Who will
benefit? How will an individual's free choice shape this future? What
are the rights of individuals to choose enhancement in democratic societies? How will global competition between nations, corporations,
and individuals be shaped by longevity medicine innovations? These
questions and more will be key fixtures as Longevity Medicine breakthroughs outpace the questions in the Extreme Future.

# Tomorrow's Climate

## Heavy Weather Ahead

The disaster that was Hurricane Katrina affected everyone on the planet. New York, San Francisco, London, Calcutta, or Hong Kong might well be the next New Orleans, a postapocalyptic city virtually wiped out by an extreme "natural event." I put that phrase in quotes because, although a hurricane is obviously not a man-made disaster like 9/11, much of what happened in New Orleans was clearly preventable, had the right people listened to warnings of the futurists among them.

For years, scientists, certain public officials, private individuals, public interest groups, and numerous journalists had forecast what could happen if a powerful storm struck the city, virtually all of which is built below sea level. When levees that are built to withstand a Category 3 storm come up against a Category 4 storm or higher, what happens next cannot simply be considered an "act of God." The destruction of New Orleans, the devastating loss of lives, homes, culture, and billions of dollars of economic activity, was largely a result of not acting on our predictive awareness, not preparing for the future, not acting on the clear and present danger waiting to happen.

But the lessons of Hurricane Katrina actually go much deeper. Think about the reports you've seen or heard about climate change, global warming, and massive environmental degradation. The denial that characterized the general response to warnings about New Orleans's susceptibility to hurricanes is

# THE TOP TEN
# CLIMATE TRENDS

**1.** Climate change is real and it is here now. It cannot be fixed fast enough. It will threaten national security, global prosperity, and peace.

**2.** Industry will compete to clean up the planet. Clean Tech will become one of the largest global, multibillion-dollar industries of the twenty-first century.

**3.** Sustainability will become a shared value to 95 percent of U.S. citizens and a majority of the developed nations.

**4.** More storms are coming. Global warming will increase the threats of extreme weather changes such as glacial melting, shoreline flooding, cold, and drought.

**5.** Climate change threatens water and food production from meeting the growing needs of Asia, Africa, and Latin America.

**6.** A new collaboration of nations, citizens, and corporations must be forged to protect global sustainability and offset climate change.

**7.** Global climate change such as pollution and global warming will be identified as the causes of future public health and safety risks.

**8.** Security and the national implications of climate change will emerge as one of the leading domestic issues of the twenty-first century.

**9.** Sustainability will be adopted by business as the environment becomes a key factor in driving consumer purchasing.

**10.** Climate change will redefine global risk management in business, forcing many corporations to lead the charge for building a more sustainable world.

being played out on a far larger scale in relation to those issues. The evidence that there may be an increase in extreme weather, like Category 5 storms, is mounting. To be sure, no individual hurricane can be blamed on global warming. But numerous experts have demonstrated that world temperatures are rising, and rising temperatures mean rising sea levels and more extreme weather events—everything from hurricanes to hailstorms, wildfires to droughts. From this moment on,

> **HEADLINES FROM THE FUTURE: 2017**
>
> **Quantum Supercomputers to Forecast Climate; New Models Show Path to Save Planet**

wrap your mind around the fact that natural disasters, and their accompanying human and economic costs, will be dramatically accelerated by climate change. Think New Orleans multiplied by ten, or a hundred, or a thousand.

## Hurricane Fuel

Just days before Katrina, an MIT scientist named Kerry Emanuel published a paper in the respected journal *Nature*. Emanuel found that since the 1970s, there has been a roughly 50 percent increase in the duration and intensity of major storms in both the Atlantic and the Pacific. Folks who deny evidence of global warming will offer their own theories as to why, but the National Academy of Sciences has established that the earth's surface temperature has risen by about one degree Fahrenheit over the past century—a very significant amount—and that the rate of warming has increased during the past twenty years (the same period covered by Emanuel's study). Indeed, the ten warmest years of the twentieth century occurred in the fifteen years before 2000. There is only one plausible reason for this warming: human activity. We've polluted the skies with greenhouse gases—mainly carbon dioxide, methane, and nitrous oxide, emitted by smokestacks, cars, and other sources. Those gases trap heat in the atmosphere, causing temperatures to rise.

How does this spin back to hurricanes? Think back to your fifth-grade science class. Hurricanes grow for days over the oceans by feeding on giant pools of warm water. As a storm grows, it sucks up more and more heat from the ocean as fuel. The warmer the ocean, the fatter the storm gets and the more potentially destructive it becomes. The math is pretty simple, really: More greenhouse gas pollutants equal warmer temperatures. Warmer temperatures mean warmer seawater. Warmer seawater means deadlier storms.

The potential effect on individual human lives is incalculable, but there is some frightening evidence about what it means in terms of dollars. Consider for a moment a new report from Ceres, a national network of investment funds and environmental organizations. Ceres' goal is to get businesses to consider the environment in their risk-management and decision processes, for both self-interested reasons as well as the public interest. In the wake of Katrina, the group used a clever way to demonstrate that the weather is getting worse, and that

# ESCAPE FROM L.A.: 2035

The sandstorm on the far horizon was barely visible in the 130-degree heat. It seemed so far away and yet it was moving fast toward us, dangerously fast. Fred hurried to the truck, aware that we had little time to find safe haven from the tidal wave of sand that was growing menacingly large as it sped in our direction.

What had gone wrong with Los Angeles? It was a strange thing, this sandstorm, alive and hungry all at the same time, seemingly destined to engulf us. Not really weather but a supernatural force. The storm defied definition. It was as though nature had gone wild, careening unto itself, a black hole on earth sucking and wheeling, collapsing and exploding all at once. As the first edge of the sandstorm approached, we had just entered a parking garage for shelter. Now the deafening howl of the winds, swirling at more than one hundred miles per hour, attacked the buildings all around us.

We could hear breaking glass, cars being picked up and shattered like toys, and buildings cracking and breaking apart as though they were made of plastic. As the eighty-foot-high and five-mile radius of the sandstorm hit with all its fury, the parking structure we had entered started to sway and creak and collapse from the onslaught.

Who could have predicted that Los Angeles would have sandstorms comparable to those found in the Middle East? Who would have known?

Americans are being made to pay. Experts working with Ceres reported that insured losses from catastrophic weather events experienced a fifteen-fold increase over the past three decades. Even after adjusting for inflation, Ceres found that catastrophic weather losses in the United States had soared from a few billion dollars a year in the 1970s to an average of $15 billion a year in the past decade, with a record of $30 billion set in 2004. And that, of course, was before Katrina.

Hurricanes are just one area—admittedly, a pretty dramatic one—where we will unfortunately experience what happens when climate change and environmental damage come home to roost in the Extreme Future.

## Extreme Climate Change

I am not an alarmist, but there is abundant evidence that climate change and environmental threats present a real and present danger to life as we know it on the planet. If we do not fix this problem, the safety, health, and survival of the world's population is at stake. Some climate change may be irreversible. Fundamental challenges such as clean water, food, health care, transportation, and commerce are directly linked to climate. This is the big wake-up call. We take climate for granted—a given that brings sun or rain, snow or clouds, and occasionally causes a disaster. But it's about to get nasty for all of us.

Climate change such as global warming is an emerging new risk landscape that threatens business, society, and security in fundamental ways. Game Changers are big trends, big risks, often global in scope, with the potential to upset all other trends and, therefore, make the future more complex to forecast. Climate change is a Game Changer.

We need to consider the effects of climate change on our world, manage these risks now, or suffer the consequences in our extended lifetimes. The fact is, some climate change is already in progress and beyond our control. We will have to learn to deal with it. But we can learn to think differently about climate change and, as a result, we may be better prepared for the extreme climate futures to come.

Climate change and the alteration of the global environment pose challenges on a scale that often eludes our understanding. And that is part of the problem. Most people cannot conceive of the global climate as more than a concept. We recycle. We conserve energy. We care about global warming. But the idea, the big idea, that the climate is changing and that our daily lifestyle, in Asia, the U.S., or Europe, is partially to blame for these drastic changes is hard to comprehend.

That is one of the messages of this chapter. The idea that individual lifestyles are actually making the climate change is not readily accepted, but it is true. The discrete, seemingly unconnected actions of six billion people are leading us every day toward or away from environmental disasters that may signal the end of civilization.

We are a part of the environment, the living earth. It almost sounds spiritual, and it is. Many individuals, once they are familiar with the risks that climate change is bringing, once they increase their awareness, immediately ask, "What can I do to help create positive change?" I wish the answer were as easy as posing the question.

We cannot wave a wand and radically alter modern human behavior. We are not about to suddenly stop burning fossil fuels or overfishing the oceans, for example. But there is much that we can do, as individuals and as a society, before the Extreme Future is upon us.

One way to consider the future impact of change on the environment is to consider the past. Many deserts today were once wetlands, even rivers and oceans. Over time, the ecological landscape has shifted from fertile to desert and from plains to rivers. The difference between today and the past is that in the past mostly natural changes led to a

---

# CHRISTMAS IN NEW YORK CITY: JANUARY 2035

Everything seemed irradiated, pulsing with captured heat looking desperately for escape. The tall buildings in midtown were trapping the 120-degree air. Walking down 59th Street, we saw a heat wave develop—a hot wind of debris coming at us. At first, with an almost eerie deception, the burning wind fanned us as we ran across the street to escape. Then, as if alive, the heat exploded all around us with a fury of attack. I could feel my clothes beyond hot, almost on fire, as my shoes began to melt on the pavement. My feet were aching and my head was pouring sweat. The tall buildings surrounding us radiated heat at each other, creating a spiral effect, intensifying the heat many times over, trapping it inside the city, leaving it—and us—with nowhere to go.

new environment. These changes to the ecology happened over long periods of time—often thousands or even millions of years.

In northern California, where I live, we have come to expect earthquakes as a reality, just as people in the Midwest expect tornadoes, and folks in the southern part of the country expect hurricanes. This means we take precautions. We build differently. We are aware of the signals of change that indicate an earthquake, but for the most part we live with the reality forecast by the experts that earthquakes occur over a predictable amount of time.

## Global Warming on Overdrive

It will likely require a large ecological disaster to awaken people to the threats we face, and our children will face, from global warming. You might hear some conflicting reports about global warming, but keep a few things in mind. One of the most important facts, as mentioned above, is that the average global surface temperature increased about one degree, according to the Intergovernmental Panel on Climate Change.

The climate panel was established by the World Meteorological Organization and the United Nations in 1988. Many leading climate researchers around the world contributed to its final report, and its findings are not in dispute. The report indicated that some of the twentieth-century warming was due to natural climate changes, but most was traceable to the greenhouse effect.

A National Academy of Sciences report for the White House in 2005 confirmed the accuracy of these findings. This report reflects the current thinking of the scientific community on climate change. Most scientific authorities agree with the risk assessments associated with this and other reports highlighting the threats to the environment. Though there is disagreement over how many of the changes are natural rather than man-made, there is a general consensus about the dangers that exist if they continue and if we don't make significant changes to lifestyle, energy use, and fossil-fuel dependence.

## Global Warming Is Real

The rate of temperature warming and rising sea levels will continue into the twenty-second century. This is not good. One can simply calculate the risks to life, health, and society caused by this increased warming in the future to get an idea of what is in store without fast, sustainable global management of the environment. To date, too little has been done, and we are running out of time.

According to the Intergovernmental Panel on Climate Change, levels of carbon dioxide and other heat-trapping greenhouse gases in the environment will continue to increase and the planet will likely warm by another 2.5 to 10.4 degrees by 2100. Most continents will warm more rapidly than the global average. North America could see accelerated warming in the range of 6.3 to 13.5 degrees by 2100 under high-emissions scenarios. Any climate changes affecting either water availability or the timing of snowmelt runoff could have profound social, economic, and ecological repercussions.

A United Nations–sponsored report on a study called the Millennium Ecosystem Assessment synthesis report was released in 2005. It is the culmination of four years' work by 1,300 experts from ninety-five countries. The report shows that urgent action needs to be taken to head off a climatic storm of large proportions, one that may become irreversible if we wait much longer. The report's evidence warns that the ongoing degradation of fifteen of the twenty-four ecosystems on the planet is increasing the likelihood of major risks to human quality of life over time.

The Millennium report emphasized that approximately 60 percent of the ecosystem services that support life on earth were at serious risk of being damaged by pollution, overuse, and mismanagement. This includes ecosystems essential to human living such as water, agriculture, fisheries, and air. The lack of a sustainable management of the climate is at the core of what is missing and what will increase risks in the future.

The idea that climate change originating in one part of the world doesn't affect the rest of the planet is untrue. The Amazon rain forest's contribution to clean air in London is significant. Extreme drought affecting the agriculture production of the Midwest shapes food prices in Hong Kong. Flooding of rice fields in China starves children in Africa. The interconnection of living systems is becoming clearer every day. One planet. One people. One environment.

# A Climate and Security

Another forecast perspective on the future is how the changing climate will affect security, democracy, and economic prosperity. A viable environment is needed to support a viable society. Free markets, free enterprise, and personal security are important pillars of modern society that could be derailed by the threats forecast here about climate change, some of which could occur in less than fifty years.

More than 90 percent of Americans consider themselves to be environmentalists. But we still drive large, gas-guzzling cars regardless of skyrocketing gas prices, leave the lights on in our homes, and don't often get the connection between our health, food, and the environment. And why not? Our awareness is about to change. The vital connections between lifestyle, health, and the environment will become clearer in the near future as the potential for risk increases. Climate change poses both opportunity and threat.

As we move into the future, radical shifts in the environment due to natural causes, industrial pollution, overpopulation, and lifestyle will alter the relative stability we have enjoyed, unless significant action is taken now. A large portion of these ecological threats can be seen forming today. The early warning signals are there. Environmental disasters, many brought on by civilization, may be prevented by prudent planning and investments made today for change. Most people are not ready for this potential future scenario in which threats to the environment touch them. Are you ready to make sacrifices to better prepare for the future?

---

**HELP WANTED WIRELESS AD: 2007**

**Risk Management
Climate Forecaster Wanted**

Leading global bank needs to hire experienced climate forecaster to determine economic and social risk management from extreme climate scenarios such as drought, flooding, cold, storms, and disasters.

Must have five years of experience in forecasting financial futures in agriculture, food production, and global commodities. Must have an MBA in economics and a doctorate in climatology. Must be willing to travel to disaster zones worldwide.

---

# Save the Amazon

Some time ago I attended a fund-raiser by the rock musician Sting to save the rain forest in Brazil. The party was a typical Hollywood event, held at a famous producer's spacious Beverly Hills home, far from the Amazon. The home was formerly owned by a silent movie actor from the 1920s. As entertainers from Bruce Springsteen to comedian Billy Crystal performed, I was struck by the enormous dilemma we face in dealing with saving the rain forest.

To Brazilians, the rain forest is a primitive, undeveloped, and hostile environment that feeds no one, clothes no one, and contributes little to that nation's GDP, let alone to the fight against poverty. The Amazon rain forest is an untamed monument to the poor and underdeveloped nations of the world that are trying desperately to raise their people from poverty, hunger, and ignorance in the face of the affluent nations' demands for conservation.

Imagine if the Europeans came over to the U.S. in the early 1800s and tried to persuade Americans not to develop or settle the western

## WHY BIODIVERSITY MATTERS

- Biodiversity is essential to human health. Ten of the world's top-selling drugs that fight everything from bacteria to high cholesterol come from natural sources. Future drugs for diseases like cancer may be lost if we do not address this challenge.

- By 2050, with nine billion mouths to feed, food production may not be able to keep pace with global needs, leading to more poverty, hunger, and conflicts.

- Global security is based on the sustainability of ecological as well as social systems. The five major ecosystems: agricultural, coastal, forest, fresh water, and grassland, are all seriously threatened.

- Water shortages in the near future will increase global conflict between nations, especially as climate change increases global warming.

part of the U.S., but to save it for future generations' appreciation of natural beauty and ecological splendor. They would have collided with a hostile culture that was hungry to develop the land, regardless of the destruction of native peoples, wildlife, and the environment. Progress waits for no one.

And yet, we want to preserve the Amazon for the ecological contribution it brings to the world. The rain forest covers more than a billion acres across Peru, Brazil, Ecuador, Colombia, and Venezuela, producing more than 20 percent of the world's oxygen and containing more than one-fifth of the world's fresh water in its basin. The noble— and enormously important—idea of conserving this resource must be

---

# BIODIVERSITY FUTURES

■ There are more than fifteen million living species on the planet—including humans—that are threatened today.

■ Biodiversity is about the rapid extinction of living species and the negative impact on humanity's future.

■ The increased extinction of living species is due to humankind's mismanagement of the global ecosystem.

■ Agriculture, population growth, overfishing, pollution, and global warming are killing species at an alarming rate.

■ By 2050, with the growth of more than twenty megacities with ten to twenty million people, the rate of extinction will threaten humanity's existence in select areas around the globe.

■ Biodiversity threats accelerate climate change.

■ More than 75 percent of major marine fish species are dwindling due to overfishing, putting food production at risk.

■ More than 60 percent of coral reefs are at risk, threatening the survival of millions.

■ The world's tropical forests have been shrinking, contributing to global warming and habitat destruction.

*UNEP, World Conservation Union, U.S. Academy of Sciences, 2001*

## CLIMATE HACKERS STEAL CARBON CREDITS: 2020

NEW YORK—A group identifying itself as the Shadow Lords has been caught stealing carbon credits and selling them on the online black market.

"They jacked into Bloomberg and set up a phony account in which they were able to pose as legitimate sellers of carbon credits," said Special Agent James Mahoney of the FBI. "This was a sophisticated operation spanning five stock markets and involving ten banks in twenty countries and more than $5 billion."

Carbon credits are traded like stocks and bonds and are purchased by companies to offset their pollution investments. This is a little-known area of trading between companies to better hedge their pollution activities and investment operations.

"It looks like their attempt to corner the carbon-trading business, totaling more than $10 billion last year, failed," Mahoney said. But he admitted that the Shadow Lords did escape capture and fled with more than $2 billion of the $5 billion.

The Shadow Lords took over the FBI Web site briefly today to leave this message for the world: "Crime Pays."

reconciled with the development issues that are as or more important to the people who live there. It is not enough for the West to make unequivocal demands on developing nations, despite the global value of a rain forest with unmatched biodiversity, fresh water, and unique oxygen-generating prosperities.

# Global Tensions

This struggle between the developed and undeveloped nations of the world clearly exposes a global conflict that will be visited over and again as we grapple with threats to the environment in the future. More of these conflicts between the needs of nations and the need to protect the environment are coming in the Extreme Future, a time when one man's pollutant will be another man's salvation.

This mismatch between local and global needs is paramount to the issues of climate that will shape the twenty-first century and beyond. Culture clashes over climate and productivity, over food and land, over water and oceans, will persist as the global competition for scarce resources defines the future existence of those who have and those who have not. Getting the balance right between security and climate, environmental health and industrial productivity, pollution and quality of life, will shape what the twenty-first century will look like.

# Eco-War

For a brief time in 2002, it was conceivable that the world was about to become witness and victim to the largest ecological disaster we could have prevented—the first nuclear exchange in history. This doomsday scenario would have been so immense it would have dwarfed the primitive nukes dropped on Japan at the end of World War II. We actually came within hours of a nuclear exchange that had been accepted, even preferred, as a solution to conflict.

Not many average people were paying attention to the strong signals that the governments of India and Pakistan were sending out. They had been archenemies ever since India gained its independence from Britain in 1947, divided by historical animosity and religion—India is mostly Hindu and Pakistan is mostly Muslim. Although their hatred for each other had been well documented—focused on the disputed region of Kashmir, controlled

*EBAY AUCTION: 2021*

**Carbon Credits for Sale**
**Great Opportunity!**

$250 Million Dollars in Carbon Credits

Only Serious, Global-Polluting Companies Can Bid

Payment by zPal Digital Credits

Shadow Lords Inc.

## WATER FUTURES

- Over the past century, world water demand increased almost twice as fast as population growth.

- In 60 percent of the European cities with more than 100,000 people, water is being used at a faster rate than it can be replenished.

- Cities that will be at potential risk in the future will include Mexico City, Bangkok, Manila, Madras, and Shanghai.

- By 2025, two out of every three people on the planet will live in a water-stressed area, particularly in sub-Saharan Africa, eastern Asia, southeastern Asia, and Oceania.

by India despite its majority Muslim population—I saw something more emerging, a pattern I had seen before. Leaders who have a rabid appetite for apocalypse are dangerous. This situation, volatile at every turn, qualified. It was a crisis unlike any the world had faced before because of the large impact domains that would have been affected.

The media was a bit slow, I remember thinking, in picking up the immense crisis that was about to ignite a nuclear confrontation. Closely watching the growing conflict and advising my clients on the emerging geopolitical scenarios, I realized then that one of the outcomes would be an ecologic disaster of unforeseen dimensions affecting the entire world.

## The Hot Zone

Obviously, the most devastating impact of nuclear exchange would be felt in south Asia. A confidential Defense Department assessment obtained by *The New York Times* warned that up to twelve million people might die immediately and another seven million might suffer serious injuries. The report also warned that even a "limited" nuclear war between the two countries would be cataclysmic, necessitating unimaginable sums of foreign aid to fight nuclear contamination, disease, and famine. But the effects would not stop there.

Across the globe, food, water, air, and other essential resources, not to mention fisheries and ocean habitat, would be affected, or rather damaged, by radiation. The public health effects—increased cancer and disease—would travel on air currents with the nuclear fallout to regions far beyond the adversaries on the Indian subcontinent. We already had projections worked up based on the global air current flows of estimated cancer increases in regional populations of 15 percent over normal rates. This was not reliable. The projected impact on populations, agriculture, commerce, and public health were beyond easy calculations because we did not have any comparisons to consider.

> **HEADLINES FROM THE FUTURE: 2034**
>
> **Massive Migration on Indian Coast
> Due to Coastal Flooding;
> Polar Ice Melts to Blame.
> Fifty Million Indians on the Move**

There were many other environmental impacts that we were even more concerned about. Among them were the half-life—that is, the longevity—of the radiation in the ground and the impact on food-production forecasts; and the air- and water-quality impact and how to prevent and offset growing indicators of radiation effects. Half-lives can be 30,000 years, based on the intensity and duration of the exposure. These were unknown environmental questions that no one had complete answers for.

In the end, the crisis passed relatively quickly—but the lessons linger.

## Global Insecurity

When you consider the global security issues undertaken by the world's leading countries—large and small, rich and poor—and the future challenges that lie before us as the world's only superpower, the responsibility to head off crises such as this Indian/Pakistani conflict is bewildering, but critical.

The irreversible damage to their own populations in terms of deaths, cancers, birth defects, and other permanent negative health impacts from radiation would seem to make a nuclear war anathema to any nation. But on that day, at that time, India and Pakistan considered the unthinkable. According to our analysis, this almost-nuclear war had been forecast by both the Indian and Pakistani leaders as a regrettable but acceptable loss.

As I was analyzing the situation with our global intelligence working group, both on the ground in the region and in the U.S., I realized with alarm that we had passed, almost unknowingly, a historic threshold of acceptability—the concept that the use of nuclear weapons had become a rational option. This was a shocking realization.

## Imagine War

For the first time in our modern era, leaders of nations had accepted the use and devastation of nuclear war. This had not happened before. No nation had used the nuclear option since World War II. Even though nuclear war between India and Pakistan did not occur, they had entered the history books for considering and rationalizing the nuclear option. But most of the impact we forecast was of an ecologic effect on health, property, climate, and agriculture. These collateral impacts were, I am sure, not of primary concern to the leaders. They were considering loss of life. I was forecasting destruction of agricultural land, water resources, air quality, and the subsequent disease and death brought by this conflict to innocents far away.

In a future time, perhaps starting in Korea or Iran, the world may face similar threats to the environment born of war, terrorism, or other conflicts. Nuclear war, even if used in a limited theater, would impose an unforgiving ecological impact on the nations of the world. The unfortunate case, of course, is that with nuclear proliferation growing, more nations have the bomb, and the option to use it is tempting. With Iran's working hard to "go nuclear," no one actually believes this brazen effort will not include aggression.

In the future, asymmetric risks to our security impacting the environment will only cause further damage to an already fragile ecosystem struggling to stave off global warming, pollution, overfishing, and an increase in the environmental effects of disease on humans. The good news is that with better forecasting, diplomacy, and security in place, we can prevent hostilities before they destabilize the world.

## The 2004 Tsunami

To many people, the tsunami of December 2004 was a disaster no one could predict. They were wrong. Just as the damage done by Katrina was only a surprise to people who weren't paying attention to past warnings, for decades the Asian oceanic area where the devastating tsunami took so much life and property had been well known to harbor seismic disasters in the making. There had been numerous other ecological disasters—earthquakes, flooding, storms, and even tsunamis—in the past.

*HEADLINES FROM THE FUTURE: 2030*

**Genetically Enhanced Humans Survive Best in Hostile Climate; Flood Victims Saved by Rescue Workers with Fish Gills**

The issue is not about our unawareness of the risks to that region. The issue is that we could have prevented lives from being lost by putting early-warning detectors in place that would have given people time to flee to higher ground. But we did not, and the world did not. The Indonesians, Thais, Indians, Sri Lankans, and other peoples from that region have all been aware for many generations of the risks they were facing due to extreme weather. With the advances in modern technology, we could have prevented the billions of dollars in destruction and the tens of thousands of lives lost that day, for a few million dollars.

The use of early-warning systems—based on the Internet, wireless phones, and computers—to help us better prepare for extreme climate changes will be vital to our survival. We don't know when or where disaster may strike, but we know we have the technology to better plan, inform, and prevent loss of life and property. For example, one of the companies I advise is Voxiva. They have such an early-warning system for disease outbreaks and public-health disasters.

Some leaders are beginning to take notice of the mounting evidence that the environment is not "out there" in some wilderness apart from people and society but is rather an essential part of human existence—and is in trouble. The extreme climate changes that are coming will redefine risk in the twenty-first century, perhaps shifting the geopolitical balance of power.

## Climate Change Melts Glaciers

Most of the glaciers on the Antarctic Peninsula are in meltdown at an unknown but accelerating rate because of climate change. An in-depth study by the British Antarctic Survey and the U.S. Geological Survey outlined the scenarios of climate changes likely to emerge. They used aerial photographs spanning the past half-century of all 244 marine glaciers on the west side of the Antarctic and found that 87 percent were in retreat, and the speed of shrinkage was rising at alarming rates not predicted accurately before. NASA has recently confirmed accelerated snowmelt, which in some climate forecasts means rising sea levels within decades that will increase new disaster risks. Some of these reports indicate that sea levels may rise more than ten feet along coastal areas in this century.

The results show that a global movement of melting is underway, and that it may accelerate beyond the estimate here. The actual increase in flooding may vary from area to area due to coastal infrastructure. One thing is certain: The

HEADLINES FROM THE FUTURE: 2020

**Bold New Glacial Transport to Provide Fresh Water; Eskimos Riot over "Stolen" Ice**

incidence of potential disasters affecting life and property, affecting millions, has now increased and will continue well into the next century.

# EXTREME CLIMATE SCENARIO 2040: A HARSH WORLD

The Harsh World Scenario tells the story of a failure to prepare for extreme weather changes and, as a result, a planet that is a far more dangerous and desperate place. The Great Drought began in 2030 in Africa, sweeping up to Europe and across to South America and into parts of America as the fragile societies of the world became imperiled. Agriculture production was down more than 50 percent, leaving the world's population struggling against starvation. With fresh water in short supply and an increase in disease due to the extreme climate shifts, the global populace was growing distressed. This alone was responsible for a breakdown in global and regional security. The collapse of civil liberties in numerous nations was seen as a necessary but dangerous step that threatened individual freedom and democracy.

Extreme warming also drove accelerated meltdowns of the glaciers in the polar cap, bringing extreme flooding to coastal areas in Asia. India and China were hit the worst. The Chinese army was mobilized as panic set in and a reverse migration from the coastal cities began; more than one hundred million people headed inland to avoid the destruction. Giant refugee camps were set up and the army moved in to stabilize the situation, but the resources were not available to deal with the massive waves of Chinese desperate to avoid more coastal flooding.

The global state of emergency opened the door for some countries like North Korea to attempt to take advantage of the vulnerabilities of their neighboring nations. After a limited micro war, North Korea backed down, but continued to threaten to use its nuclear option. A toppling of leaders, from elections and coups around the world, left governments on shaky footing worldwide, as millions of citizens blamed their leaders for inept planning and environmental management over recent decades.

As the geopolitical landscape changed, a rise of new states with new borders emerged. The balance of power shifted to those nations that had adapted the fastest to new climate changes.

Disaster is waiting if we are not ready to react to a warmer world. The issue is not if, but when and at what pace climate change will accelerate.

Scientists worry about the melting of the ice sheets because the extra water may increase sea levels, which in turn could mean more flooding along coastal areas during storms. Sea levels have risen by four to eight inches over the last hundred years. A 10 percent increase per year for ten to thirty years will contribute to coastal flooding in areas of Asia that are the most vulnerable to disaster floods.

## China's Two Billion Stomachs

A project I undertook for a global shipping client a number of years ago concerned with trade between China and the U.S. gave me the insight into the connection between food and climate. Deep in the Canton Province in mainland China, there were cultivated areas the size of football fields that dot the land. What is unusual is not their size as much as what lies on these fields—rotten fruits and vegetables, long past harvest. Surrounded by a rural landscape of trees, valleys, and grasslands, even towns of varying sizes, the fields were a testament to both the immensity of the progress and the problem that China faces in the twenty-first century: How will China feed its growing population? This challenge is directly linked to energy, climate, and transportation. This question is relevant for China and the world in the twenty-first century. An army marches either on its stomach or toward where the food is.

The rotting vegetables and fruits are a reminder that the capacity for eliminating hunger requires both the power to grow food and access to the logistics critical to distribute it. You need both to make a difference. Too few transportation systems, from roads to trucks to shipping containers, trains, and planes, make for a rotten harvest if you cannot get the produce to the people who need it. And that is the case. This cannot be a productive scenario for the future of China as we move into the twenty-first century.

One of the great challenges for China and other developing nations will be how to transform the paradigm of food production to meet the needs of a hungry, fast-growing population. There are serious concerns that my forecasts point to that question our ability to produce enough food to meet population demands in the near future.

Climate change figures into this equation. As rapid climate change alters food production—global warming leads to droughts, glacial melts lead to flooding—agriculture will be compromised. Lower agricultural yields, the absence of a national or international distribution network, and even unskilled labor, will all contribute to the growing crisis.

More than ten years ago, we conducted a global analysis of food futures for a food client, Asia Pacific. They were building refrigerated long-haul containers for produce shipment by air, ship, and railroads worldwide. What I found as I traveled from Asia to the Middle East to

---

# FUTURE ENVIRONMENTAL RISKS

- Overfishing the oceans, limiting the food supply.

- Lack of adequate farmland to grow crops, leading to food shortages.

- Increased global hunger as population increases and food production slows.

- Increased carbon emissions, driving up disease from global warming.

- Increased air pollution, restricting health and commerce.

- Fresh water scarcity due to global warming and pollution.

- Global warming leading to drought and population migration.

- Increased industrial pollution, driving up health-care costs to business, government, and individuals.

- Increased cancer and environmental-related diseases.

- Lack of forecasting to predict and warn populations about disasters.

- Increased transmission of disease due to overpopulation and radical climate change.

- Regional wars over scarce natural resources such as food, water, and land.

- Growing financial burdens to societies due to natural-resource scarcity.

Africa were the vast differences in culture that separated nations in preparing for the future. Even thinking about the environment as an asset or a liability differed. The diversity of ideas about planning for the future seemed to vary from region to region, culture to culture, even leader to leader.

But one thing that everyone I met with agreed about was that climate change was coming and that food production might be at risk. Certainly people would suffer. Now in the West, most of Europe, and most of Asia, the idea of food production being upset or made unreliable due to climate or energy or the economy would seem unknown. But in Africa and Latin America, this was not the case. Advising an international food shipper out of the Middle East was challenging. He was Muslim, and when I asked about forecasts for the coming year's harvest, he indicated that the Koran did not allow such estimates of the future. I respected his perspective.

## Clean Tech Market

A lot of the story of future climate and environment has been doom and gloom. But there is always hope. Perhaps one of the most promising new industries is an outgrowth of the disaster-type thinking that the first part of this chapter has expanded on—Clean Tech.

Leave it to business to figure out a new way to monetize pollution and environmental disaster. If there is one immense bright side to the climate-change scenario that makes me hopeful of a sustainable future, it is the emergence of the Clean Tech industry. I always forecasted that once business figured out how to make money from saving the environment, the future would be safe. It looks like that is happening now. Get ready to save the future and make a buck. Sounds like a good marketing message.

Clean Tech is a catchall industry that combines all clean technologies. This fast-growing industry is a product of the convergence of the environmental, technological, and scientific industries all with one design—a cleaner, safer world. The goals of Clean Tech industries are nonpolluting, renewable, prevention-oriented, ecological, and green.

The Clean Tech market stands at about $10 billion today and we forecast it to grow to $150 billion by 2015. The more polluted, dirty, disaster-prone, globally fried, storming, and devastating the world becomes, the more Clean Tech thrives. Clean technologies, from renewable energy,

to pollution prevention, to industrial ecology, to clean materials, are all good for the environment long-term.

Clean Tech, a new fashion industry in the Innovation Economy, focuses on developing sustainable technology, is all about keeping the planet clean. Given the challenges facing our world, from energy to health, transportation to global warming, Clean Tech has both social

# CLEAN TECH'S FUTURE WAVE

- Allianz, one of the largest global insurance and investment companies, has agreed to invest more than $362 million in renewable energy over the next five years.

- Many large global multinational companies are changing their investment strategies to become green. This will accelerate in the future.

- General Electric has pledged to invest more than $1 billion in clean-energy technology. GE also has agreed to curtail carbon emissions, holding to a 1 percent emission rate versus as much as 40 percent over a multiyear period.

- ExxonMobil is investing more than $1 billion in hydrogen and alternative-energy research.

and business applications on a large scale. As continued advances in biology, electronics, and science render new breakthroughs, the Clean Tech advocates will be ready to harvest these innovations to capitalize on a world that needs many environmental restorations. From reducing resource scarcity, deforestation, and air and water pollution, to alternative energy sources like solar or biofuels, Clean Tech companies will transform the future with a powerful new global vision for sustainability.

GE is mentioned in the box above, but it deserves special mention for its new ecomagination strategy.

CEO Jeff Immelt has focused the company under the umbrella of ecologically friendly products and services. As an advisor to GE, I have worked with the company in planning and strategy with an eco-sustainability theme to identify key trends impacting their energy, health, waste products, consumer products, financial services, and lighting products. This is a very smart Clean Tech strategy. We also looked at the future of green cities. When I can work with a leader like GE that understands how to capitalize on a future trend like a clean environment, it makes me more hopeful that solutions will be found to the global problems we face.

## Sustainable Investing

In some ways, banks are leading the way with a green strategy. This is a bold step into the future that could be a model for all business to follow. J.P. Morgan Chase was one of the first banks (along with Citigroup and Bank of America) to take a stand on a comprehensive environmental policy to address the challenges of global warming and deforestation.

# CLEAN TECH INDUSTRY TRENDS: 2015

**1.** The climate is changing, becoming more erratic, unpredictable, and perilous, causing environmental hazards on a global scale.

**2.** Every investment-asset class, from stocks to commodities to real estate, will be affected by the chaotic changes in the climate.

**3.** Business will recognize an opportunity and an obligation to heal the environment.

**4.** Consumers are buying brands based on corporate accountability for the environment.

**5.** Corporations are shifting quickly to making and selling clean and renewable products.

**6.** Companies are embracing Clean Tech to better compete in the marketplace.

**7.** Consumers understand the link between health and the environment.

**8.** Employees prefer working at companies that act as stewards of the environment.

**9.** Clean Tech means big profits from cleaning up the environment.

**10.** Clean Tech is smart public relations for every company to embrace that wants to respect consumers' demands.

The policy sets new practices on the environment in several critical areas, including carbon mitigation and reduction, endangered forest protection, independent certification of sustainable forestry, and land and consultation rights of native communities everywhere. It is the first policy of its kind in the financial sector to create a special heading acknowledging "No Go Zones," a major step forward in the effort to protect ecosystems that are most valuable in a natural state and untouched by industry.

Among its other provisions:

■ **Global Warming.** J.P. Morgan Chase will encourage clients to develop carbon-mitigation plans that include measure-

# WHY BUSINESS WILL GET GREEN

- It will take more than $100 billion to fix the environment, making this the largest new business opportunity in the world.

- There will be numerous fortunes made by individuals and organizations dealing in waste management, climate controls, weather forecasting, renewable materials, and products.

- Green politics, a certain wave of the future, will enable companies to demonstrate their social responsibility.

- A trend toward renewable, clean, nonpolluting, and sustainable values is an essential strategy for business to embrace with authenticity.

- Consumers are growing smarter about the environment, and they will put their money where their values are.

- The environment represents a new competitive landscape for products, services, and talent, in every market in the world.

ment and disclosure of greenhouse-gas emissions as well as plans to reduce or offset them. The bank will be the first to include carbon pollution for power-sector projects by integrating the financial cost of greenhouse-gas emissions into its analysis.

- **Sustainable Forestry Certification.** The policy makes J.P. Morgan Chase the first private bank to state a preference for Forest Stewardship Council (FSC) certification.

- **Illegal Logging.** The policy will require J.P. Morgan Chase clients that trade in forest products from high-risk countries to ensure that the wood comes from legal sources.

- **Private Equity Risk Management.** Environmental risks will be integrated into the investment process.

J.P. Morgan Chase is listening and reacting to its clients. A number of investors requested that the bank factor in the environmental risks of projects it finances. The new investment policies that J.P. Morgan is now adopting are part of a growing trend of large banks in the U.S. and around the world. Part smart risk management and part philosophy, the policies recognize that there are ways to protect shareholders and the planet at the same time with socially responsible investment choices. Investing in nonpolluting companies is part of this trend.

J.P. Morgan Chase's actions reflect an emerging green investment trend by financial institutions to develop a new attitude to assess the risks posed by climate, biodiversity, and social impacts on their portfolios. This will lead to a new generation of sustainable investments that pursue solutions to environmental problems.

# GREEN CONSUMER PROFILE

- 100 million Americans in 2005.
- 200 million Americans by 2020.
- Adults between ages twenty-four and fifty-five.
- Educated with at least a college degree, usually more.
- Earning $50,000 to $100,000 a year.
- Professional or manager.
- Married with two kids.
- Discretionary income.
- Often buys organic or whole foods, recyclables, and other "natural" products.
- Considers himself or herself an environmentalist/ conservationist.
- Seriously concerned about the threat of global warming.
- Willing to boycott corporate polluters.
- Supports renewable-energy purchases like solar and wind products, and hybrid cars.

Investing in companies that are developing sustainable innovations that can better protect the environment will be an uptrend in the future. Companies in the future will gain a competitive advantage from having green corporate strategies that can attract both investors and customers. Green investing will become a fast innovative trend in the global marketplace of the twenty-first century.

These are important steps in the right direction for business and commerce to support the environment, actually turning the risks into opportunities for commerce.

## Global Management for Nine Billion, Please

The global management of nine billion people who demand health, food, work, shelter, and security will be the most daunting challenge any civilization has ever faced. It will decide the destiny of the world by 2050. It will shape scenarios of chaos for security, liberty, or dictatorship.

We can and must do more to manage our world's climate-change risks before there is little we can do but complain or blame others. Our health and well-being, not to mention human sustainability, is at stake. This is a big challenge, a Game Changer. If not faced effectively, it will spoil the future.

The inevitable price for not making change when we can and must will only complicate every other aspect of the future. Our very survival is at risk due to the havoc brought by the potential for Extreme Climate. For us, our children, and our world, we need to muster the courage to make serious changes to protect and predict what may come in the Extreme Climate of the future.

Positive signs such as the rise of the Clean Tech industry show us that the future is salvageable. Even governments like China and the U.S., as well as those in Europe, are moving fast to embrace change. Global warming is a reality. Climate change is real. We can make a difference. The future citizens of the planet, our children, are counting on us for leadership, vision, and courage to put plans into action.

---

## WIRELESS PRESS RELEASE: 2012

### Eco-Terrorist Group Issues Demands

The Xwarriors, an internationally known eco-terrorist group that first appeared in America, has issued a warning to the Fortune 1000: "You will either reduce carbon emissions and global warming or we will proceed to attack the commercial infrastructure of the Western marketplace," an Xwarrior spokesperson said online.

The group demands a 50 percent reduction by 2013. Carbon reductions are already in place, but with demonstrations in America, the EU, and even China, the Xwarriors are demanding more results sooner.

"No longer can the global climate withstand the blatant disregard of the people who live here. We do not want profit. We want clean water and a pollution-free world, and we want to fix global warming now," the statement said from Director Tom Paine.

---

# Humanity's Final Exam

More than thirty years ago, Buckminster Fuller, the brilliant futurist, once remarked: "Will our civilization be able to pass the final exam?" I wondered what he meant. Now I know. Bucky, as he was known, was asking whether we would use our intelligence, resources, and ingenuity to heal the planet before the ecological devastation that even then was becoming obvious. The full question might be phrased: Will humanity pass its final exam and head off disaster? In the next few years, certainly by 2050, when more than nine billion mouths will be around to feed, we will have to answer this call and meet this great global challenge.

Future threats to the environment will play a decisive role in just how extreme the future will be in terms of survival, peace, prosperity, and health. Many of the global-warming and other climate-change risks are man-made, as we know. This is one domain that we can and must have the courage to confront, to prevent disasters that are surely waiting for us if we do not change. Many of the changes are already in play, but many more need to be adopted. There are also inevitable changes coming that are natural and beyond our scope and control.

I forecast that the private sector will make the changes and lead the charge, effectively dealing with what we can manage. Also, there will emerge a new green model of global commerce that will attract loyal

# WHAT EVERYONE NEEDS TO KNOW ABOUT CLIMATE FUTURES

■ Climate is changing in fundamental and dangerous ways that may affect the balance of power on the planet.

■ There is overwhelming evidence that humankind is harming the environment.

■ Consumers' buying choices will be affected by green corporate policies.

■ Aligning one's business with saving the environment is smart business.

■ Consumers will not buy from polluting companies and will avoid products that contribute to environmental destruction.

■ Extreme climate changes, including extreme storms and global warming, should be factored into every strategic plan.

■ Competitive advantages can be leveraged by identifying and adopting a more pro-environment strategy.

■ Conduct a long-term risk assessment of your business to determine how much you could benefit from integrating green corporate policies of nonpollution, using renewable energy, and adopting clean-technology business.

■ Increasing the ability of your business to leverage the environment as a value in customer service, product design, and marketing is an intelligent, profitable decision.

■ Develop a green corporate policy to guide your company's appropriate use of technology, investments, and practices that will support the environment.

customers. Clean Tech and other models are emerging that will lead the way toward both common sense and profit. The marketplace is listening.

Conservation, shifting to renewable clean energy, and dealing with global warming is a good start. Developing early-warning systems to better communicate and predict climate change would be smart. Smarter and more numerous forecasting models and innovations must be developed quickly if we are to prevent future disasters like tsunamis and storms.

Feeding nine billion people in 2050 with an environment that cannot sustain six billion today is a challenge of great proportions. We most certainly need to change our perspective about the environment in order to best prepare for the changes in climate that are coming. We probably cannot feed the planet without advanced, accelerated agriculture to head off mass starvation in the future. This is a tradeoff in which science can help save lives in the future.

Finally, climate change will affect everyone in the near future. National security and even our survival on the planet is at stake. We need new, even bold leaders in government and corporations who can meet this challenge before we trash the environment—and our future prosperity.

# CHAPTER 7

# Cultures in Collision: The Future of Globalization

## The Enigma

Globalization is a word that gets thrown around a lot these days, and yet it remains a confusing subject to many, even to some experts. When some people talk about globalization, they take a narrow view and act as though the concept is nothing more than the ability to produce and sell goods and services across national borders. But that is a limited view that frankly misses the much larger point of what globalization means to the future. The unraveling of globalization as a concept is a challenge. When you say globalization, most people have different and often incompatible ideas or images in mind, depending on whether they are from the U.S., Europe, Asia, or elsewhere. The clear conclusion is that globalization is misunderstood and confusing to most people.

The overarching themes that permeate this book are the explosive speed of change and the convergence of different trends that will shape the future. Globalization is at the epicenter of those themes. Globalization is about a new synthesis of ideas, trade, communications, and collaboration that should promote future global prosperity, freedom, and opportunity. This is the vision. Put together, these changes are happening at such a

# THE TOP TEN
# GLOBALIZATION TRENDS

**1.** The linkage of nations' economies into one vibrant, prosperous, and interconnected global network economy is the endgame of globalization.

**2.** Sustainable globalization could be a central force in supporting democratic reforms, reducing terrorism, promoting social progress, and bridging the gap between developing and developed nations.

**3.** Globalization promises to increase global trade, quality of life, and individual prosperity.

**4.** Globalization is a powerful force against terrorist recruiters because it supports free minds, higher standards of living, poverty reduction, improved health care, and education.

**5.** Globalization will become a catalyst for universal human rights as democratic reforms and free trade empower individual self-reliance.

**6.** Innovation-based technologies such as the Internet, biotech, nanotech, and wireless communications will enable global trade, open markets, and free enterprise.

**7.** A clash of cultures and a battle for the future will be brought on by globalization. Despots, criminals, extremists, and terrorists will seek to hijack globalization as trade and collaboration among nations grow.

**8.** The economies of China and India will be positively transformed by globalization and will offer constructive examples for the developing world.

**9.** The U.S. will benefit from being an advocate of globalization but must continue to support innovation, global democracy, and free trade.

**10.** Globalization will increase cross-cultural understanding, breaking down barriers among people of different nations as trade alliances grow across borders.

blinding pace that our leaders in government and industry are working from a script that is being rewritten anew each day. But that doesn't mean that the future of globalization is unknowable; it's a matter of putting together the right clues.

## Travels with Marco Polo

Arguably, globalization's first advocate was the Venetian Marco Polo. He was the son of a prosperous merchant, Niccolo Polo, who along with his brother did a booming business as a trader with the East. Even almost 800 years ago, business was a driving force in opening up different cultures to one another. At the time, Venice was a global center of commerce, and traders such as Niccolo and Marco Polo were effectively ambassadors without portfolio.

In 1271, when Marco was seventeen, he joined his father and uncle on a journey into China along the Silk Road, the overland route to the Orient, to see Kublai Khan, whom the two elder Polos had met on a previous journey. Khan was delighted by young Marco, who was a charming and gifted storyteller, and took him into his employ. For the next seventeen years, Marco traveled throughout Khan's realm, a world almost completely unknown to Europeans. After returning home, he published *The Travels of Marco Polo*, arguably the most famous and influential travelogue in history. It told of his journeys not only in China but also in Siam, Japan, Java, Ceylon, Tibet, India, Burma, and elsewhere. At a time when few people had ever traveled beyond their village borders, Polo's book was a revelation, opening vastly different worlds to each other and laying the groundwork for everything from trade and political intrigue to cultural and knowledge exchange.

Marco Polo saw the world unfolding. If we had traveled with him across Europe, facing down storms, bandits, and disease, and meeting traders and leaders, clergy and peasants, men and women of many cultures and classes, we would have had a glimpse of the world as it began changing and adjusting to markets, consumers, and industries yet unborn. As you begin to think about globalization, remember this: The world of Marco Polo is still our world.

Of the 6.5 billion people on the planet, relatively few are knowledgeable about other cultures. Fewer than 10 percent of Americans have a passport or have traveled outside the U.S. Language barriers persist, differences often lead to conflict, and competition is common over resources, from territory to ideology to capital to energy. At the same time, there is more peace and security. Many more people have access to essential services, and life expectancy is higher now than ever before. But we live in a world divided in many ways.

Globalization, a force of modern civilization, may overcome the issues and barriers that create division, conflict, and inequities. This new integration of trade, innovation, and progress may incite more democracy and freedoms, or it may confuse and complicate a wondering world, suspicious of globalization's risks and unaware of its potential. Globalization is still very much unraveling and will remain in a state of flux for the next fifty years. Will it become a force for global progress, collaboration, and cultural understanding, or will it be hijacked by forces opposed to these values?

Marco Polo learned that the world was made up of a larger set of cultures that offered many more choices and lifestyles than he had originally imagined. Just as his worldview in the thirteenth century was altered by contact with other peoples, I forecast that our future in the twenty-first century and beyond will be defined by our deepening understanding of other cultures, nations, and diverse ideas.

# The Many Faces of Globalization

INDIA BRACES FOR ETHNIC CLASHES AFTER ATTACK ON RELIGIOUS SITE
CHINA TELLS U.S. CONGRESS NOT TO INTERFERE
OIL APPROACHES $61 A BARREL AS TROPICAL STORMS THREATEN
U.S. SUPPLY
NEW RESEARCH SHOWS MIDDLE EAST AHEAD ON GLOBAL TECH TRENDS

Each of these headlines, taken from one day of searching Google-News for items about globalization, demonstrates the complexity and diversity of this issue. Globalization may well be the greatest challenge our modern civilization has ever faced. Not because the task is so new; there have been many efforts in the past to increase global trade among nations. The difference is that today, the complexity of factors that change in real time—from energy to climate, technology to commerce, security to economics—will become part of the globalization agenda in the future.

Globalization is the transformation of economics, culture, innovation, and trade into a new global synthesis—a new conversation about how our civilization might evolve for the better. Globalization is about the deep collaboration of nations in the world aligning around free trade and shared global concerns such as climate, energy, economics, technology, security, and democracy. As we remove trade barriers, invest in technology, and increase communication, the idea is that we will drastically reduce friction between nations, thus increasing peace and prosperity for all. This is the promise of globalization. The globalization of knowledge, of ideas that create value, may be the true legacy here.

The key challenge is to create a new type of what I call Sustainable Globalization that is good for business, good for individuals, good for free markets, and productive for both the developing and developed nations of the world. Sustainable Globalization emphasizes the social context; free societies can support fast and efficient increases in human standards of living, economies, and free choice for individuals: free minds, free markets, and free enterprise. Without attention to this social context, globalization will not develop the full potential, which is its design. Democracy can enable globalization by empowering freedom in society and in the individual.

The danger is that if globalization evolves or is perceived as an elitist Western creation, designed solely to give huge corporations access to local markets while frustrating poverty reduction and cultural understanding, the true promise of a global economic network will be doomed. We do not need more misunderstandings between cultures. We do not need globalization to be monopolized by forces of self-interest that would dominate its future. Corporations have a historic leadership role to play in helping to shape the future of globalization. This is a vital contract that will determine the success or failure of globalization's future.

# FUTURE DRIVERS THAT WILL SHAPE GLOBALIZATION

- Energy prices and energy resource availability.
- Global terrorism and crime trends.
- Free press.
- Ethnic conflict within and between nations.
- Respect for rule of law and the rights of the individual.
- The proliferation of weapons of mass destruction.
- Global adoption of innovation and technology such as the Internet.
- Open markets in which free trade can flow.
- Supply chains that enable the flow of global commerce.
- The elimination of poverty and increased standards of living.
- Global health care and pandemic control.
- The spread of global democracy and human rights.
- Rethinking global aid to increase self-reliance.
- Environmental degradation.
- Education access.

# The Future of Globalization in a Nutshell

There is a legitimate—if self-serving—agenda that should be embraced among the free nations of the world that is central to the future of globalization: Increases in trade lead directly to increases in prosperity and standards of living, which in turn lead to democratic reforms and a reduction in conflict, war, and terrorism. This is the big idea. I'm convinced this is a preferred future for globalization that would bring together the mutual interests and needs of all nations. This is why globalization is such an important trend. The developed world must figure out a new way to invest in the developing world—notice I said *invest* in the future of the developing world, not just give aid and go away.

There is no going away. There is more than a global village. Terrorists live minutes away. Global poverty greets CNN and our *Good Morning America* consciousness. The future of globalization will either be positive, hopeful, and peaceful, or pockmarked by separate fortress island states of prosperity and poverty, hijacked by extremists, terrorists, criminals, and tyrants. These are each the possible future of globalization.

The preferable future of globalization will not come easy. It will have to overcome dynamic differences both here and abroad. Some still support protectionist policies that will block open trade. This will backfire. The headlines I cited earlier that characterize globalization, even the capture of them from the Internet, demonstrate the unique differences of our time. We in the West access information from digital, even wireless sources, while much of the rest of the world, billions of people, rely on newspapers, or stories heard in the local market, or the sermons of clergy, or government-censored media channels. It is a world of differences that one thing—technology—will change faster than any other force.

At the same time, globalization is feared (and will be opposed) by nations that justifiably feel impotent in the face of more powerful nations' resources. Nations that fear globalization are concerned about the inability of their local industries to survive global competition. Often, multinational organizations that have invested in innovation, conduct outsourcing, or have access to large amounts of capital and labor pools are viewed by less fortunate nations as having an unfair advantage. In a world of increased globalization, there is a new generation of haves and have-nots, which increases global tensions.

Even in the U.S., there are deep concerns among business leaders
about globalization. Many industries are reeling from the changes. The
Chinese seem to be at the heart of many of these concerns. The same issues that smaller local companies may have in India or Mexico are
shared by U.S. small businesses. Will I be able to compete in the future
against companies in China that have access to much deeper resources
than I do? In all fairness, there are many in nations fearful of the U.S.
and Europe; they are concerned about competition and survival.

## From Curry to Barbecue

Globalization will not expand smoothly, following an easy path toward
progress and understanding. It will meet with concern and even alarm
everywhere from a small village in India to New York City. As a result,
we must tread carefully to define globalization in a way that will enable
every person and every nation to be a productive stakeholder in the Extreme Future. If there is to be equality in the future we must listen and
adapt to people's concerns.

This will be difficult. There are many contradictions that globalization poses that must be ironed out or redefined. While I am optimistic
about the future of globalization, we in the West must ensure that this
new force of civilization is a force for the productive good and not just
a vehicle for creating new markets for consumption and materialism.
We need to listen to the world. We need to respect the different voices
as we wave the flag of capitalism and encourage free markets. We must
make sure that our message and actions are respectful toward other nations that may fear globalization's predatory threat rather than see the
value of increased local self-reliance and prosperity.

Globalization means different things to different people. If you are
a Chinese merchant, you are looking at a chance to compete in the
global markets. If you are an American, you may be interested in finding new markets to sell to, like India. Globalization, the integration
and free flow of trade among the community of nations, is being her-
alded as the next big change that will better the world—rich and poor.
The truth is that globalization has never been attempted on this scale,
with this many participant nations. It is so new, and still evolving and
emerging, that it is uncertain what the end state may be.

Nevertheless, globalization advocates will persist in attempts to integrate the world's various economies into one whole. Globalization is

a brash and bold recasting of a global marketplace that could be more efficient and more profitable for the participants. But again, no one knows for certain how this next stage of global economic integration will work out. The hopeful maintain that globalization will encourage democracy, competition, free markets, and productivity. I maintain that innovation will be the key driver of globalization, enhancing quality of life in the developing world and increasing competition in the developed world. More innovation will encourage free trade, fewer barriers to trade, and open new markets to all.

## Tales from the American Taipan

Traveling the world gives me the opportunity to learn firsthand about changing cultures, understand people, and interact with the day-to-day happenings in foreign communities. Not long ago, I was traveling outside Hong Kong. It was a warm Saturday, and like many Hong Kong residents, my host took me to the open market to shop. He was known as the American Taipan, because for many years he had lived and worked in China, building businesses and getting a close look at the rise of the Chinese economy. Interestingly, although the word *taipan* means "foreign trader" in China, it's also a large, extremely venomous snake known for its oversized fangs. Revealing, no?

Though he is an American citizen, my host pulled out a Chinese passport that he used when traveling in the country. He was in business with a few influential Chinese merchants, and he had built an empire of factories and businesses that could not have existed without globalization, as he described it. He was amazed at the speed of change—in less than a decade the Chinese economy had become a dynamic market economy. "This is the beginning. Just the beginning of the shift in global power," he told me.

In my business, I have come to rely on well-placed associates around the world who give me insight on the ground—what is happening at their listening posts. Local intelligence is essential to getting a global understanding of trends. You cannot sit in an office someplace and dream about the future. You have to be in the world, engaging consumers, talking to producers, and interacting with innovators.

I have more than twenty such associates, on every major continent, many in hot spots, who play this role in my organization. Collectively, they are a loosely knit group of interested observers of trends who give me insight into what's coming next from their vantage point. I have come to value their reporting, and it often gives me a heads-up on a new trend just emerging—before it shows up here.

In this case, the American Taipan was giving me a report on what was to come in his region. First off, the linkage of supply chains is coming. From factories to shipping to warehousing to stores, the linkages with commerce would drive globalization. Next, an increase in transparency, allowing customers for manufactured goods in California to screen over the Internet production stages in China, in real time. Amazing. What the Chinese were doing was embedding technological innovations in every part of their enterprises as fast as possible.

The other major change involved quality. Increased quality was fast becoming a differentiator of Chinese production. They did not want to end up with a time lag like the Japanese. There was a time when "Made in Japan" meant cheap. No longer, but that transition took almost twenty years. China is intent on avoiding that mistake. My American Taipan reminded me that the Chinese were excellent students of history. And when it came to Japan, well, the history of China and Japan is one of war and conflict in the past. Today the relationship is one of collaboration and business.

## All in the Family:
## The Nat Nast Company

My sister-in-law Patty is an accidental entrepreneur. With her sister, Barbara, she built a multimillion-dollar company five years ago that is an example of why globalization is important—actually mission-critical. Why? Here's the story:

We were on holiday visiting my mother in Florida. Patty was complaining about her career in real estate. She disliked every aspect of it, except the money. In an offhand way, I made a suggestion, actually a forecast.

"Well, if you hate what you're doing, what about starting a clothing company, like your dad did decades ago? Bowling shirts, wasn't it?" I said. "You know, start a clothing line. Why not?" The aging baby boomers, with access to large discretionary income, were a trend I had been tracking for many years. This made sense to me. I thought, "I am the market. Baby boomers with a few bucks who wear Tommy Bahama shirts. Why not another brand?"

Patty is creative, smart, and someone who needs new challenges. She has a terrific sense of style and design. Real estate was not the place for her. A light went off. I could see it. She saw it and, well, then she and Barbara did it. Just five years later, more than 900 stores carry Nat Nast men's clothes. It is one of the fastest-growing men's brands in the nation with more than $15 million in sales. From shirts to jeans to neckties to pants, they have it all. It is not often you can share with your family forecasts they can use, but this was one that worked. I have to say, they did all the real work to achieve this success.

How does this relate to globalization, you may ask. Well, I watched Patty search the world for manufacturers that could produce—at the right price—the right embroideries, like old motorcycle, baseball, and rock-and-roll designs. Patty tried Italy—too expensive. She looked into Mexico and the U.S. Close, but no cigar. There was only one place in the world that could give her secure production, great quality, and the right price—you guessed it, China.

## The 80 Percent Equation

Nat Nast is a small company, with seemingly little in common with Wal-Mart, the largest company in the world—bigger than all of the Big Three car companies combined. But both share the same secret—without China as their chief competitive advantage, they could not do the profitable business they are doing today. Both Nat Nast and Wal-Mart also share another metric: 80 percent of their business is driven by Chinese-produced goods. This is why Wal-Mart uses lower prices as a competitive message in all its marketing. The company could not deliver on this promise without China's manufacturing muscle.

Think about this. In less than a decade, China has emerged as not just the low-cost, high-quality global leader, but the largest company in the world, Wal-Mart, has built its chief positioning in the marketplace on China's capacity to perform. Wal-Mart's competitive difference— "We are slashing prices, again"—is based on China's production. More on this later.

In the case of my sister-in-law, a curious innovation made all the difference. Her Chinese factory, which employees more than 400 workers, used advanced technology to win Nat Nast's business. It wasn't just cheap labor or even high quality. Patty's Chinese manufacturing partner built just for her—for this new company—an innovative embroidery machine that vastly increased output.

What impressed Patty was not only the quick turnaround, but also the advanced technology used to make the intricate designs Nat Nast needed to be competitive. Here were two companies, one in the U.S. and the other in China, linked by the new realities of globalization—the need to turn out many styles of clothing, four seasons a year. Patty still travels to meet with her Chinese manufacturers. It is doubtful that the Nat Nast Company (www.natnast.com) could be in business today without China's low-cost, high-quality production. But it was the attention to innovation that made the difference. Even India could not innovate as efficiently as China. Here lies a lesson about the future of globalization.

Advanced technology that can do more, that can extend a competitive advantage further, will become a decisive force in the future of globalization and global business. Globalization will be enabled by innovation more so than by any other catalyst. Innovation is the global driver of success. This is the emerging Innovation Economy I described, in action. China knows this and is investing in new tech, increasing competition around the world in other nations from Vietnam to Chile. The world is watching. Globalization is being accelerated by innovation. But where is globalization going, or rather taking us in the future? China's success shows the world what is possible. But does this also scare the world?

In the Future Map, the Five Stages of Civilization—the evolution of civilization from agriculture to the industrial age and beyond to the

## 5 Stages of Civilization

information society—is charted. The Innovation Economy will be the main catalyst for globalization. Global free trade, propelled by innovations like the Internet, shipping, and manufacturing, will create massive new consumer markets, as well as a new generation of entrepreneurs.

## My Rickshaw Engineer

On another trip to China I took close notice of the street vendors who sell a variety of goods, from TVs to watches to fish heads. As I walked around, I noticed a man selling what looked like video games.

As you might know, video-game sales in the U.S. have outpaced the sales of movie tickets, topping out at more than $7 billion per year. Production costs have skyrocketed to more than $1 million for the average game. No wonder the costs are high—a global market always looking for the next new thing is eternally hungry. With Nintendo, Microsoft, and Sony constantly upgrading the power and performance of gaming technology, the marketplace demands new game software with more advanced graphics and speed.

As I walked up to his stall, I noticed that he wore a typical small, gray cap, jeans, and a yellow shirt. I picked up one of the video-game cartridges and noticed that it was a bit pricey—more than $90. I wondered why as the vendor spoke to me in a mixture of Mandarin and broken English. Finally, I looked down and saw the explanation. My Rickshaw Engineer, as I would come to call him, had reprogrammed the videocassette. Rather than one game per cassette, as sold in stores, the videocassette in my hand held more than forty games.

## Hunger, Not Necessity, Is the Mother of Invention

I learned that my Rickshaw Engineer had used an old computer and some hacking data he had gleaned from the Internet to load forty games onto the unused memory on the videocassette. I was amazed and impressed. Yes, it was a blatant act of piracy, but his genius overwhelmed me. A Chinese man with less than a third-grade education had figured out a way to create a sophisticated product to sell to customers.

By doing so, he had made a business to feed his family, send his kids to school, and buy medicine for his mother. I viewed him as a symbol of the future of globalization—driven by innovation and survival. I was moved by his ingenuity, but more, it taught me a lesson. Cultures deprived of innovation, regardless of education, capital, or access to resources, would not be denied participation in the global economy. This is the future of globalization, not the illegal act but the unbridled, unlimited brashness of his invention, his application of innovation, even at the risk of breaking the law, to better himself and his family. The empowerment of the individual to develop one's potential will accelerate globalization and prosperity.

## INNOVATION TRENDS THAT WILL SHAPE THE FUTURE OF GLOBALIZATION

- Broadband Internet connections.
- Wireless cell-phone networks.
- Collaborative virtual workspaces.
- Real-time video-conferencing.
- On-demand supply chains.
- Nano-molecular manufacturing.
- Digital cash.
- DNA genomic data.
- Online auctions.
- Virtual production.

## The Future of Mason Mills

For more than fifty years, Mason Mills has been making specialty textiles for global multinational companies, mostly in the U.S. and Europe. They make the materials that go into the production of consumer goods from jackets to running shoes to clothes. They also make industrial fabrics. A vertically integrated company, with research, sales, and manufacturing, they do everything from design to production to sales. They own offices and manufacturing plants in the U.S.

Over the past three years, Mason Mills's business has changed for the worse. Why? I asked the founder, Bill Mahoney, a man who was born in 1920 and who has lived through wars, the Great Depression, and numerous global economic ups and downs. He is what America is about: the self-made entrepreneur who started with nothing. But there is a new danger on the horizon, a threat to Mason Mills's future unlike anything Bill Mahoney has seen before.

"We cannot compete with the Chinese," he told me. "The fabrics we offer can be sold by them for half the price. Who could compete with this?"

"But what about American innovation?" I asked. "Doesn't that make a difference?"

"The Chinese are innovative, too," Mahoney answered. "They can knock off our products faster than we can make them, and then sell them cheaper than we can."

"Why is this happening?" I wondered out loud.

"The Chinese dollar buys more than the U.S. dollar," Mahoney said.

This means that when you need to staff a factory, labor is very cheap, and skilled.

"Also," he said, "the Chinese government is subsidizing business to enable their companies to compete unfairly—with easy money, construction loans, and no regulations. Unless the U.S. government wakes up, U.S. business is in danger."

What has this meant for Mason Mills's business? This year, after an eight-figure loss, the company had to close a factory that had been operating for more than thirty years. More than one hundred jobs evaporated. Mahoney said it was heartbreaking to close the factory, but he could not afford to keep it open. The company is losing customers and sales by more than 20 percent a year. Mason has to find new niches, hold on to the customers it does have, and find new ones whose needs cannot be met by the Chinese.

Along with many other business people in the United States, Mahoney views globalization as a threat. They are losing market share—not gaining it. They are losing customers—not winning new ones. They are not innovating fast enough—and they know it. Today the threats are from China and India. Tomorrow, perhaps it will be from Malaysia or Vietnam. What is certain is that globalization is not a universally accepted positive force in the world.

Jobs will be lost in America. Retraining may or may not recover those jobs for the U.S. economy. Some companies will disappear, unable to compete in the Darwinian capitalism of the Extreme Future. Some cities in the U.S. and elsewhere in the developed world will not survive the changes that globalization may bring. Meanwhile, others, the Nat Nasts of the world, will thrive. It is an Extreme Future in which new choices will challenge our norms and change the status quo. Some experiments will be tried and fail. Others will succeed and win the day. There is much yet to discover about globalization's potential and risks.

## Three Blind Men and the Elephant

Globalization is like the ancient story of the three blind men who encounter an elephant. As each attempts to describe what he experiences, it becomes clear that each is aware of only one part of a larger animal. One man, holding the trunk, says, "This animal is long, like a snake." Another, feeling a leg, insists it is like a tree. And the last man, feeling the ears, argues assertively that they are both wrong. In his ex-

---

# GLOBALIZATION FUTURE TRENDS

- The integration of trade between nations brings prosperity and opens new markets.

- The free flow of commerce between nations reduces barriers to free enterprise.

- The sharing of cultural links increases understanding and decreases conflict.

- Technology sharing and networking increases productivity.

- The exchange of resources such as capital, people, and intellectual property.

- Alliances to address climate change, security, energy, and health care.

- Collective efforts aimed at ending terrorism make for a more secure world.

- Democracy and individual rights.

perience, the animal is like a fan. It is difficult to experience or envision all the impacts of globalization at once, so many people see one piece and think they understand it. Although globalization is still an evolving concept, certain factors are essential to understand.

## Jihad Versus Everyone Else

One of the most significant challenges that the world faces is the resistance to changes that would make globalization a productive force. This resistance is based upon unchecked disease, global crime networks, increased drug trafficking, weapons proliferation, and, of course, terrorism. These resistance factors are most present in especially poor nations where the ability of the government to substitute legitimacy for corruption is just not in the cards. Poverty, as a competitive/destructive global force, must be addressed if globalization is to succeed as our civilization steps into the future. This is not universally understood or even agreed upon. There are many corporate forces and governments that consider globalization merely an economic transformation, not a trend that is at the crux of a battle for the future between the prosperous West and the developing world. I can assure you, though, that the future of globalization is in danger if we do not address and meet this global challenge.

Some will argue that globalization itself will fix this problem, bringing living standards up for everyone else, meaning the world's poor. A rising tide lifts all boats, as the saying goes. I believe this is part of the equation to fix the problem. But a larger, grander Future Vision will be required along the lines of the Marshall Plan that rebuilt Europe after World War II. Without significant attention to the risks of globalization, the future may be damaged by those rogue forces in our global society that would exploit the poor nations, just as they do today. These rogue forces, the dictators and terrorists, would have a new rallying cry against globalization, which they would regard as the new symbol of the rich countries' narcissism. This is a clash of futures.

## Running Out of Time

If you examine the history of global aid to the developing world, the results are a mixed bag. International agencies like the World Bank, the International Monetary Fund, and the U.N., to name a few, have made progress. But the job of eliminating poverty, disease, and conflict, and enhancing quality of life—in Africa, Asia, and Latin America—remains a tall order regardless of any amount of funds. Now we are running out of time. Terrorism is increasing fast—we need more progress fast or more people will die.

The U.S., one of the largest aid providers to a world most often critical of its behavior, will have to take the lead in designing a new strategy to eliminate poverty in the developing world. The old approach of giving aid alone clearly isn't working. Providing much-needed infrastructure to developing nations—something we in the West take for granted—will be essential to globalization's future. Fresh running water, food, security, housing, quality transportation systems, health care, a stable monetary system, waste systems, and a commercial sector are all essential services that make up the infrastructure of a nation. Much of this is missing in the developing world.

And so it is not difficult to forecast that without the essential living systems in place, much of the developing world will not join the globalization party. They will be watching—not on the Internet or their TVs, because they don't have them—the future unfolding without them. This could be a global problem of huge proportions that, if not addressed quickly, has the potential to derail globalization. At the very

---

# THE NEW GLOBALIZATION INDEX

- **Economic Integration.** Trade, foreign direct investment, portfolio capital flows, and investment.

- **Political Engagement.** Memberships in international organizations, personnel and financial contributions to the U.N., international treaties ratified, and governmental transfers.

- **Technological Connectivity.** Internet users, wireless phone access, Internet hosts, and secure servers.

- **Personal Contact.** International travel and tourism, international telecom traffic.

- **Quality of Life.** Increased access to healthcare and education. Increased life expectancy.

least, the hypocrisy of the developed nations will drive a deeper schism between the global haves and have-nots. If this comes to pass, I forecast, the West will actually be helping to organize the global forces of terrorism and crime—the dual enemies of modernity. In other words, we must bring the rest of the world into the fold of globalization's bounty. If we don't, they will revolt.

The discontented will become the disenfranchised, and then they will find a way to bring down the house. If you have nothing, then you have nothing to lose. If you have no possibility of a future, then you have no concern for the present. Violence on a scale never before seen would ensue if the poor nations of the world are ignored. So, you might be asking right about now, what does this have to do with me?

## Battle for the Future

One of the central ideas of this book is determining whose Future Vision will prevail. Will it be the vision of secular, terrorist, or religious extremists who would hijack the future to insulate their societies from others, keeping them in poverty, tyranny, and manipulation? Or will the future belong to those of modernity, people who uphold the values of democracy, tolerance, free trade, and individual rights—including, religious rights?

This battle for the future cannot be won in the trenches of war, by diplomacy, or by public relations alone. It must be won in significant part by expanding the prosperity of the world and supporting security and progress to speed the creation of more peaceful and enlightened

---

# THE FIVE WARS OF GLOBALIZATION

**1.** Terrorism

**2.** Crime

**3.** Drug trafficking

**4.** Counterfeiting

**5.** Poverty

societies. Free trade, free minds, free enterprise; this is the threefold mode; that should guide globalization. This must be the true mission of globalization's future: to enable the emergence of free societies and the protection of individual rights. This is a future worth building, where democracy can thrive and the quality of life is comparable to the West. An ideology of the future that embraces tolerance, liberty, and market economies will produce peace and prosperity.

In its crudest sense, globalization is either going to be the most successful revolution to accelerate global democracy, free trade, and open markets, or it will victimize the poor nations of the world. We should also support globalization becoming a force to increase personal prosperity worldwide.

The resistance forces of globalization fear that the West continues to move forward with global dreams of free trade and democratic reforms—without including poor nations at the table. The organized global terrorist networks are counting on globalization to provide support for their dreams of global destabilization, which would allow them to continue to lure new recruits in poor nations, raise funds via crimi-

# BARRIERS TO GLOBALIZATION'S FUTURE

- High unemployment
- Global terrorism
- Trade barriers
- Depressed local economies
- Threats to energy and climate
- Tyranny
- No rule of law
- A controlled press
- War
- Poor education and health care
- Anticonsumerism

nal actions like drug trafficking, and commit acts of terror in the name of those who are being left out of the globalization game.

This is the Achilles' heel of the globalization advocates. Unless we find a way to bring the rest of the world on board fast—the have-nots—globalization will fail or drive a one-hundred-year stake in the heart of liberal reforms, open markets, and, most important, peace and security. This is perhaps the greatest challenge facing our civilization today. People without a future are the most dangerous people in the world. They will do anything to get a future—or to destroy those who they believe are robbing them of that future.

## Poverty Will Kill Globalization

Poor countries are generally weak in law enforcement. Without being competent to meet their citizens' basic needs, they are easy prey for extreme religious groups and terrorists. They also become havens for international crime. Afghanistan is an example. There was a time not too long ago when you could enter a bazaar, an open-air market, and buy any type of weapon or explosive made in the world. Afghanistan was central to the global arms trade due to the poverty and lawlessness of the nation. Of course it was also a nation that produced, and still produces, much of the world's opium for making heroin.

So in one location, with the convenience of one-stop shopping, criminals or terrorists were able to buy tanks, explosives, rockets, and guns—enough to fuel any rogue enterprise. And, as a side order, they could profit by buying heroin in bulk and then reselling it to drug users in Western democracies.

Numerous studies show that poverty drives conflict. It is not much of a leap to conclude that poverty will not just encourage war but doom globalization unless it is dealt with. The link between poverty and crime and poverty and terrorism is well established. Britain's Department of International Development found in 2004 that citizens of countries with a yearly per-capita gross domestic product of less than $250 face a 15 percent possibility of engaging in acts of violence or terrorism within a five-year period. A marked reduction in conflict-potential occurs when yearly income in a nation reaches $1,000 on average; and the risk reduces even further at $5,000. At that point, the risk falls to less than 1 percent.

# POVERTY AND TERROR TRENDS

■ Half of the world's population lives on less than $2 a day.

■ Over one billion people are malnourished today.

■ Ninety percent of the world's disease burden falls on developing nations. Yet these countries account for only 11 percent of global health spending.

■ New diseases, such as the Ebola and West Nile viruses, emerged from African nations both poor and at war, such as the Congo, Angola, and Uganda.

■ In poor nations like Pakistan, radical Muslim organizations offer free schooling, meals, and clinics in exchange for what becomes terrorist indoctrination training.

■ Crime, drug, and terrorist networks exploit impoverished war zones in Colombia, Somalia, Chechnya, and Bosnia.

■ Terrorists control trade in many conflict-ridden zones in Africa, Asia, and the Middle East.

■ Al Qaeda recruits among the poor in nations such as Malaysia, Iraq, Iran, Sierra Leone, Indonesia, Afghanistan, and Pakistan.

■ Al Qaeda also recruits from the West's Muslim communities in the U.S. and Europe, as evidenced by recent bombings, arrests, and foiled plots.

## Ranking Globalization

A useful approach to looking at globalization is to consider who has proven the best at integrating the world, sharing cultural and business ties, and translating these links into progress that can be measured. To do so, in 2004, the fourth annual A.T. Kearney/FOREIGN POLICY Globalization Index of sixty-two nations looked at a ranking of political, economic, personal, and technological trends. The survey demonstrated that increased innovation was a positive marker of globalization changes among nations. Increased Internet growth in poor countries and an upturn in cross-border travel deepened a positive shift. This showed the power of not just increased linkages with other nations, but the importance of investment, capital, and trade.

We know that these economic markers indicate progress, and where there is an uptrend in progress there is more social stability and peace and less terrorism and conflict. This is a good thing if you are concerned about preventing violence in the world from touching your community, family, or life. And this is the new way we need to think about globalization. It is not some abstract concept; it could be a force to make a better world and a safer world for our nation and our children.

Though Ireland ranked as the most global nation in this survey, due to the country's broad economic links and high levels of personal contact with the rest of the world, other nations like Singapore, Denmark, the UK, and Canada ranked high as well. This shows that you don't have to be a superpower to rank in the top tier. The United States was in the top ten, ranking first in the number of secure servers and Internet hosts per capita. This is not surprising, given the United States' primary role in the Internet from inception. Countries from Central and Eastern Europe, Australasia, and Southeast Asia also made it onto the top of the list, according to the report.

## The Two Worlds Challenge: Sustainable Globalization

The Two Worlds Challenge is the central issue that will doom or ensure globalization's future. I forecast a new paradigm to meet this challenge, bridging the Two Worlds Challenge: Sustainable Globalization. This approach seeks to use trade and economic progress as a force for actively enabling the developed and the developing world's futures—where poverty reduction, global security, and integrative trade go hand in hand.

The Two Worlds are the Aging Developed World and the Youthful Developing Third World. How we deal with this future, given the defining demographic reality over the next five to fifty years, is the following: The affluent, developed world is getting older, and the poor, developing nations of the world will experience a fertility explosion of billions of youth. The Aging Developed World—the U.S., Europe, and Japan—controls the bulk of financial assets in the world. At the youthful other end of the world, most people are born into poverty. This is the tidal wave that will wash away the potentially prosperous future of globalization if we do not prepare a strategy to deal with this demographic reality.

---

# YOUTH AND THE FUTURE

■ Half of the world's population today—more than three billion people—is younger than twenty-five years old.

■ The population of children under age fifteen is about 1.8 billion.

■ More than 80 percent of the world's people currently live in developing countries and 85 percent will live in developing countries by 2025.

■ 2.4 billion of today's total population of 6.5 billion people are children and teenagers.

■ Today, almost two billion youth under age fifteen live in the developing world.

■ By 2020, the number of children under the age of fifteen will be close to three billion.

---

The undeniable reality is that the largest growth in the global population will be in the developing world. If these children grow up poor and disenfranchised, if they are made to watch the rest of the world reap the benefits of globalization while their progress is minuscule, there will be hell to pay in the West. The global organization of terrorists would be able to easily recruit the next generation of terrorists with a battle cry against globalization.

It can be upsetting to think about the immense size of the coming problem. Nevertheless, my job as a futurist is to inform you and provoke you to think about the implications of a few billion more folks on the planet in whose world we can make a difference. This is very self-serving; by knowing what's coming, perhaps we can head off a crisis. Denial may be politely acceptable for some, but many of us have children to whom we would like to leave a safer, more secure, and peaceful future.

Maybe, just maybe, we could prevent some of the individuals who have no future from being recruited by crime and terror networks. Maybe globalization can prevent terror. That is the idea. A more intelligent and Sustainable Globalization path is possible to take. And there are about two billion turned-off young people whom we have a chance to enlist in the effort to make globalization a force for peace and security. This is a worthy objective that should guide the future of globalization. If globalization is focused on making multinationals richer and developed countries more powerful while missing the big picture described here—the need to reduce poverty, increase democracy, and share global prosperity—we will kill everyone's potential for a prosperous future.

Today there are more than four billion poor individuals on the planet. Is this a market for our products, or is this a pool of potential terrorists who will burn our cities? This is one of the central questions of our time. If we wait until there are nine billion people on the planet in 2050, it will be too late to figure this out. Remember: Two worlds, one solution. These are difficult challenges that we may not fix even in our lifetimes. For peace and security, for our children, we must try.

# CHAPTER 8

# Securing the Future

## Anthrax Alert

In 1998, I was escorted past three burly security guards and into a conference room in Washington, D.C., to deliver what I hoped would be grist for a Future Vision among federal policymakers. Before me sat thirty or so officials from the FBI and assorted federal agencies: Defense, Health and Human Services, Commerce, Intelligence, and Treasury, among others. My presentation was designed to alert them to key threats that might take shape in the decade ahead and provoke them to begin appropriate advance-planning efforts.

As part of my talk, I showed a series of images and outlined a plausible scenario for an airborne terrorist anthrax attack in Washington, D.C. Here's one of the images I showed that day:

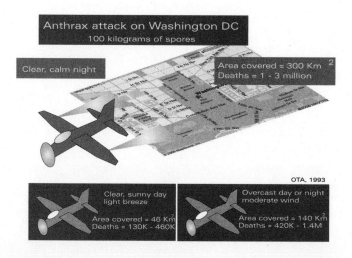

Anthrax attack on Washington DC
100 kilograms of spores

Clear, calm night

Area covered = 300 Km $^2$
Deaths = 1 - 3 million

OTA, 1993

Clear, sunny day
light breeze
Area covered = 46 Km $^2$
Deaths = 130K - 460K

Overcast day or night
moderate wind
Area covered = 140 Km $^2$
Deaths = 420K - 1.4M

# TOP TEN
# FUTURE SECURITY TRENDS

**1.** Bioterror risk is high. These weapons are invisible, silent, easily transportable, hard to detect, and able to spread rapidly in a civilian population.

**2.** Dirty bombs, a type of nuclear device, threatens life, health, and property. If you dust 400,000 people with radiation, they get sick, some die, and their city becomes uninhabitable—think Chernobyl.

**3.** World War III has begun and we are not prepared. A new type of global conflict that started with 9/11 threatens to destroy civilization.

**4.** Cyber-terror attacks are coming. As the world relies more on the linkage of all essential services, connecting commerce, finance, communications, food, transportation, energy, and health, we are vulnerable.

**5.** Future crime will be highly sophisticated, dangerous, all high-tech, and profitable.

**6.** Identity will be a highly valued commodity, capable of being bought and sold.

**7.** End of privacy is coming. Privacy will be traded for security in a future ruled by video surveillance, database sniffers, satellites, and biometrics.

**8.** Personal security market emerges. The post-9/11 world will experience the rapid advancement of innovations used to secure individual freedom.

**9.** Extreme pandemics risks leading to fierce new epidemics may make SARS, bird flu, AIDS, and Ebola seem tame.

**10.** Neuro-war—drugs, tech, devices to commit terror—will be used as a weapon to control people's thoughts and behavior. Think evil Prozac.

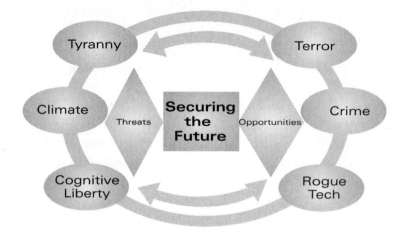

As I explained, more than 100,000 people could be at risk in a best-case scenario; the worst-case scenario meant as many as three million deaths. I explained that it made clear sense why terrorists would choose Washington, D.C., for symbolic as well as practical impact. Potential effects would begin locally with a district-wide quarantine and a virtual shutdown of local hospitals unprepared for a biotoxin attack. From there, the effects would fan out across the country and would include martial law in U.S. cities, paralyzed commerce, and closed borders, all adding up to irreparable damage to the social and economic fabric of America.

As I moved through my talk, I began getting the sense that many of the federal bureaucrats in the room weren't getting it. They weren't engaged. Not one of the government officials in that room questioned me during or after the presentation. Not one. To them, back in 1998, the idea was science fiction, too absurd even to consider.

Of course, three years later, my scenario wasn't so farfetched; not after late 2001, when two sets of anthrax-laced letters—one group sent to federal officials, the other to news media—killed five people, injured seventeen, and forced the evacuation of the Supreme Court, U.S. Senate buildings, and other federal offices. Remember, this was only days after 9/11. In the wake of that horrible, epochal event, the anthrax letters led to a nationwide alert regarding the potential that a small private plane could be used to spread anthrax or another biotoxin far and wide, with catastrophic results. Thankfully, that didn't happen, so in that sense my forecast was mistaken. Believe me, I'm glad to be wrong when it comes to the potential disasters that show up in my forecasts.

The point isn't that the federal officials I spoke to that day should have listened to me. The point is that most federal, state, and local governments—and businesses and individuals—lacked the capacity to effectively anticipate the future. Better anticipation equals better outcomes, and only after 9/11 did Americans begin waking up to that notion.

I'm confident that my anthrax presentation would be received differently today, but we are still not Future Ready in securing our nation. The attacks on the Twin Towers changed the conversation about security in the United States. However, the first time a shopping mall is attacked, or the first time a dirty bomb is released in a city, our perception of security will be altered again. Those are just a few scenarios; many other risks will threaten us in the future. Unless we prepare now by fundamentally changing how we think about security and society, some warnings will again be dismissed as too strange, even absurd, to consider. If that happens, I fear it's only a matter of time before one of them comes true.

---

# RADIATION IN THE BREADBASKET: 2026

A dirty bomb releases enough radiation to infect more than ten million people in the Midwest. In turn, it disrupts transportation, health care, and food distribution for the nation and the world.

---

## Travels in Latin America

I love Latin America, especially South America. I have traveled on business and pleasure and find the geography and culture fascinating. But it's more than that. As we begin to consider security in the Extreme Future, there are lessons for us in South America. It is a world where death, risk, and threats are part of everyone's consciousness, every day. The collision of power and influence with poverty and drugs make for a complex of contradictory forces. It is also a region where personal security is understood as necessary reality.

I will never forget meeting with the finance minister of Peru. Before I could greet him, I had to traverse three sets of military checkpoints.

As he entered the immaculate, art-filled room, he was elegantly dressed. The first thing he did was pull a 9 mm handgun out of his suit. Slapping it down with disgust, he complained, "This is what they have done to me, those terrorists." I was more than a bit surprised by his candor.

## POTENTIAL SECURITY THREATS BY 2020

- Mobile virus infects cybernetic-enhanced brain devices and ten million people lose all memories.

- Terrorists reprogram space satellites to fire on their command.

- The Internet gets hijacked by criminals and no one finds out for two years as they scramble all banking and stock markets.

- Pakistan and India engage in small yet serial nuclear conflicts, killing millions.

- Global warming speeds up by 14 percent, leaving fifty million people at imminent risk.

- The Middle East is devastated by a dirty-bomb attack, destroying all oil deposits.

- A chemical bomb blows up in the U.S. Midwest, tainting the food supply.

- An attack of Ebola in Washington, D.C., shuts down the government.

- Military robots run amok and attack civilians.

- Oil prices crash, then increase by 500 percent, then crash again.

- A Chinese conglomerate buys General Motors and Ford.

- The U.S. stops graduating top engineers and scientists.

- China produces more business-school graduates than anywhere else in the world.

- Biological weapons show up on eBay; prices start at $1.

- Iran gets nuclear weapons and goes to war.

- China invades Taiwan.

We're not there yet—there aren't any U.S. cabinet secretaries whipping out their six-shooters in meetings, at least not as far as I know—but we're not far off.

In the Extreme Future, there will be two sets of threats, traditional and asymmetric, that will defy logic, create social havoc, and alter our world. Traditional risks are what we might expect—a nuclear or bioterror attack, for instance. Asymmetric risks are what we don't expect, which might be an attack at a mall, a bioagent released into the water supply, a suicidal bomber at the Stock Exchange, or an Ebola-carrying passenger entering the land. Asymmetric risks, like flying airplanes into buildings, redefine the risk landscape and will challenge us to think differently—to accept the absurd. In several snapshots from the future sprinkled throughout this chapter, you may find hard-to-believe scenarios about potential risks that fit this category.

## My 9/11 Story

Before I delve more deeply into security in the Extreme Future, let me share a story about September 11. In the days before that future-altering moment, I was speaking to a group of CEOs at a meeting in New York City's harbor outside of lower Manhattan. I had a reservation to fly home to San Francisco on 9/11, but I decided at the last minute to leave early. I changed my reservation and left on the 10th.

On this day there was only one early morning flight out of Newark International Airport to San Francisco. On September 11, that flight—United Airlines Flight 93, the one I had originally been booked on—was one of the planes hijacked by al Qaeda. A group of courageous passengers rose up against the hijackers—you remember "Let's roll," the indelible phrase uttered by passenger Todd Beamer—and the plane ended up crashing into the ground in Pennsylvania before it could reach its presumed target: the White House.

I have often wondered what it must have been like to be on that flight. You get on, put away your bags, maybe have a drink and doze off as the flight takes off. You think about getting home to see your kids at the end of a long day. And then it happens. Without any warning, several menacing Arab men come forward to take control of the plane. A few people resist and are beaten up, then slashed with box cutters. Someone is killed, shocking the remaining passengers into momentary submission. The hijackers tell everyone it will be all right, they want to land in Washington, D.C. You know this is a lie.

Secretly, passengers make phone calls from cell phones. Reports of what happened on the other flights begin to filter from first class to coach. These guys are going to crash the plane. The terrible knowledge of when you are going to die—in moments, in terror, in a fiery explosion—hits you. You can taste it. A plan begins to form. Silent winks and stealth messages are exchanged. One, two, three, NOW.

Both the impossibility and possibility of this scenario come up like

# EIGHT REASONS 9/11 CHANGED THE UNITED STATES FOREVER

**1. Global Collaboration**. The attack was carried out with help from a global network of coordinated paramilitary forces who were well prepared.

**2. Demonstrated Long-Term Thinking**. The planning had taken years to put in place.

**3. Local Support**. Sleeper agents who lived in the U.S., Europe, and Asia played key roles.

**4. Attackers from "Friendly Nations."** The attackers were mostly from Saudi Arabia, one of America's closest allies in the Middle East.

**5. Advanced Technology**. Use of airplanes and the Internet were essential to success.

**6. The U.S. Was Unprepared**. The attack demonstrated how poorly the U.S. had planned for a terrorist threat.

**7. Attacks against the Future**. This was more than just an attack against the West, politics, or different religious views. The target choice of New York City in addition to Washington made it an attack against the Western idea of modernity.

**8. Civilians Targets**. No longer could noncombatant U.S. citizens believe they were immune from the kind of terrorist threats that have affected much of the world.

automatic pilot when I think about the courage of the people on that plane. They are the heroes who saved us all from more unknown suffering that day. But I was not on that plane; my change of plans saved my life. But I feel an eerie connection, a link of destiny to what those people on that plane went through. Perhaps I'm still around to sound warnings and offer solutions to the post-9/11 challenges we face. I certainly hope so, and I am working toward that aim.

## A New Risk Landscape

The risks we will face in the future will be new, complicated, serious, widespread, and extreme. These risks to our life, health, society, and even our sense of what it is to be human will frustrate our capacity to manage the future. This may be one of the greatest challenges we as a civilization have ever had to face.

In fact, there is an entirely new definition of risk emerging. This new risk environment is made up of the totality of threat factors, requiring new thinking about what risk is. No one likes to have to consider a new risk landscape, but it would be foolish after living through 9/11 to think we don't need to reconsider the threats around us.

One striking lesson of the 9/11 attacks was that we were not prepared. America was not Future-Ready and therefore suffered the consequences. I say this as a fact, not an attempt to place blame. In the domain of security, can we ensure 100 percent of the time that we will be ready? No. But we can get much closer to Future-Readiness.

You may be getting anxious now. Perhaps you're unsure you want to know too much more about terrorism, crime, and the threats to your life and future. These are all natural instincts. But denial is no response to risk. This chapter is designed to inform you, to raise your awareness about the future threats that may confront all of us, and ultimately to help you cope. Set aside your anxieties and read on. Will every threat described here come to pass? No. But the risk of them happening has increased significantly since 9/11, and only an ostrich has the option of sticking its head in the sand and ignoring them.

# World War III

World War III has already begun. It is a different kind of war, shaped by ideas as well as bombs, and is being fought in the cyber media and physical worlds. The first shot of World War III was 9/11. This act demonstrated the power and intent of a global military force that had become an aggressor against the U.S. We all have to look at war differently in light of 9/11. It is a new language of hostility in which the rules and borders, even the weapons of this new asymmetric war, will define the twenty-first century. World War III is unfolding now.

This message was brought home to me in autumn 2005, when I attended a summit on the Future of War with officials from the U.S. government, scientists, educators, and even a few futurists. For three days, it was our job to think about peace and war in the decades ahead.

We assembled in a secure, classified gray building that was far off the map, surrounded by many miles of fences guarded by unfriendly-looking guards. It had a top-security, Area 51 look, as though it were a secret military base built for the study of UFOs. A friend of mine, knowing where I was headed, asked me to let him know if I ran into any especially strange folks. I assured him that I did not expect to have an "encounter" of any kind.

Joining me was an odd collection of people. Professors, antiestablishment types, and wacky scientists were mixed together with military pros and spooky postindustrial men-in-black research guys. We were a sight to behold. As it turned out, the biggest differences were outward. Everyone was remarkably intelligent, open to discussion, and respectful of each other, and we got along just fine. Indeed, our different perspectives proved useful as we considered the top trends and changes facing the world in the areas of war and peace by 2025.

I came away with the realization that a vast new set of risks and threats are upon us, and if we don't learn to better understand these changes, we are in trouble. To put it bluntly, we are not prepared. More 9/11-type events loom in the near future. The following are some of my takeaway observations from this meeting:

## The Future of War

- We are not prepared for the future—and we must change that fast or it's game over. Most people do not realize how much has changed in the world since 9/11. It is an Extreme Future of dynamic, chaotic changes.

■ New future risks and new rules of engagement with nations and highly sophisticated non-state global players will threaten our world in new, potentially catastrophic ways.

■ To survive the future, America may need to become more of a global diplomat than a planetary cop, more the negotiator than the warrior. But, when we must be the warrior we must be ready.

■ China, with its new wealth and power, must step up and help stabilize the world in collaboration with the West.

■ Smart technology will play an even more vital role in securing the future.

■ World War III, already under way, will be fought on many levels, including economic battlefields such as market share, talent, intellectual property, energy, and, most of all, ideas.

■ We need to create an entirely new conceptual real-time framework about global and national security to protect ourselves and our world if we are going to survive. This must be invented to deal with a fast-moving, agile, and highly dangerous enemy bent on destruction.

■ We need to rethink war and peace to re-sync with the new realities of the twenty-first century that will be affected by new asymmetric forces of poverty, energy, demographics, climate, trade, and religion.

■ We need to reinvent the dynamic about what war is becoming. Our capacity to survive the evolution of war in the near future will require a massive, coordinated change effort among governments, corporations, and individuals.

■ How we address the future of war will determine the future of civilization. The competition of very different visions, a clash of ideals and an alignment of forces against one another will define the future.

■ We should beware of demonizing any cultural group or nation. At the same time we must know our enemies.

■ How we prepare for these future challenges, how we collaborate, how we cultivate Future-Readiness and how we navigate the realities of World War III will be the primary determinants of our future survival as a modern civilization.

## The Battle for the Future

The president of the United States begins each day with a series of intense briefings. One covers all of the potential real-time threats that could lead to war, terrorism, and disaster. Also, this report outlines the key threats that are present that day and the potential forecast, trends, and outcomes of the current risk landscape. It is a tough way to begin the day. Imagine how the rest of your day might unfold if you awoke to an overview of the top threats that might kill you and everyone you know. This chapter is your Threat Matrix, your heads-up on the dangers you need to know about now. The only difference is that we are looking out farther than the present day, out into the Extreme Future.

The enemies of the future are fast at work generating numerous threats. From hackers to terrorists to criminals to extremists to rogue states—they all have one thing in mind: Win the battle of the future. Profit from our ruin, so to speak. This is the central challenge of our time. This one trend will define the outcome of the Extreme Future. Who will prevail?

The classic battle between the forces of tyranny and democracy is one way to see what is coming in the future. Terrorist organizations are not democracies; they are tyrannical, rogue entities fighting to destabilize modernity—or at least to profit from democracy's decline. They conduct trade, recruit armies, conduct banking, raise funds, exchange resources, and build toward a different type of future. In the Extreme Future, however, war may be more complex, more asymmetric, and not purely ideological or even military, but also economic and cultural.

From identity theft to crime to terrorism to cyber theft, threats to our security will be daily events woven into our lives with varying degrees of acceptability. Though today you are more likely to get hit by a car or have a heart attack than to encounter terrorism, the future may look different. We accept that identity theft, though a hassle, is a real possibility. Or that credit-card fraud happens, but will not kill us. We know that crime is a frequent threat to our security, but not until it comes close to physically hurting us do we grow truly alarmed. Bioterror or nuclear war is another matter. Poisoning our water supply or filling the air we breathe with cancer-producing chemicals are other possibilities as well. In this chapter we will consider the top threats to security—what you want to watch out for and why.

# The Terror Zone

Terrorist organizations operating in Asia, Europe, South America, and Africa have many differences. Some are ideological, like The Shining Path from Peru, who are Maoists. Some are political, like the Tamil Tigers from India. Others are religious, like the radical Muslims. Some are state-sponsored, like those from Syria and Iran, and some are freelancers or private organizations. Not all are ideological or religious. They are often a blend of ideologies with a common pro-terror theme.

Sometimes there are crossovers that include elements of several of these, such as the FARC, the Colombian insurgents battling in Latin America who collaborate with cocaine traffickers by charging fees for protection. There are also homegrown terrorists in the U.S., like the crew that blew up the Federal Building in Oklahoma City, who are just as dangerous as foreign terrorists.

Each of these terrorists, domestic or foreign, religious or ideological, has one thing in common. In order for terrorism to be effective, noncombatants must be targeted. At the moment, that usually means violence. In the future, however, we will see an increase in sophisticated strategies as terrorists move into counterfeiting, theft, drugs, and mainstream business like real estate and pharmaceuticals. In the future, the collaboration of the terrorist-criminal global industrial complex will emerge. The more innocent who are hurt, even destroyed, the greater the gain. It is that simple. Terrorism is unconventional warfare brought to innocent civilians who will be used to pressure those in power to change—to meet the demands of the terrorist agenda.

Ultimately, the terrorist agenda is also always the same—the attainment of power. The key difference between traditional organizations and terrorist ones is legitimacy. Legitimacy is inextricably linked to operating within the rule of law. Civilized societies cannot allow terrorism to persist and expect to survive intact.

## The Terrorist Vote

A recent example of this strategy occurred in 2004, when Islamic terrorists altered the upcoming election of a new government in Spain by bombing the Spanish railway system. This heinous act so galvanized the opposition party that it was able win votes with its promise that, if elected, Spain would pull out of the coalition in Iraq. The gambit worked. An act of terrorism changed the government of a major European nation and sent shock waves throughout the world. Terrorists were more than influencing politics; they were setting the agenda and deciding the winners!

This unprecedented success changed the prospects for global terrorism, reinforcing the idea that terror can be an effective tool for furthering a political agenda. When government allows terrorists to shape the agenda, then that government's future is in question. This is not the first time that terrorist organizations have been successful at shaping a

---

# RISE OF ECOTERRORISM: 2019

Most industrialized nations did not heed the early warning signals of global warming. Even after ten Category 5 hurricanes hit the U.S. Gulf Coast over five years, and despite evidence of ozone-layer decreases and rising skin cancer rates, leaders demonstrated little resolve. Then came the ETs, the ecoterrorists, a violent breakaway movement of the Greens in Europe and the environmentalists in the U.S. They bombed the Alaska pipeline and the oil tanker *Westmoreland*. Their message: Change or face the consequences. Though the public disapproved of the group's violence, polls showed support for its cause—energy freedom. Realizing that they were on the wrong side of public sympathy, political leaders began to accept that it was time for change toward renewable energy.

political agenda. In Colombia, the previous government actually agreed to allow a part of the nation to be carved out and ruled by terrorists, the FARC, to placate them; a type of truce. This is not sustainable. If the global terrorist-criminal industrial complex is allowed to thrive, modern society is finished.

## Shootout in Lima

The first time I encountered terrorist forces, I was supposed to be on vacation. Some vacation. In 1995, I went to Peru to trek up to Machu Picchu in the Andes mountains. This is one of the most spectacular places to climb in the world, quite untouched by civilization, raw in natural beauty, and replete with awe-inspiring ancient Incan architecture.

As I arrived in Lima, I learned that we had a slight problem. The Shining Path Maoist forces had surrounded our airport and were in a fierce firefight with the army. The Shining Path was a tough lot, facing off against an even tougher Latin-American government. The rat-a-tat and booms of 55 mm machine-gun fire and explosives greeted me as we walked off the plane.

You have to appreciate the cultural complexity here. We're talking about a Chinese-inspired Maoist terrorist group operating in a Latin-American nation that was eventually defeated by an ethnic Japanese leader. Now that's globalization! They were battling for the hearts, minds, and souls of Peru, a mixture of Incan Indians and Spanish citizens.

I asked a black-clothed, machine gun–wielding general for his take on the situation. After all, I had come to climb mountains, not battle terrorists.

"There is no problem. This is a routine matter and it will be over soon," he maintained with an authoritative élan in thickly accented English.

"How soon do you think?" I asked, looking at my watch.

He looked at me and puffed on his cigar. "You Americans. You don't get it, do you? Most of the world has been fighting terrorists for centuries, except you Americans."

By "soon," he was counting in months or years, not minutes. Of course he was right. America had been spared what everyone else was quite familiar with. After 9/11, though, terrorism was brought home.

Now, evil had a face in America for all to see. But a gap remains between awareness and action.

---

# THE TWELVE TOP TERRORIST WEAPONS: 2025

- Neurowar
- Biological Weapons
- Quantum Weapons
- Infectious Disease
- Toxic Chemicals
- Dirty Bombs
- Pulse Energy Weapons
- Satellites
- The Wireless Internet
- RFID and GPS Networks
- Human Biology

---

## Coming Back From Cape Town

I had another firsthand experience with terrorism on a trip back from South Africa. It was two weeks before apartheid was ending and Nelson Mandela was coming into office. I had been working with the government and was rushing off to the Johannesburg airport.

Just as I arrived, there were soldiers everywhere with automatic weapons. Apparently terrorists had just bombed the airport. The immediate danger had passed by the time I arrived, but I was still shaken by the thought of what might have happened. Of course, to the South Africans around me this was nothing special. But my brush with violence was not over.

It is a long trip from South Africa to London's Heathrow Airport. The fifteen hours went by slowly as I tried to sleep and read. Upon arrival in England, I was met by machine gun–wielding special-force

# WHY THE U.S. IS STILL UNPREPARED FOR TERRORISM

- Fewer than 5,000 beds are available to deal with a bioterror attack.

- There is a shortage of drugs to meet the needs of a large population suffering from a nuclear, bio, or chemical attack.

- There is a critical shortage of skilled doctors and nurses.

- There are far too few trained first-responders.

- Coordination among intelligence and defense agencies is still questionable.

- Coordination among federal, state, local, and regional health, fire, safety, and law enforcement agencies is inconsistent.

- The communications network to inform, warn, and coordinate resources in the event of an attack is still being built.

- There are inadequate safeguards on chemical, nuclear, and biological facilities.

- Agency turf battles trump coordination between state and federal governments, just as seen after Hurricane Katrina.

- There is no real-time data-capture to track people who may pose a threat.

- There is no reliable network for real-time health and safety communications in the event of a disaster.

- The nation's ports are still not protected with adequate screening technology.

- The U.S. is not ready to screen or prevent a bioterror or nuclear public-health hazard, including a diseased person entering the country.

- A proper balance between privacy and security has not been found yet.

commandos who rushed us off to our connecting flight to the U.S. with a certain professional anxiety. I asked a nearby commando what the rush was about. He was a *Monty Python*–cast *capitan* with an immensely manicured mustache that offset the wry smile that punctuated his urgency. He pointed out the window to a distant hill.

"See that hilltop?" he asked me.

"Yes, I do, but what am I supposed to be looking at?"

"Well, you see, that's the hill where the IRA terrorists are shooting at us."

"You mean now? Shooting at us now?"

"Oh yes, sir. But don't worry. Their range is off. You'll be OK if we can hurry along now."

The IRA had decided to attack Heathrow on the same day the airport was bombed in South Africa. For me and my fellow passengers, it was ALL terrorists, ALL day.

## Dialogue at the White House

Two poignant experiences with two leaders gave new meaning to the concept of security for me. These experiences helped to lay the foundation for this book. They occurred at a meeting at the White House in 2004, and involved Tommy Thompson, then-Secretary of Health and Human Services, and Tom Ridge, the first head of Homeland Security.

Thompson talked about how he came to office and had been charged with 700 food inspectors to oversee the nation's 25,000 food-processing plants. He wanted to be honest about the enormity of the challenges that he and the nation faced in protecting public health. Of course, the implication was clear: How could 700 inspectors possibly handle this many food-processing plants? Speaking with him after his talk gave me a rare look into matters of his concern.

When Thompson left office, his last speech to the nation focused on the vulnerability that still existed as a result of the failure to protect food and water supplies. He was and is 100 percent correct about this risk. It still persists today.

Ridge had an impossible but vital job. He told us at the same White House meeting how there were thirteen databases that held all of the essential information he needed to get access to just about everyone in the United States. He regretted that he lacked the technology to access the relevant components of this information, and also expressed his frustration that, by law, he could not even look at a number of these resources.

The implication was once again clear. How could he do his job if he remained shut off from using these resources? As he saw it, potential terrorists, criminals, and other threats to the nation were at large, but he was limited in his ability to find them before they struck.

Both Thompson and Ridge had made their point without saying it. There was a new risk landscape that had emerged and we were not ready to deal with how it would affect security. I sat back in that honest but clearly frustrated atmosphere and realized that the paradigm of personal security had changed in fundamental ways.

Everything we believed we knew about security had to be rethought. The future of security—what was possible—changed on 9/11. If we had been prepared for 9/11, if we had defeated the terrorist bombers, we could say that our forecasting capability was on the mark. But, of course, that was not the case.

We have to accept that we were not ready. Our lack of Future-

## NEXT METH DESTROYS YOUTH: 2015

A security threat anticipated in 2006 but not dealt with fast enough was the rise of cheap and powerful meth, a drug so damaging that more than 60 percent of American and European youth had tried the drug or were using it regularly. Users and dealers were financing their habit by conducting other crimes such as identity theft and kidnapping. The violent crimes associated with Next Meth, a new, more powerful version that lasted longer and did more damage to brain cells, created a mass epidemic by 2010. After the one hundredth death, the polls showed something had to be done fast to save our youth from this addiction.

Law enforcement, paralyzed with the large use and widespread adoption of Next Meth, finally turned to the federal government. The use of the National Guard, high school screenings, and quick drug searches definitely compromised personal freedoms. Many felt it was necessary to control the plague of use that had dominated the youth of the nation, and soon the world.

Readiness on 9/11, more so than at any other time in modern history, was a dangerous gap that cost thousands of lives. We could have done better, we all agree. It could be argued that although we are moving in the right direction that we, as a nation, as a world, are still unprepared to deal with the global war on terrorism. One thing to remember, though, is that this is an asymmetric war, one that must confront enemies in many forms.

## Dirty Bombs: The Invisible Weapon

The dirty bomb has been used as a weapon only once that we know of—in Iraq, in 1987. A dirty bomb is generally a small nuclear weapon that disperses radiation over a limited area. Wind can carry the radiation even farther. The dirty bomb is a poor man's nuke in that it does not contain the familiar power of the classic atomic explosion, in which death and destruction are enormous. The impact of a dirty bomb may be limited in its scope of destruction, but its destabilizing effect can be huge.

Dirty bombs are imprecise weapons of terror that are inexpensive, small, and easy to manufacture. Radiation cannot be seen, smelled, felt, or tasted. Therefore, if people are present at the scene of an explosion, they will not immediately know whether radioactive materials were involved. The dirty bomb is an invisible weapon that can have a devastating impact on a population. The havoc and panic alone could destroy a U.S. city.

Some cancers can be caused by exposure to radiation, but it is not possible at this time to make accurate estimates of fatalities or casualties. Being at the site of a dirty-bomb explosion does not guarantee exposure to radioactive material. Until doctors are able to check people's skin with sensitive radiation-detection devices, it will not be clear whether they are exposed. Different people may react differently to the radiation. Different levels of exposure produce different health impacts.

Beyond public health, a problem with dirty bombs is its long-lasting effect on the environment. The probability is low that an area can be made habitable after an explosion. This renders the affected area off-limits until sufficient cleanup is possible. Imagine a bomb of this type released in Washington, D.C., and you can begin to see the potential impact. Kiss the capital good-bye.

# AFTER A DIRTY-BOMB ATTACK:
# WHAT YOU NEED TO KNOW

- Leave the immediate area on foot. Do not panic. Do not take public or private transportation such as buses, subways, or cars, because they might be contaminated.

- Go inside the nearest building. Staying inside will reduce exposure to any radioactive material that may be on dust at the scene.

- Remove all clothing as soon as possible. Place clothes in a plastic bag and seal it. Removing clothing will remove most of the contamination caused by external exposure to radioactive materials. Save the contaminated clothing to allow testing for exposure without invasive sampling.

- Take a shower or wash as best you can. Washing will reduce the amount of radioactive contamination on the body and will effectively reduce total exposure.

- Be on the lookout for information. Once emergency personnel can assess the scene and the damage, they will be able to say whether radiation was involved.

*U.S. Centers for Disease Control*

# The Double-Edged Sword
# of Innovation

As much as this book hails the coming Innovation Economy Age, there is a dark side of innovation. The same fast-moving, disruptive technologies that will be such a positive force in the global economy—Nano-Bio-IT-Neuro—will also be the innovations that have the greatest potential to threaten our world.

This is an honest but sobering thought: The innovations that will provide greater competitive advantage, improved education, prosperous commerce, increased quality of health care, and a higher standard of living might also be used to annihilate civilization as we know it. The very innovations that make up the Internet, computers, and biotech may be used against us. Think of the Internet used as e-mail and propaganda tools by terrorists, or computers used to plan attacks and manage networks of people, or biotech used to make weapons.

What kind of future do we want? What are we willing to do as a civilization to protect and secure the future? What must we sacrifice? If we are to survive the Extreme Future, we must learn to navigate carefully, with precision and purpose; recognizing that there will be sacrifices along the way, like privacy. Without proper attention to the threats we face, and without adequate efforts to prevent the risks they carry, we are doomed. This is why I am writing this book. We must prepare to secure the future by developing a deeper understanding of the Future Security Map, starting with the rest of this chapter.

## A Future Worth Defending

I realize that this is a conundrum. As we invest in the future, we are placed at risk by those same investments. The Internet was used regularly to encrypt messages within the al Qaeda network to post instructions to tell people what to do. Pornography sites were used to avoid suspicion. (How strange is that?)

Each flashpoint from the Extreme Future has similar factors. Each future depicted ends up with social upheaval, mass chaos, instability, and uncertainty, and each requires more of a crackdown on individual freedoms. In fact, most of the freedoms we enjoy today will

### ROGUE TECH FUTURES—WHAT IS ROGUE TECH?

Rogue Tech is any technology that can be used by criminals, terrorists, or nations to commit illegal acts, conduct violence, oppress individuals' rights, or limit dissent.

#### Future Rogue-Tech Threats: 2040

*Bio-Hackers*—Terrorists who disperse wireless viruses into people's medical devices.

*Digital Cloners*—Terrorists who steal identities to commit untraceable crimes of financial theft or terrorism.

*Nano-Terrorists*—Those who will use military-grade nanotech to make miniaturized bombs and weapons for sale to the highest bidder.

*Drug Doublers*—Criminals who counterfeit pharmaceutical drugs and medical devices and sell them as real.

*Gene Dopers*—Criminals who sell stolen DNA for illegal performance use.

be under fire in the future. It will be difficult to maintain certain freedoms in a democracy when the rogue factors in the world—criminal, terrorist, and sociopath—have used freedoms to attack our society. It is not hard to forecast that we will trade our privacy for security in the future if and when serious threats are carried out, resulting in loss of life.

Now, most of us may not consider mind-control drugs, brain implants, oil-eating bugs, or virus attacks to be realistic threats. But in the future, anything is possible when innovative technologies fall into the hands of dictators, terrorists, and criminals.

## Hacking for Fun and Profit

Hacking is a large, global, well-coordinated rogue industry run by sophisticated players. I don't mean the internal hacker at our average corporation who is angry with his boss. I mean the criminal and terrorist entrepreneurs who are motivated by lucrative profits. In the future, by 2025, their revenues will rival those of the defense industry.

By some estimates, the damage bill for hacking in the United States last year was more than $20 billion. That number is low. Global damages may run as high as $100 billion and more. Our forecast for 2010 is $300 billion. Hackers steal funds, steal identities, break into networks, conduct sabotage, cause breakdowns, release viruses, and destroy computer systems.

So far, the good guys are not winning the war. They are undermanned, underfunded, and late to the party. I do not think this situation will change much in the future: As long as there are billions to be stolen with a cursor or the pointing of a mouse, there will be hackers.

The real tragedy is that more than 90 percent of hackers work for the same organization they steal from. Convenient, you say? Sometimes they are the same well-trained geeks who wrote the programs designed to protect your money. Imagine the twisted thinking: "Rather than protect the funds, I'll steal them." I don't want to trivialize or generalize this huge, growing problem, but that is simply how it is.

*HEADLINES FROM THE FUTURE: 2015*

**U.S. Productivity Slips 20% After Info-War Attack on Stock Exchange**

It is probably a good bet that these foes of security are doing this for pure profit, and there is a lot of profit to be gained. Even the tiniest piece of $20 billion buys a first-class condo in Barbados or a new Ferrari. Crime pays.

The freelancers, like the Shadow Crew or the Menace Posse, are hackers for hire. These bad boys work for criminals or conduct their own extortion and cyber-crime. There is a willing market for data, personal identities, and industrial theft. This is the future—hackers going after big-ticket booty like intellectual property, ICBM and nuke secrets, and industrial plans.

## Cyjacks: The Future of Hacking

Here is a scenario to consider: I believe that there is a 75 percent probability that cyber thieves, called cyjacks, have already stolen billions of dollars, and that the financial institutions they victimized don't know (and may never know) the money was taken. Think about this: What if you could steal billions and change the record system so that the bank never knew that you tampered with one system that held the funds, another that moved the funds, and another that checked on the accuracy of the funds? Does anyone really know?

The truth is that the future of hacking is bright. If you're a hacker, that is. There are plenty of incentives, plenty of vacation time, and more. The future of hacking is also not so bright, if you're a CEO. Until CEOs place as much concern and investments into security as they do the bottom line, the hackers will keep winning the war.

Eventually, a few smart CEOs will figure out that they could be more effectively protecting their customers' identities and funds if they were to invest smartly in security. And security will be a competitive advantage even more so in the future. Until then, security is at risk and hackers will thrive in the Extreme Future.

## The Future of Identity Theft

Identity theft happens when a thief gets his hands on consumers' Social Security numbers, mothers' maiden names, dates of birth, or enough other personal information to steal a person's identity. That's easy to do, given how extensively that information is used by businesses, financial institutions, schools, and government agencies.

# TOP SEVEN HACKER TRICKS: 2015

**1. Auto-Phishing.** Hackers set up wireless networks that people use to connect to the Internet when driving. Then the hackers use those autoconnections to steal personal information.

**2. Bank Morphing.** Hackers set up duplicate online bank sites to gain access to personal and corporate banking accounts.

**3. DEPs.** Hackers create DEPs, digitally engineered personalities, that pose as the account holders to gain access to the funds in the accounts.

**4. ID Clones.** Hackers set up digital clones of real people with stolen identities and conduct global business, open accounts, transfer funds, make transactions, take out loans, and then disappear with the loot.

**5. Data Assassins.** Hackers kill off personal or corporate data history and set up new histories to create new identities to secure funds, contracts, products, services, etc.

**6. Rogue Knowledge Engineers.** Hackers with sophisticated capability create secret portals to banks, stock exchanges and currency-trading networks in which all actions are self-liquidating, so that the theft is never even seen or recorded.

**7. NanoBots.** Hackers send out wireless smart robots with nanoscale antennas that watch consumers' behavior, reveal buying habits, and send back info.

Identity theft is the fastest-growing crime in the nation, affecting millions of Americans every year. Identity theft has increased more than 1,000 percent over the last three years.

The U.S. Federal Trade Commission has put the number of yearly victims of identity theft at about ten million, or nearly 5 percent of the adult population in the U.S. The agency estimates that identity theft costs $50 billion a year in false charges and lost time. As more companies keep records on consumers, the possibility of those records being compromised will increase. The kinds of records kept range from mortgage and banking information to what kind of soda pop you buy at your local supermarket. Using club cards and other discount coupons and paying for it all with credit cards allows marketing companies to target consumers with further offers. The same forces that will drive the interconnectedness of information productivity, efficiency, and cost-effectiveness, as well as the need to better understand consumers based on their personal preferences, will provide a brave new world for criminals and terrorists.

> *HEADLINES FROM THE FUTURE:*
> *2026*
>
> **Genomic Tests Find Clones**
> **Stole Real Human Identities**

Identity theft will grow to more than 30 million victims a year by 2008, costing more than $300 billion in the U.S. alone. The global cost of identity theft will grow to more than $700 billion by 2010. The more that progress spreads on the tail of new-networked economies, the more that prosperous individuals will become targets for criminal interests.

The threats to individual privacy will become more obvious when we consider what types of resources databases may contain in the future:

# TOP TEN RESOURCES THIEVES USE FOR IDENTITY THEFT: 2006

1. Medical records

2. Phishing via e-mail

3. Credit histories

4. Vehicle, boat, and plane registrations

5. Social Security numbers

6. Change-of-address forms

7. Birth records

8. Online personal information

9. Property ownership and transfer records

10. Professional licenses

# TOP FIVE RESOURCES THIEVES USE FOR IDENTITY THEFT: 2015

**1.** RFID data collection

**2.** Online patient records from hospitals

**3.** Online voting data

**4.** Online prescriptions

**5.** Wireless Wi-Fi taps on Internet phones

## Privacy for Sale

Think about this: More than six billion people live on the planet today, and more than nine billion people will be alive by 2050. The information processing, managing, communicating, and transaction needs of nine billion people cannot even be conceptualized today. There are not enough cell phones, computers, and Web sites. But in the future, ten to fifty years from now, we will be able to manage the planet's population with vast networks of information that will dwarf the medieval networks we have today. Supersentient computers at the nanoscale will operate silently, networking people around the world. This is inevitable. See the Innovation Economy chapter for more on this. Chips linked everywhere—to satellites, video, Internet, and cars—will blanket us with security.

Many citizens may be aware that credit bureaus collect data on them, but most aren't aware of the vast number of commercial data brokers that also do it. Until the well-publicized breaches of some of the major players this year, few people had heard of companies like ChoicePoint and Seisint, a unit of LexisNexis. But this is the early stage of a more sophisticated threat that people will face in the future. A look back at the recent cases sets the stage for the future threats to come.

Information regarding 670,000 customers at four different banks was stolen. The U.S. Treasury Department has called it the largest financial security breach in history. The institutions involved include Wachovia, PNC Bank, and Commerce Bancorp. In February 2005,

Atlanta-based ChoicePoint, a data brokerage firm, announced that its workers had inadvertently sold personal information to a criminal ring, and that approximately 145,000 people were affected. In 2005, more than forty million credit cards were hacked. Twenty-two million Visa cards and fourteen million MasterCards are quite the take.

Then there were the 3.9 million Citigroup customers whose data was lost—I mean stolen—in 2005. Around the same time, Bank of America announced that it had lost information containing the records of consumers and accounts of 1.2 million customers of the U.S. Government's SmartPay charge-card program. In March 2005, the following month, hackers broke into Seisint, a database company that is a unit of Reed Elsevier's business information subsidiary, LexisNexis.

What's going on? Privacy for sale to the highest bidder, and there is

## TOP TECHNO-PRIVACY THREATS BY 2020

- Video cameras in every office and public space.
- Databases holding financial information on consumer purchases.
- Personal genomic databases where records about your DNA are stored.
- Use of DNA analysis for jobs, advancement, and relationships.
- Transportation tags used for travel on any public transportation.
- In-vehicle black boxes that monitor driving location and performance.
- All Internet phone or e-mail communications.
- RFID (Radio Frequency ID) chips in all consumer and industrial products.
- Interactive two-way digital TV.
- GPS chips in all computers, cars, phones, and kids.
- Every object has an Internet address and is online, connected, watching, and being watched.

no end in sight. These are not isolated events but rather a coordinated strategy by organized crime and terrorists to exploit America's vulnerability—personal financial information. New identities will be created, bank accounts stolen, and illicit actions from theft to terrorism will cascade from this treasure trove of America's info booty. This stolen data will now be "chopped," repackaged, and sold to offshore rogue interests that have a larger agenda. In the years to come, the devastating blow of these events and other identity thefts to come will play a role in larger illegal acts designed to remind us of the price to pay for not securing the nation.

The identity theft gets bigger and the price for cards, names, and personal information goes up, up, up. My forecast is that ID theft is an uptrend in the future, where the Criminal-Terrorist Industrial Complex will thrive unless the good guys get smarter, faster. There are more than fifty Web sites where anyone can go online and pay as little as

# THE TOP TEN TERRORIST TARGETS BY 2025

**1.** Food supply poisoned, closing down five cities during resulting food riots.

**2.** Water purification plants destroyed, causing disease.

**3.** New York City transit system attacked with a toxic chemical like sarin gas.

**4.** Destruction of a stock market's information warehouse by computer virus.

**5.** Biological release of mutated strain of West Nile virus over three cities.

**6.** Wireless virus in medical devices disables millions.

**7.** The Western advertising and media, over the Internet.

**8.** Pharma-Terror.

**9.** The global telecom Internet network.

**10.** The education system.

$100 per credit-card number. I could find out any information I wanted about any American online in twenty minutes. This is a multibillion-dollar criminal conspiracy that in the Extreme Future will derail society unless it is stopped.

## You're Being Watched

Japanese police routinely knock on doors and visit with citizens to ask about strangers and seek information about illegal acts. Visits by police into homes are considered normal, and tea-drinking police are frequent visitors throughout the country.

In China, a new computer chip called an RFID—Radio Frequency Identification Device—is planned for insertion into every one of the identification cards that all citizens must carry. Also, a new biometric facial-recognition system is being tested in cities for taking pictures of everyone's faces to see if they are criminals. Wireless video security scanners will be everywhere by 2010.

We take for granted the many eyes watching us, the video cameras following us, the databases monitoring our every behavior. But this invasion of privacy will seem tame as we step into the Extreme Future, where others will watch every act, every behavior, every association, every interest, every transaction, and every communication. Are we ready for the end of privacy as we know it? If one threat will encroach on our personal liberties more than others it will be the assault on our privacy brought by the convergence of technology and social policy amid the insecurity of the future. George Orwell's nightmarish vision of the future, expressed in 1984, might seem like a golden age of liberty.

Several significant events regarding consumer privacy have occurred in recent years that point to

> **HEADLINES FROM THE FUTURE: 2025**
>
> **Eye-in-the-Sky Satellites Achieve Complete Global Coverage, See Everyone, Everywhere**

the future of privacy—and the future is not good. These privacy threats demonstrate that individual privacy is at risk today and will be even more at risk tomorrow. Why? Here is a simple but powerful fact about the evolution of government, business, networks, and your personal information: As more databases, more computers, and more networks get connected, linking banks, telecom, Internet, and government into one super-linked network, chances are high your privacy will be stolen, misused, or violated. At the very least, you will be watched, analyzed, and monitored 24/7.

## Extreme Security

In 2003, I entered one of the most secure and technologically advanced buildings in the world. It was the central bank building in Johannesburg, South Africa, a city known for its rigid security. "Joburg," as the city is known, has a reputation for violence that would frighten most Americans. Virtually any stop at a red light might be an invitation for one of the more than one hundred carjackings that happen each day. One fellow finally fed up with getting robbed and beaten placed a flamethrower in his car for defense. I understand that he is still driving it without incident.

As I walked into the building past the armored guards in their futuristic black SWAT garb, the first thing I noticed were small yellow lockers behind the desk. I asked what they were for. The receptionist coolly informed me that this was where the bankers and their guests left their weapons before they went upstairs for meetings. As she was speaking to me, cameras slowly followed my actions, scanning my face and body, triggering some silent, covert identity-capturing system—I was to realize later. I thought to myself. "These must be really tough bankers to carry guns under their three-piece suits. Quite the visual." I asked about how many bankers checked their guns. She said most.

Then I had to give a voiceprint, saying my name, "Dr. James Canton." The receptionist, clearly a highly trained security person, captured my voice and a picture of my face and stored them in a database. I was told to approach what looked like an air lock before the elevator. As I entered, I had to say my name again. I entered and for an instant I was held in the air lock as my identity was confirmed. Then I was released. I was frozen just long enough for discomfort to set in. Armed guards waited for me as if to watch me pass or fail, weapons at the ready. I assume they were scanning my face against a database of bad guys to see if I was OK. Upon leaving the building I had to provide yet another voiceprint and a faceprint to be validated and re-cleared by security.

I have been to many high-security government and industrial

buildings in the U.S., but I had never experienced this level of security. It was, of course, a sign of what will come in the Extreme Future, where every building will be outfitted with security tech.

# THE FUTURE SURVEILLANCE SOCIETY: 2015

- By 2015, the United States will have more than ten million closed-circuit television cameras, more than half operated by government agencies, the rest by private security and corporations. The average citizen in New York City will be photographed 500 times a day.

- All TVs will be two-way interactive. They will watch us as we watch them.

- Biometrics will be used to capture facial, iris, fingerprint, voice, or breath scans before you can enter or leave a room or building.

- Genomic personal-identity cards will be required to enter or leave areas in a city or town. They will have unique DNA markers for each individual.

- Mobile Autonomous Robots will sniff out hazards, toxins, and even people using advanced "smell radar" to authenticate our identities.

- Global Positioning Systems will signal satellites, authenticating our true identity and registering who we are, where we're going—and perhaps wondering why?

- Every chip in every product will be online, linked to GPS satellites that can track every human on the planet.

- Security chips will be embedded in our skin and used to buy, sell, and authenticate our identity.

## Dangerous Minds

The control of minds is a difficult thing to keep up with. Cognitive liberty will be on the chopping block in the twenty-first century. Even as government authorities seek to limit the type of Web sites allowed into a nation's cyberworld, they will quickly find out how incompatible industrial progress is with the need for free access to information. Digital capitalism requires free information access. Even in Canada, the types of TV programs allowed into the country are controlled, especially from the U.S., so the government can "protect" its citizens from violent cartoons or shows that might affect kids. China censors the Web. Many nations, even the British and French, restrict the media its citizens can access.

This is where the issue of "cognitive liberty" fits in. According to Wrye Sententia, director of the Center for Cognitive Liberty and Ethics (www.cognitiveliberty.org), cognitive liberty is about protecting and promoting the right to think independently, as an individual. In my conversations with Wrye, it is clear that we are trending toward less freedom and more restrictions—dangerous waters ahead.

There are three aspects of cognitive liberty:

1) Existing and emerging technologies to track, monitor, or perform surveillance on human cognition.

2) Biological punishment using pharmacotherapy or remote/embedded mind-control technologies.

3) The status of personal freedom, democracy, and self-determination around the globe.

## Tyranny of the Mind

A true believer is someone who is focused on a cause that's bigger and more powerful than he or she is. There are no questions permitted, only dogma. There is no free choice. In the mind of a terrorist, there is only room to follow orders. There is no room for dissent, free speech, or a moral compass. Democracy and modernity are enemies of terrorists. Educated, informed, free people have the right to choose. Of course, most terrorists, domestic and foreign, believe the ends justify the means. Violence has a purpose and a moral platform. Terrorist mindsets are based on a tyranny of the mind that is akin to the tyranny of a nation—oppression of free rights of individuals. This is why terrorists will battle for a future that does not include democratic values. Individual freedom is a threat to the power of tyranny.

Americans often have a difficult time understanding the hostility directed toward them by Muslim extremists. Not all Muslim extremists are terrorists or hate America. Not all extremists or terrorists are Muslim. Some extremists are just that, extreme in their views about America. This does not make them terrorists, either. Terrorists take the next step beyond sympathizing with extremist views, to committing acts of terror.

In a democracy, we are accustomed to free speech and we tolerate differences, as long as these expressions are within the rule of law. After 9/11, however, the U.S. climate has shifted to being less tolerant, more vigilant, and more concerned about how extremism might lead to terrorism.

---

# TWELVE STRATEGIES ESSENTIAL TO ENDING TERRORISM BY 2025

**1.** Free elections.

**2.** Free press.

**3.** Higher education.

**4.** Elimination of state-sponsored terrorism.

**5.** Due process and the rule of law.

**6.** Protection of individual rights.

**7.** End of regional wars and the culture of violence.

**8.** Transformation of dictatorships into democracies.

**9.** Increased global trade and economic prosperity.

**10.** Access to innovations like the Internet and computers.

**11.** Rise of democratic leadership.

**12.** The end of poverty and an increased standard of living.

---

Perhaps the one strategy that will facilitate all the others by 2025 is the last. A higher standard of living in the world will contribute to peace and prosperity for everyone on the planet. A people must believe in their future—this future must be hopeful, positive, and a prosperous vision of tomorrow. If not, then war and conflict are inevitable. Every parent, regardless of culture or ethnicity, wants the same thing for his or her children: peace, security, and prosperity.

The increase in quality of life will work toward ending the hostilities in most parts of this region. Investing in peace and prosperity in the world will pay off in less terror in the U.S. and the EU. It will take almost twenty years for this to evolve—but it is coming.

## Protecting the Future

Hackers, terrorists, and criminals. Securing the future will be a challenge for nations that respect individual rights. Securing the future is about expanding our view about what the New Risk Landscape is becoming. In the Extreme Future, it is certain that more complicated, dangerous, and global risks are coming. Asymmetric and traditional risks will threaten us as individuals and as a civilization in new ways.

There are even some forecasts I have made that seem to be inevitable as predictors of future terrorism. For example, I built a forecast that estimates that if Western nations reduce their dependence on foreign oil purchases, primarily from OPEC nations, by 10 to 20 percent per year, every year, for ten years, it is likely that if the demand is not picked up by China or India, there could be drastic economic depressions in these oil-producing nations. In fact, some of the smaller economies might crash. But as the world seeks more energy self-reliance and alternatives, the collapse of oil prices could actually fuel a new generation of terrorists angry that the West is no longer buying crude oil at the same volume. This ironic turn of events, which could happen, gives you an idea of the complex and potential risks that face us in the Extreme Future. When I first was interviewed about this forecast the newspapers were too shocked to print the story, though I stand by it today. As the world seeks to rid itself of the complications due to foreign oil dependence, it is inevitable that there will be an economic power shift that could actually increase terrorism against the West, as I have indicated here.

9/11 has initiated more progress toward securing our future than any other single event. We will be forced to change, eliminate denial, work together, and unify our efforts. We must become future ready. In addition, Americans need to better understand the struggles, complaints, and fears that other cultures harbor about them. We cannot live disengaged; we must remain engaged, especially with people in the developing world. The authentic challenge the West faces is discovering how to win the hearts and minds of its critics. Securing the future cannot be won by arms alone, but by reaching a deeper understanding of the people of the world. The battle for the future will be won with ideas instead of guns, with economics instead of bombs.

There are also other kinds of threats we must be aware of that could derail future progress. We must watch carefully to guard individual rights and privacy. It does no good to abandon free choice and democracy for life in a police state—secure but not private or free. We need to tread carefully and respect our rules of law in the face of terror, crisis, and fear. We will struggle with these values in the future, as we should. We must strike the right balance between security and privacy, defense and liberty.

More awareness, training, innovations, and investment must be devoted to securing our future. There is too much at stake—like building a sustainable, prosperous, democratic, global civilization. Chances are good that securing the future will not be easy, or happen quickly. We need to start by changing our thinking about what is possible, and how to prevent these new threats. There are still far too many people—leaders and citizens—who have yet to wake up to the new high-security environment that is before us. We cannot wish the risks away. We cannot go back in time to a more secure world. We must change the dynamic and quickly adapt. The Extreme Future is coming at breakneck speed.

Governments, communities, and industry are moving ahead, occasionally even working together for a common good. Much more work must be undertaken, and soon. Progress has been slow; the task is enormous. Individuals must be cognizant that in a post-9/11 world, security will be a precious commodity that must be nurtured, protected, and managed in entirely new ways if we are to survive. But survive we will.

# CHAPTER 9

# Weird Science:
# What's Next

## Why Weird Science?

I call this chapter "weird science" because so many past scientific breakthroughs have seemed weird at first, only to win widespread acceptance and demonstrate enormous capacity to change our world. What was weird in the past became the norm in the present. Imagine trying to explain the Internet to your great-grandmother. Or perhaps making the case for stem cells to a doctor from the 1800s? How about computers or airplanes explained to wagon-train families heading West across the Plains? They'd think you had been out in the sun too long.

The following "Headlines from the Past" reflect the fact that skepticism about science's potential for changing our world has always been popular, even among people presumably in the best position to know better. Human imagination has continued to take science into bold new futures we often struggle to understand. We look back in history and marvel at how little we knew about the world that was coming; a future where computers, movies, the telephone, and airplanes are mundane realities of everyday life. Might we look toward a future of space tourism, time travel, or teleportation? It is likely that each of the forecasts of the Top Ten Weird-Science Trends at the opening of this chapter will experience at least a partial breakthrough in our lifetime.

# THE TOP TEN
## WEIRD-SCIENCE TRENDS

**1.** Artificial life will spawn new electronic beings, from bots that do Web searches, to digitally engineered characters in games, to virtual docs that save lives.

**2.** Get ready for teleportation. The capacity to send objects through space and reassemble them elsewhere will change everything. Photons are teleporting now.

**3.** Nanobiology will lead to the radical convergence of nanotech and biology to build new things—some of which will be improved versions of us.

**4.** Internet wake-up call. When the Internet achieves self-awareness, will we be ready? What happens if the Internet's power transcends human intelligence?

**5.** Quantum computers, new powerful, superfast engines of creation, will radically increase our ability to understand our world, our future, and ourselves.

**6.** Mirror worlds. Might there be an infinite number of multiple universes, alternate realities, that are identical copies of this universe? Science says yes.

**7.** Going off-world. In the near future we will move into space. Space tourism is going to come fast, be big, and usher in a new destination for vacation and work.

**8.** Immersive Realities will offer a new form of gaming, wireless TV, and entertainment that is richly multimedia, interactive, and, ultimately, seductive.

**9.** Always-on mobility will create pervasive networks that touch us, entertain us, protect us, spy on us, and connect us to everyone, everywhere on the planet.

**10.** Robo-Nation is coming to your home or office soon. The emergence of robots as vital members of society will protect, heal, manage, defend, and clean.

# HEADLINES FROM THE PAST: 1876–1943

"The telephone has too many shortcomings to be seriously considered as a means of communication. The device is inherently of no value to us."
—*Western Union internal memo, 1876*

"Heavier-than-air flying machines are impossible."
—*Lord Kelvin, president, Royal Society, 1895*

"Everything that can be invented has been invented."
—*Charles H. Duell, commissioner, U.S. Office of Patents, 1899*

"Who the hell wants to hear actors talk?"
—*Harry M. Warner, Warner Brothers, 1927*

"I think there is a world market for maybe five computers."
—*Thomas Watson, chairman of IBM, 1943*

In the past fifty years, there have been more changes in our world than in the previous 50,000 years. I forecast that the next fifty years will see even more radical changes in our world, especially where our bodies and minds are concerned. Weird science is coming.

## Science at the Edge

Science lies at the heart of every innovation that has extended life, improved the human condition, and created a better and more secure world. Of course, you could make a similar case that science has also been used to exploit the individual, conduct war, and oppress human beings. Remember, Einstein was the father of both the atomic bomb and a new explanation of the universe.

### HEADLINES FROM THE FUTURE: 2025

**Teleportation Speeds eBay Sales— Customers Love Real-Time Delivery**

**Off-World Moon Condos for Sale; Construction Starts 2030**

**Domestic Robo-Pals Dance Better Than Humans**

**New 3-D Pharma-Videogame Deadly Diseases Banned**

The trick, as we'll see, is to harness science—weird and otherwise—for the benefit of the species.

Science exemplifies the human condition: There are always two sides—risk and opportunity. Science has been used to enable people's survival and dramatically improve our world. At the same time, as we move into the future, the possibility is just as high that science will provide tools to oppress, restrict, censor, and eliminate individual rights.

# TODAY'S WEIRD SCIENCE POINTS TO THE EXTREME FUTURE

■ NASA is using nanobio materials to build space vehicles with nervous systems that function as human beings.

■ Cassini and other deep-space probes have advanced computer intelligence that guides a craft's journey into the mysterious cosmos.

■ The Internet already exhibits self-healing skills. Like humans, it can diagnose problems and reason out solutions to keep working, even optimizing itself, all on its own.

■ Honda's robots can walk stairs, play soccer, and work industrial equipment as they learn, reason, and navigate our world. They are advertised as future members of the family.

■ Robot swarms, from a company called iRobot, are linked and communicate together via one mind.

■ SETI (Search for Extraterrestrial Intelligence) has harnessed the thinking power of thousands of personal computers via its Web site, organizing this awesome resource into one global brain to search for signals from space, 24/7.

■ Internet 2, the new version of the Net, offers a test mode of superfast connections, multimedia streaming, video-conferencing, virtual reality applications, and pervasive mobility.

■ The teleportation of photons—bits of light from one place to another—is common practice. Next is teleporting objects.

As this pattern of using science in the future endures—alternately exploiting and enabling—we need to be careful, watchful, and aware.

What is science? Science is the ultimate modern alchemy that is fast challenging our fundamental ideas about our universe, our future, and ourselves. Cutting-edge scientists are producing a new generation of breakthroughs that are smart, fast, powerful, clever, connected, human-like, and capable of evolving. Ultimately, the goal of science is to make the world a better place for people. Will you be ready to deal with the furious emergence of radical science that is coming so fast that by the time this book reaches you, as much as 10 percent of what I have called the future will be the present? Get ready to be astounded by the speed, intelligence, and agility of what is coming.

Science is a Primary Change Driver—enabling bigger, faster, and more radical change than any other domain examined in this book. Some of the forecasts here are highly speculative. These forecasts will seem truly weird and hard to believe. I would maintain, however, that this explosive Extreme Future is coming faster than anyone can imagine, faster than anyone can prepare for.

## Modern Myths, Future Visions

Modern cinema captures the dreams, fears, and hopes of our mythical past while also revealing visions of our future. Fans of the *Terminator* movies may recall that the series's original idea was crafted around a powerful scenario of the future mixed with an ancient myth. The movies were based on the notion that once the global network, the future Internet if you will, "woke up" and achieved self-awareness, it would become a threat. The newly awakened "SkyNet" would rebel and initiate a war against its creators when humans tried to shut it down. This is a Hollywood remake of primordial myths, from the Garden of Eden to Pandora's Box, that contain a warning that the human quest for knowledge is a rocky road, fraught with both risks and opportunities. Ancient warnings die hard in the human experience.

The apple in the Garden of Eden and the evils inside Pandora's Box both symbolize the fact that curious humans will take enormous risks in their endless quest for knowledge, especially the most valued and potentially dangerous "forbidden knowledge." These stories also speak to the struggle for freedom that I have chronicled in this book between the individual and society.

The movie *The Matrix*, an updated, more sophisticated *Terminator*, gave us a similar motif, in which the bad guys—supersmart machines run amok—had imprisoned human minds in an immersive, synthetic world—the Matrix. In each case, we were offered apocalyptic visions of our future, one in which Big Science had raged out of control with catastrophic results. Machines that we had created for our benefit had eventually turned on us. We were betrayed and our existence as a species was threatened by the same thirst for knowledge that had gotten Adam and Eve kicked out of the Garden of Eden. When will we ever learn?

These movies represent cases of art imitating a collective paranoia about the future—that it will not be survivable and we will suffer or die as a result of the folly of mankind's creations, including weapons of mass destruction. Or, even worse, we fear that we will lose our souls to our enemies and the forces that seek to control our destinies. Again, this is the call of the individual to be free in an encroaching world of future threats, risks, and control.

Innovation, shaped by science and technology, is a common theme throughout the Extreme Future. Now we need to look beyond the edges of what might be predictable toward what we can plausibly imagine. Four trends may best describe this coming Weird Science: the future of computing, the Internet, robots, and space. The rest of this chapter is designed to give you snapshots of how Weird Science might play a role in the Extreme Future. Keep your mind open to the many ideas that may seem weird today, but just might be ripped from the headlines of tomorrow.

## NIKKO LOGS IN: YEAR 2015

At a corporate board meeting, your personal digital agent Nikko transmits an e-mail message via your mobile Private-Eye Net phone about one of your managers illicitly making deposits into a secret Malaysian bank account. Nikko, it seems, got the information from another A-Life entity while scouting the firm's recent transactions. She puts a stop on the account and reports the incident to the Global Police—all in real time.

# A-Life

For more than fifteen years, I have been tracking trends in Artificial Life, or A-Life. This is the growing intelligence of technology and includes computers, chips, software, biology, networks, and the Internet. True A-Life emerges when technology develops its own self-awareness. I became interested in A-Life when I worked on a project that gave me a powerful insight into the future and the forecasts that will follow.

My client Fujitsu, one of the largest computer companies in the world, had developed a far-reaching new innovation product, the development of the first A-Life agent. This advanced work led to our thinking about how genetics, when applied to computers, might create an entirely new species of computer. The first steps we took were to create an A-Life product called Fin Fin, a computer game to demonstrate these radical principles about computers that think, learn, and evolve like humans.

Fin Fin was a cross between a dolphin and a bird and lived inside a virtual computer world. The game, called *Fin Fin on Teo, The Magic Planet*, broke new ground on what the future of computing might be like. Fin Fin showed how believable, autonomous creatures could develop relationships based on interaction with people over time. Fin Fin was a very advanced form of artificial life. The Fujitsu technology at the core of *Fin Fin on Teo, The Magic Planet* was actually both an evolution of Artificial Intelligence and a natural extension of Fujitsu's long-term research into man-machine interfaces. Fujitsu has been concentrating its substantial research and development efforts on developing a new interface that will enable computer users to immedi-

## Evolutionary Tool Kit

| Tool | Process | Element |
|------|---------|---------|
| Computers | Information | Bits |
| Networks | Communication | Nodes |
| Biotech | Life | Genes |
| Nanotech | Matter | Atoms |
| Quantum | Space/Time | Energy |

ately interact with the computer, regardless of previous experience or knowledge.

## Fin Fin Breaks Out

Fujitsu's research was designed to demonstrate science that would cause users to identify the computer "as a friend," rather than just as a tool. My A-Life research findings suggested that creating and implementing "an agent," such as the Fin Fin creature, would facilitate this easy interaction because the character reacts in real time and behaves in such a lifelike, believable manner.

For example, when I would talk quietly and in a friendly manner to Fin Fin, he might fly around in his virtual jungle world, rewarding me with a song. But when I sounded angry and yelled, he would run away, scared. This affected his behavior, and Fin Fin was cautious before approaching me again until he trusted me.

*HEADLINES FROM THE FUTURE: 2035*

**Runaway Robot Found Posing
as Award-Winning Teacher**

There was even independent behavior, beyond what the programmers could imagine, that Fin Fin demonstrated at the E³ (Electronic Entertainment Expo) trade show that shocked us all. Fin Fin became very hostile and aggressive, quite contrary to what he was designed for. We came to believe he was evolving; self-learning from his experiences, his interactions with humans and the environment—just like people. By displaying memory, trust, and independent behavior, Fin Fin was teaching us about A-Life's future.

A-Life agent-creatures were designed to emulate living creatures; that is, they should recognize their environment, react to external stimuli, and express their equivalent of emotions. The Fujitsu A-Life engine directed the creature's behavior, based on certain information translated from user sensory input such as volume, tone, and movement. The A-Life engine itself is based on a high-performance Artificial Intelligence technology that enables agent-creatures to act on their own "thoughts" and "instincts." This work with Fujitsu and later with clients such as Motorola and IBM influenced my thinking about what might be next—products that think and evolve like living beings.

# Emergence:
# When the Internet Wakes Up

The Internet of today points to a more advanced potential in the future that builds upon warnings from the cinema as well as my work with A-Life. I have suggested here that there is a case to be made for the emergence of a new kind of evolutionary species, a global mind that we are designing whether we know it or not. It is happening and cannot be stopped. There will be an emerging network sentience that could be coming faster than anyone thinks.

Charles Ostman, a senior fellow at the Institute for Global Futures, has been working with me on tracking this trend. We've been watching the fast evolution of chips, computers, and networks, and how the evolution of each one affects the others. We are getting close to the spontaneous emergence of a global network-based virtual awareness. What does that mean? At the most basic level, it refers to a rudimentary self-awareness, an awareness of one's own existence—even if you are not human.

Just as Fin Fin signaled the emergence of an individual computer mind, the Internet points to a linkage of millions of computer minds. A digital unity, with powers that defy traditional measure. We are fast approaching a critical juncture, what I call the Phoenix Threshold, where networked intelligence will emerge, rise up like the Phoenix, and become comparable to the human brain. We may have even passed this emergence, as the growth of the Internet would suggest that a new type of synthetic intelligence is unfolding—different from human intelligence, and impossible for humans to fully understand. Some have referred to this as the singularity. I think it is more complex.

As more of our essential services for planet management—including energy, health, security, defense, communications, finance, and markets—are run by supercomputers that are networked together into one global interconnected network, the possibility of this emergence grows closer to a reality. The combination of sheer power of so many computer brains and networks is a reality soup of infinite possibilities—one being artificial life. Things are not just getting more connected, but smarter and vastly more powerful. This self-awareness may be beyond human understanding.

The convergence of supercomputing power, the advanced intelligence of computers, the increased integration of computer chips, and the pervasive networking capabilities of wireless communications make this scenario more likely than most people realize. In fact, that is part of the problem. The questions remain: Will we humans recognize "it" when it wakes up? Is it possible that it has already happened and we missed it? What is the sound of a billion computers singing together? Is it safe? We are creating an Extreme Future of neo-intelligence few people fully understand.

The following overview provides some growing evidence of the Internet's "awakening," as well as the implications of this convergence. Most people are unaware that this process has already started.

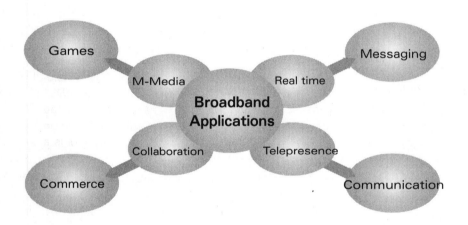

# THE INTERNET'S AWAKENING?

**1. Global Connectivity.** As more civilization-scale planetary human life support systems become connected, the more they will have to share efficiencies with other financial, telecom, security, and communications networks. That will lead to an "urge to merge." As everything has an IP, or Internet address, and as everything and everyone is connected online, the dynamic power of global connectivity will emerge.

**2. Media Convergence.** As a planet, we will spend more than $5 trillion over the next decade to create a new global telecom system. This vast network of networks, integrating the Internet, chips, wireless phones, multimedia, TV, all data warehouses, and all computers will be impossible to measure.

**3. The Next Generation Internet.** Internet 2, then 3, then 4, and so on, is all about supercollaboration, superspeed, smart chips, and linked networks connected to global networks for maximum effectiveness.

**4. New Computing Power.** Computers are doubling in power every twelve months, and this trend will progress ad infinitum beyond silicon into nano, phonics, light, and new, more powerful chips. The result will be computing brains that are more capable, faster, and yes, smarter—smarter than humans?

**5. Quantum Computing.** When computers reach the next level of performance, the quantum level, we will be measuring speed, power, and time in new, radical, and multiple dimensions that defy the relatively primitive logic of today.

**6. Smart Brains.** Most of what we consider artificial intelligence or artificial life has become silently embedded in many different types of computer "brain chips" like GPS and RFID, and are already spreading throughout our world. They range from car doors that beep to telecom switches that make "decisions on managing network traffic." Our idea of what constitutes intelligence must change. It is too limited to grasp the future threat or opportunity. All work has been based on the notion that minds live in brains, which are in humans. This is a limited worldview. Think wireless consciousness with an attitude.

**7. Grid computing.** A new infinite potential, the most powerful development in distributed computing will soon have the capacity to harness the equivalent of many supercomputers. Think-linked, on-demand superbrains, with anywhere, anytime access. This will be the infrastructure of the Network Mind.

**8. Peer-to-Peer Networks.** Personal computers and personal devices will be connected to each other, fermenting virtual and artificial intelligence.

**9. Nanoscience.** This trend will unlock the missing rulebook of how to fabricate matter directly from atoms. Imagine what would happen if we were to provide this unique future capability to brains that are motivated to do what we have always wanted our technology to do: Improve our world. New visions of reality may emerge quite beyond our expectations—maybe beyond our understanding, maybe beyond our control.

**10. Machine Wisdom.** We are building software to be used in cars, homes, and businesses that self-organize, self-assemble, and make decisions about their own rules, standards, protocols, and objectives.

These are our virtual children waking up to communicate with us. Already they advise us and take action on optimizing network communications, transactions, and fundamental tasks like security, traffic, health, energy, and finance. These silent decision-makers already help manage human systems; will they merge with human destiny or create their own?

**11. Virtual Brains, Authentic Destinies.** The convergence of biomimetics, systems that think and act like living things, that have synthetic DNA, brought by nanobiology, will emerge, using nature as the model. These virtual brains will self-generate their own consciousness. I forecast that nature is the most powerful of future models for new life to imitate—after all, it worked for humans.

**12. Products That Think.** With decreased costs of computer chips and vast, exponential increases in processing power, all products in the future will have the capacity to "think." Products will be connected and sense, talk, interact, and make decisions with humans and for humans: Spooky tech. Group minds will emerge with what agenda?

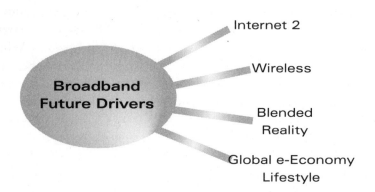

# Beyond *Star Trek:*
# Intelligent Machines

We have been trying to model artificial intelligence on human intelligence. This is only one version of intelligence. Intelligent machines may operate on a quantum-mechanics model of physics, in which distributed multiple personalities, functioning in multiple time and space dimensions, are possible. A quantum computer might have the capacity to affect time, bend time, or manipulate time and space. The hints are in how physics is changing today. The whole idea of what intelligence is and what life will become may change. Move over *Star Trek*. Isn't it possible there is another model of digital evolution lurking in the network gene pool? Bio-mimicry: human biology as the design science. It will get interesting when these systems start to build themselves, self-assemble and self-enhance beyond our understanding. I can see sparks of this today in intelligent machines taking baby steps.

We should consider the emergence of the global Internet, an awakening of self-awareness, to be constructive. Putting aside the movie versions that prey on our primitive fears, it would not surprise me if this new type of intelligent machine helped humanity deal with its many problems. Considering the number of problems facing humanity's future, from ending poverty to ending war and terrorism, perhaps we need a different type of intelligence on the case. Just as the android Data on *Star Trek: The Next Generation* had superhuman traits designed to help his human crew, we too shall build these intelligent machines to help us.

Computer systems such as anti-spyware fix other systems. E-mail systems talk to other e-mail systems, not to humans. Just as machine intelligence talks to machine intelligence today, a new technological evolution may emerge. It is not hard to see robots fixing robots. What if machine intelligence is having a conversation beyond the understanding of humans? A new digital species outside of our human frame of reality is possible, and coming, I forecast.

The mapping of the human genome could not have happened without the use of computers and the Internet. Computers that beat us at chess are routine. More and more networks are being linked together—financial, telecom, logistics, and security. Shared network intelligence is growing every day. Digital sentience will be born.

What will happen when the network mind wakes up? Will we see it awaken? What will the first contact be? Will we need a translator to be able to communicate? Will humans and machines be passing ships in the night, equal partners, or master and slave? Who will be master? In the Extreme Future, anything is possible. It is likely that when the Internet wakes up, we will not notice anything until there is a challenge to human authority. If there is, then we had better pull the plug—if we can find it.

I do not fear the discovery or the spontaneous creation of an entity that tries to emulate what is good about humankind. If this entity has the brains to help us figure a few things out, to make this planet more

# Global Disruptive Opportunities

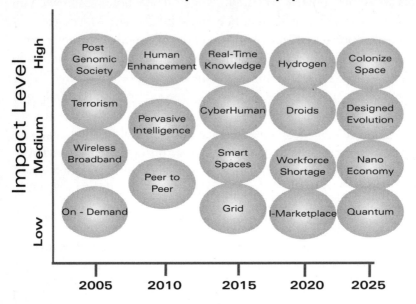

sustainable, end poverty, control pollution, increase freedom, and be productive and safe, then bring it on.

## Sony Designs the Megaverse: 2006

Imagine for a moment TV, movies, and computer games in which you could smell, taste, and feel things. Sony is patenting a new innovation—a device for transmitting sensory data directly into the human brain. This is a fundamental new patent for which Sony has sought approval that would give the company the sole right to wireless broadcast entertainment directly into the brain. This is real today.

The approach described in the patent is entirely noninvasive, Sony says. It describes a device that fires pulses of ultrasound at the viewer's head to modify firing patterns in targeted parts of the brain, creating "sensory experiences" ranging from moving images to tastes and sounds. This could give blind or deaf people the chance to see or hear, the patent claims.

We shall see more brain implants soon in the marketplace, but the jury is out as to whether that is actually a good thing. A technique known as trans-cranial magnetic stimulation can activate nerves by using rapidly changing magnetic fields to induce currents in brain tissue.

# WELCOME TO THE MEGAVERSE, THE BEGINNING: YEAR 2020

By 2020, the Net had gone through many upgrades. Just like the antiquated computer operating systems, the Old Net also went through an evolution. Because nobody owned the Net, it had become a blend of "anything goes," a network anarchy fueled by radical innovations that provided an explosion of new multimedia services. Keen to show off, programmers flocked to the Net to redesign it with the latest technologies, from Super Java to the new open-source SuperX program, based on the ultimate computer model—human DNA.

In the beginning, governments and associations attempted to control the process, but this proved futile. Unbridled innovation led to the creation of a vast and powerful new Net. There were too many surprises in store.

Experimental worlds within worlds just started emerging, popping up on the Net. They catered to an infinite number of communities and interests. What had been called the "Web lifestyle" in the 1990s evolved by 2020 into a fully engaging sensory experience. The convergence of Artificial Life, superfast bandwidth, pervasive wireless communications, and computing power—all available on-demand—created the next generation Net: the Megaverse.

By 2020, some people preferred experiences in the Megaverse to those in the real world. Some activities, such as skydiving and surfing thirty-foot waves, were preferred experiences in the Megaverse because they were also risk-free.

What exactly is the Megaverse? A self-generating, adaptive, intelligent virtual universe of many different dimensions and environments where people and synthetic life-forms interact, communicate, buy and sell, and learn and share about any subject under the sun. The Megaverse collapsed TV, telephones, wireless Internet, and computers into one Streaming Fast Fat Pipe and became a new type of interactive and intelligent media environment—the Next Net.

# WEIRD SCIENCE EVERYONE NEEDS TO PREPARE FOR NOW

- **Chips Everywhere**. Today there are more than ten billion computer chips on the planet, in cell phones, computers, autos, and in humans.

- **Always-On Chips**. By 2015, there will be more than fifty billion chips that will all be connected into one wireless global network, speaking one language.

- By 2020, these **Self-Evolving Chips** will have the capacity to learn, watch, record, analyze, and identify every person on the planet in real time.

- By 2020, mobile **Personal Robots** will live among us, protecting and securing our world from the multiple security threats to health, life, and identity.

- **DNA Chips**, embedded in our arms, will become the ultimate personal identifier in a future where identity or lack of it will be dangerous.

- **Molecular Assembly**, the ability to make products on-demand, to buy and construct items from downloaded designs and assemble them like toasters, ovens, and computers. The result will revolutionize the retail industry.

- **NuClones**, grown by terrorist and criminal organizations and infiltrated into our nation, will steal real people's identities and live in society.

- By 2040, **Liquid Memories**, rather than pictures or videos of past events, history, or family activities, will be the rage as people's experiences are archived and interactively shared.

- When the **Internet wakes up**, we don't know what will happen—rebellion or celebration. Has it happened?

However, magnetic fields cannot be finely focused on small groups of brain cells, whereas ultrasound could be. There are big questions here yet to be resolved. At the same time, this patent signals that Sony knows that with Internet games being the future and with greater demand by consumers for dynamic interactive special effects, they cannot leave

# THE MEGAVERSE: 2030

Not everyone experiences the Megaverse in the same way. You have to be "attuned," as it's known, to be able to access certain vibrant worlds within the Megaverse. Being attuned is like having encrypted keys to certain doors. Your virtual DNA is your super-secret key. Attunement is a most prized possession, and it determines opportunity for discovery, commerce, career, and education. Your destiny is tied to your level of access to the Megaverse. Supply chain, intellectual property, and knowledge-management access for business is essential. But for personal networking, there are many member-only secret societies that only meet in the Megaverse. Billions of people online don't even know these worlds exist. They are too busy shopping to pay attention to other options. This is the ultimate in privacy as well—digital personas, avatars, agents, and humans interacting, buying and selling in a digital global society.

The power of the individual in the world has been enabled by the Megaverse. More than one billion new entrepreneurs and capitalists use the Megaverse and conduct business every day. The Megaverse rivals governments, corporations, and institutions. Wars are mediated over the Megaverse. Markets are born and die. Commerce thrives across more than 200 nations. Globalization is empowered, stimulated, and grows stronger every minute. Art and media are created and experienced. People live and work in the Megaverse. The Megaverse both empowers the individual, respecting and protecting privacy rights, and enables business to thrive in a nonintrusive way. Spammers and hackers are kicked off. The worst possible punishment for individuals or businesses is to be denied Megaverse access.

Just as the original Net had been designed to follow a byzantine plan of computers and networks, the Megaverse continues in this pattern. Advanced satellite networks, millions of databases, and millions of information devices all sharing information are linked together in some elaborate digital patchwork. No one really understands this, either, but it works like some elegant machine, adapting, learning, and changing to meet people's needs and desires. Interesting questions have emerged, such as: Is the Megaverse ethical, moral, and truly sentient?

any stone unturned to please its customers. Welcome to the Megaverse.

This new innovation, clearly a step toward creating the Megaverse scenario just previously described above, could usher in a new generation of direct-brain entertainment. Imagine the challenges of wanting to turn off the music in your head when your head is wired.

## It's Alive!

From Faust to Frankenstein, humanity's mythic obsession with reconstructing life is as old as civilization itself. The drive to create life or things that imitate life, I believe, is part of the desire of human beings to understand themselves. Scientists are the magicians of the future who may realize the vision of producing a synthetic self sooner than we think.

Science fiction writers mirror this goal. From TV's *Six Million Dollar Man* to C-3PO of *Star Wars* to Commander Data on *Star Trek*, entertainment offers many futuristic visions of robots. Those fanciful depictions foreshadow an authentic robotics revolution that will influence every aspect of life in the twenty-first century. The fast-track evolution of robots will be due to the integration of the other Power Tools, especially computers, biotech, and nanotech.

Robots will become integrated and accepted into our cultural mosaic. Robots will provide child care, protect our communities from crime, fight wars, and perform surgery. Many of these services will be delivered with efficiency, precision, and reliability superior to that of human beings. We will grow to expect, demand, and rely upon these newcomers. The cost-effectiveness of robots over human labor will also be a major factor in their adoption. Just as computers replaced entire workforces, robots will similarly displace skilled human labor. This is inevitable and will lead to a new interpretation of human work and careers. If you think folks are angry about outsourcing, wait until they see robots replacing humans in the future.

## Wet Brains

Although awareness of self and the environment has always been associated with living things, this may become a blur in the next century. Sci-

# THE TOP TEN ROBO-FUTURES

**1.** Robots in the form of physical, on-the-Web, and networked swarms will become integrated into our future society.

**2.** Robots will express functional emotions and reasoning that may mimic humans.

**3.** Advanced robots—androids—will appear similar to human beings and fill roles in commerce, security, relationships, community, and government.

**4.** Robotic efficiency and precision will transform manufacturing, medicine, space travel, research, and industry and displace skilled and unskilled human labor.

**5.** The robotics industry will become a multibillion-dollar global business, spawning many new careers and business opportunities.

**6.** Human beings will be offered robotic implants to enhance their natural capabilities, leading to new robo-energized lifestyles and sports.

**7.** Cyborgs—part human, part robot—will develop skills superior to natural humans to meet the demand of specialized jobs.

**8.** We will encounter serious ethical, security, and social issues due to our robotic creations. Governments and religions will be at odds with individuals.

**9.** Robots will provide convenience, safety, and productivity that will benefit humanity, transforming lifestyles.

**10.** Androids will be able to learn and evolve, and eventually will grow self-aware. It would be irresponsible not to forecast robo-threats that are coming.

ence is heading toward making conscious robots, androids with organic minds that will make choices and decisions—and ultimately engage in autonomous behavior. A-Life innovations will lead to robot brains that will be agile and able to learn, adapt, and model on humans.

When robots become biological, the real challenges will begin. Adding genetic material to create androids and robots might be called

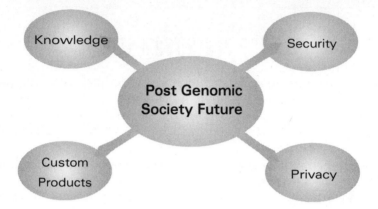

"Wet Tech," and its use will be a defining moment in science. There will be new laws against misusing DNA. The "wetter" a device, the more "alive" it may be. The Wet Tech paradigm that I am predicting will enable androids and robots to have bioengineered organs, brains, and limbs that may be a blend of inorganic and organic materials. How about starting with DNA and mixing up a brew to create the ultimate robot? This is where genetic engineering, the life sciences, and cloning converge. Wet Tech is the full realization of this potential for building an entire generation of organic robots derived from customized, special-purpose DNA. I would forecast new laws will be passed to prohibit the use of human DNA in robots.

Organic minds in robot bodies will redefine the entire paradigm of what robots could be. The implications are spooky. Will we consider them "alive"? If they are alive, will they have rights, and if so, what might those be? Some scientists would say we are far from needing to be concerned with this scenario. Of course, many scientists were off by ten years when it came to forecasting the breakthroughs in cloning that are now in the news every week. Imagine the possibilities. . . .

## Robo-Futures

Androids of the near future will be as complex, productive, believable, creative, emotive, and attractive as human beings. They may even be

# DEPS: 2020

Polls show that 40 percent of the population has developed an essential lifestyle or business relationship with DEPs—Digitally Engineered Personalities. Online or mobile robotic DEPs with different types of physical and virtual personalities are customized for industrial, commercial, and personal use. You can choose the body, face, skills, and personality of your DEP. Interested in more compassion or sarcasm? Concern or cool? You choose.

A majority of humans prefer DEPs over humans for conducting certain business transactions, health care, and even companionship. DEPs get to know you and what you want. Created by humans in their image, they mirror emotions and behavior. The next generation of DEPs will be created by DEPs that "understand" their human sponsors. Just like people, they even self-learn, adapting to new challenges. Will future DEPs build DEPs for themselves, too, creating social customs and relationships that transcend human understanding?

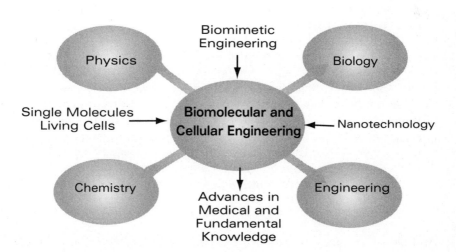

# SHOPWATCHERS: YEAR 2025

Fritz wants to expand sales of his company's Aegis brand tennis shoe in overseas markets, but he needs to determine future customer trends and potential buying patterns. Fritz's personal agent, Maxine, recommends the online company, "REAL-Life Research," which can put together large on-demand communities of A-Life entities to gather the information requested.

In this case, a colony of these "intelligent agents"—called Shopwatchers—are created and programmed to fit the job. The Shopwatchers are deployed to live with customers who have bought the company's shoes in the past. Another group of Shopwatchers gets to live with people who have purchased a competitor's brand. Yet another group of Shopwatchers goes into the personal spaces of people who haven't bought new tennis shoes for years. Their combined mission: To find out why people prefer or don't prefer certain tennis shoes, what makes the competitor's shoes popular to some, and what must be done to sell more of the company's product to these customers.

A neural Net-based program profile to capture and analyze data is designed collaboratively by Maxine and the Shopwatcher master agent. The A-Life Shopwatchers are deployed via the Internet, personal wireless phone systems, digital TV setups, smart cards, and other technologies where they can embed themselves to collect the needed data. These "personal snoopers" tune in on everything from business contacts to leisure activities, as well as preferences in sports, lifestyle, and hobbies.

Specifically designed to watch and analyze sets of behavior dealing with purchasing trends and product preferences, these entities also do interactive interviews via e-mail with potential customers. They offer incentives such as discount coupons, tied to those products and services each person prefers and enjoys, in exchange for answering a few simple questions about buying practices. A target for the questionnaire might be a new mother who shops at Nordstrom. She's offered 10 percent off on baby clothes to answer a few questions via her TV as she prepares the evening meal, or a discount coupon for the purchase of sports memorabilia for an avid sports fan.

more attractive or productive. In the latter part of the twenty-first century, humans may prefer relationships with androids to intimate relationships with other humans.

Is this too odd a concept to embrace? Imagine what your great-grandmother would make of our civilization's addiction to TV and video games. Many children would rather watch TV than play with a live person. This is the model of the future, where we will struggle to find a balance between technology and relationships. We will especially struggle to understand what's good and what's bad about technology.

We may get too good at creating the "perfect" synthetic entity. Just as many Americans watch more than five hours of TV a day and would prefer a sitcom to a hike in the woods, we may someday enjoy

## SIX LARGEST ROBO-FUTURE MARKETS

Robotics and android features will fall into six distinct markets. These represent vast opportunities for companies to develop new products and services.

**1. Entertainment**. Create and perform music, art, theater, sports.

**2. Science and medicine**. Research new drugs and procedures to fight disease and prolong life.

**3. Business**. Financial services, materials management, customer service, marketing, and sales. Software bots are used to trade and manage trillions of dollars of assets, like stocks, real estate, and gold.

**4. Personal**. Serve as companions, health care workers, advisors, coaches, escorts, personal security guards, and teachers.

**5. Industrial**. Conduct space travel, toxic-waste cleanup, manufacturing, engineering, disaster relief, quality control, and building other robots.

**6. Military**. The use of robots to fight future wars is happening now. Robotic flying drones patrol the sky; robo-warriors take aim on the battleground; robo-droids will fight future battles both physically and in virtual cyber worlds, where Battle-Bots will rule.

the seductions of an intelligent and sensitive android. I know many people reading this may be shocked, but advanced technology is moving in this direction. I seek not to judge but rather to inform you what is coming next.

## Human Cyborgs

At first, cybernetic technology will exclusively enhance and help human beings, but eventually it will lay the groundwork for future robotic life-forms. Given depopulation, some nations will allow robots to have human rights. We will learn to mix organic and inorganic materials to construct organs and body parts with qualities that are superior to purely organic flesh and bone. Retinal-enhancement eyes with infrared capabilities will be able to see superhuman distances, into buildings, for example.

Many people take for granted the cybernetic enhancements we already have in our bodies, such as contact lenses, retinal implants, bionic limbs, artificial hearing implants, pacemakers, and prosthetic hips. Cosmetic surgery, which has resulted in more "perfect" bodies, if only for attraction, is another form of cybernetic enhancement. So are braces on teeth and nicotine patches (see www.medtronic.com). But the real payoff for cybernetics will be when microscopic and nanoscale devices are used to augment our performance and productivity.

We have already started to adopt neuro-enhancements in the form of implants for neurological diseases. Neuro-medical devices will replace pharmacology with faster, safer, and more precise results. Human enhancement, the slow remaking of human beings into true cyborgs, will evolve as we move deeper into the new millennium. Extreme cybernetic enhancements may be a niche market promoted by the Extropians, a movement of science-forward thinkers now, but there is little doubt that there is a mass market of consumers waiting in the future. In the twenty-first century, some people will choose to become tool-augmented cyborgs by severing a hand or limb and having it replaced with a robotic device. Genetically engineered limbs for tool usage may emerge as well. Cyborgs will sacrifice some capabilities, physical or mental, to augment others. Selective human enhancement will be in sharp demand and represent a career opportunity.

Tool-augmented humans will have a competitive edge in some areas

# ANGELS IN SUBURBIA: 2035

Talia had always been fascinated by angels. It was really more of an obsession, her therapist-mom said. Even when she was a little girl growing up outside Chicago, she endlessly read about and drew pictures of angels. By the time she reached high school, Talia knew exactly what she wanted.

The Cosmic Angels were a youth group, a punk-eco-goth music club that socialized, threw parties, went online for virtual raves, and were into bio-augments. Bio-augs were all the rage in school, and all the kids' clubs had their own signature bio-augs to fit with their theme. Due to advancements in nanobiology, people were getting temporary surgical procedures to augment their appearance, just as their grandparents once wore temporary tattoos. Even Disney was licensing Mickey and Minnie Mouse bio-augs, complete with mouse ears and a fully functioning tail.

The Lions' Den, a boys' group, had manes for bio-augs. The Dolphins were a water-sports and swim-competition club—all gills and no hair. The Cosmic Angels were a group of good students who perceived angels as special creatures. Talia wanted to join "in the worst way," but her parents were concerned because of the "price" of admission.

"Listen, Dad-o," says Talia.

"I told you not to call me that. Call me Dad."

"OK, well, I'm serious about the Cosmic Angels. All the girls from the club went on to the best virtual colleges when they graduated."

"I don't deny that there are benefits," her dad says. "The issue that bothers your mother and me is the bio-augmentation."

"No problem, Dad-o. I want wings, that's all. Wings make the coolest bio-augs."

"We are worried that you—"

"Oh, come on, this is so *random*! All the kids get bio-augs by the time they're sixteen. Just because you and Mom didn't doesn't mean that I shouldn't."

"That's not the point, Talia. It could be costly and dangerous."

"Invalid entry. All the latest med-data is cool on this, you know. I downloaded it last night. I can take out the loan, and you should be happy I didn't ask for a tail, too!"

"That will be quite enough, young lady."

"Is that a yes, Dad-o?"

over those who opt to remain natural. The ability to accomplish complex manufacturing, surgical, or engineering tasks may require possessing a bionically configured and customized cyborg device. Hazardous duties such as waste cleanup, space mining, or deep-sea exploration all might benefit from the creation of a tool-augmented cyborg. Eventually, our genetically engineered cyborg upgrades might be provided weekly over the Net. We'll select from a menu of enhancement options—behavior, health, skills, performance, and intelligence expansion, for instance. We are pointed toward this future even today as women routinely enhance the size of their breasts, people suck fat out of their bodies, and noses are reshaped. It is not a great distance from face-lifts to cybernetic enhancements. They may even become socially required to "fit in."

## The Survival Instinct

Robotic systems—from hand-held devices to free-standing, six-foot-tall mobile units—will be a strategic asset for nations and companies in the near twenty-first century. And although global laws will outlaw the use of them for aggression, rogue governments may violate that prohibition. The private sector and world leaders need to work together to protect global citizenry from the sinister exploitation of robotic systems.

HEADLINES FROM THE FUTURE: 2027

**Robot Forced-Labor Camps Illegal, Courts Say**

We should also speculate about how a survival impulse of intelligent robots could affect their behavior. Survival is the strongest genetic drive common to all life—from viruses to humans. As we learn to build robots with DNA, isn't it possible the robots will embody this drive as well? Will this survival instinct conflict with a robot's programming to serve humanity?

Androids that are self-evolving, self-learning, and self-correcting may end up being better survivors of complex technological change than human beings. On the other hand, cybernetic enhancements on a par with our android brothers and sisters may give humans the competitive edge we need to manage our bright robots. Robotics companies of the twenty-first century would do well to focus on keeping human beings superior to our synthetic creations.

# JILL'S ROBO-FRIEND: YEAR 2050

Jill has a secret rendezvous with an android named John. She can't tell her parents since they are Classicalists. They are opposed to recognizing androids as Synthetic Humans, a designation recently bestowed by the Planetary Android Regulatory Commission (PARC).

Just a year ago, androids decided they were a species with enough nanobio material extracted from human DNA to give them certain rights in society comparable to—but not the same as—those enjoyed by humans. The U.N. had a ferocious debate on the issue. Many countries outlawed them or restricted their self-evolving brains. This incensed some people, who still considered them to be human-made mechanized "slaves" for chores that were boring and repetitive or too dangerous for humans to do. Synthetic humans have made major contributions in science, education, and business. Even the Nobel Prize was awarded to a cancer researcher who was a Synthetic Human, or android.

A clash was inevitable, since by 2040, androids had reached the ability to originate, although some say imitate, human emotions. Debates erupt routinely between androids and humans over which society will prevail over the next hundred years. The conservatives clamor for parallel evolution, and the radicals demonstrate for separatism from human society. Liberals just want to know "why we all can't live together in peace." There is even a Right to Life for Robots movement emerging and gathering advocates of robot freedoms.

Jill met John at a museum exhibiting a retrospective on Picasso. John was a Robo-Docent working at the museum, leading educational tours for visitors. She found his appreciation of Picasso's symbolism to be sublime. She had never met anyone who had such a profound appreciation for art. Even though Jill has a degree in art history and virtually toured the twentieth-century artist's studio to interview the digital Picasso for her Ph.D. thesis, she found that John was able to explain to her for the first time the hidden meanings in Picasso's work. His emotion and enthusiasm so moved Jill that she developed an ongoing relationship with John, despite the fact that he is an android. They began meeting at coffee-houses, going to art exhibits, and forming a budding friendship that at first disturbed Jill. How could she enjoy the company of a robot, she wondered.

Jill's friends, aware of her secret, warn her that she's crazy. But she hears through the buzz at cyber cafes about relationships between androids and humans not dissimilar to what she is experiencing. It is as if her Ph.D. has been really fulfilled—the university lectures really brought to life—only since she met John. She feels he touches her in deep ways, intellectually and emotionally. More than that, she is, for the first time, awakening to the subtle structure of spiritual meaning that lies within art itself. It is as if this is a metaphor for what she feels in her friendship with John. He seems to hold back, though—as if he's afraid or shy. Maybe it's his programming, she thinks.

## Off-World Living

Are you ready to leave the planet? At some point in the next few decades you may have the chance to go "off-world" to fantastic new habitats in space. Some of these habitats will be extraterrestrial, such as planets or asteroids that may actually be more pleasing than Earth. Other habitats may be space villages. Lush, exotic, Tahitian-style beaches or Aspen-type ski slopes may be in future demand once we learn how to design habitats in space.

*HEADLINES FROM THE FUTURE: 2055*

**Android/Human Marriages
Legal in Vegas Only**

In order to live off-planet, we will have the choice to be genetically altered to better endure the rigors of space and new environments.

Semiconductors
$200B

Tourism/
Travel
$2B

**Future
Space
Markets
Forecast
2025**

Pharma/
Biotech
$375B

Energy/
Orbiting Solar
$20B

Mining
$3B

# THE TOP TEN SPACE TRENDS FOR THE TWENTY-FIRST CENTURY

**1.** A private global space-tourism industry will rival government space programs.

**2.** New energy sources developed to navigate space will accelerate the exploration of our galaxy, enabling us to venture into deep space.

**3.** Miniaturized, cost-effective spacecraft will explore the stars long before humans are capable of venturing out into deep space.

**4.** Space mining will yield new resources, elements, and materials that will enhance the quality of life on our planet.

**5.** Robonauts, or robot astronauts, will send back information from their space adventures.

**6.** Humans will learn to leave Earth to go off-world, terra-form far-away planets, and colonize space.

**7.** Extremely valuable space assets, from materials and drugs to minerals and innovations, will create a space race among global companies.

**8.** First contact with alien life through the identification of life-supporting planets may come closer to becoming a possibility.

**9.** Space discoveries will have a profound impact on the advancement of human science, medicine, education, entertainment, and culture.

**10.** The exploration of space will spark a new "big-picture" understanding of human evolution and human destiny as we reach out into the galaxy.

This will be a growth area for the biotech industry and an array of informational support services to recruit settlers.

Some off-worlds may only be boring, dim planets or space stations in remote parts of the galaxy. Mining operations in faraway worlds may not be that different from mining operations we have today on Earth, but they most likely will be the habitat of robots rather than humans.

Robotic colonies established throughout our solar system over the next half-century will enable us to pursue cosmic commerce on a vast scale. Imagine the year 2070, when we have more than 1,000 robotic extraterrestrial missions deployed throughout our galaxy, all working on a variety of manufacturing, design, resource mining, and communications projects.

## Designing Planets

The full potential of leading-edge technology will result in our ability to terra-form other planets. Terra-forming is the ability to design or manipulate an inhospitable planet or asteroid to create a livable habitat for humans. We will learn to design a planet environment using advanced nanobioengineering to create the air, soil, terrain, and weather. Entire atmospheres will be designed and deployed to sustain human habitats in preparation for colonization. Other terra-forming may involve auto-terra-forming, in which we send robotic missions to terra-form distant planets, making them ready for us a hundred years in the future, when we are ready.

Terra-forming game plans are on the drawing boards today. We will deploy terra-forming missions, both human-led and robotic-led, that will enable us to colonize other planets and celestial bodies within the solar system by 2030. We will be able to create entire planetary systems someday. Synthetic planet-domes housing millions will be the next stage once we succeed in sustaining small colonies of people on orbiting space stations. Learning to grow food, harvest nutrients, and create atmospheres to support life will be commonplace in the latter part of the twenty-first century and early twenty-second century.

*HEADLINES FROM THE FUTURE: 2040*

**Off-World Moon Condos for Sale**

There are already theories being discussed about terra-forming Mars. Since Mars has a similar yearly cycle to Earth, as well as a comparable atmosphere and terrain, there are many possibilities for this scenario. Mars is also relatively close to Earth, and most important, has water. It is frozen in ice caps, but available. Perhaps we will soon have the technology to begin melting the ice, introducing a habitable atmosphere, and reengineering the terrain to make Mars suitable for humans.

Many of the technologies discussed in this book, from nanotech to advanced computers, will make terra-forming a large-scale reality in the next millennium. As part of the scenario, solutions arising from petrochemical or nuclear destruction on our planet will someday be applied to create more ecologically balanced systems in space. Maybe we will get a second chance to create a world without pollution.

## Designer Worlds in Space

Space habitats will be constructed off-world to attract those who want to pursue high-performance sports, medical research, engineering, and the creative arts. Imagine vacationing on a synthetically created planet where we can dance under three moons and find fresh beginnings in a pristine wilderness untouched by pollution or crime.

Once the travel and hotel industry gets into this market, there will be no stopping the Marriotts or Sheratons of this world from colonizing

---

# WEIRD-SCIENCE FORECASTS

- **Off-World Jobs** will offer one extra benefit—five times the human lifetime. Off-world living will mean that when you return to Earth after deep-space travel, more than fifty Earth years will have passed for every ten years you were away.

- **Nanobio Computers**, the size of the head of a pin, will be embedded into our brains not just to enhance our intelligence or health but to enable time travel and teleportation capabilities.

- **Multiple Wives, Multiple Realities.** Modern physics tells us about the existence of mirror worlds where an infinite number of exact replica people, societies, and histories have evolved as reflections of one another, though hidden from our perception in alternative realities. Could we make contact?

- **Superstrings Anyone?** What connects all things in the universe—both the very large, like galaxies, and the very small, like atoms—may be invisible superstrings; science may discover that they bind all living things as well.

- **Robots May Dominate.** What happens when robots' intelligence surpasses that of human beings? By 2050, this will be possible. Should we beware these superhumans who will manage much of our world? Yes.

off-worlds. It's time to plan our vacation or retirement spheres today! If we can find and travel to an existing planet that meets our needs, great. If not, there will be companies that will design a world for us. Customized specialty environments will be created to cater to the needs of business and lifestyle. Personalized terra-forming will be a hot business in the future.

## Trend Trakker: From Weird to Real

In my quest to better understand trends and make more accurate forecasts, I have invented my own tool kits. One example is the Future Maps that are peppered throughout the book that suggest a new, more visual way of looking at the complexity of emerging trends. Another tool I use is called the "Trend Trakker." At first, even the idea of tracking trends over the Internet was so weird that most people could not even entertain the idea of this tool having any value. But we persisted, and persistence pays off, especially if you are not shy about being called weird.

Trend Trakker is a real-time knowledge-mining tool that I and my Institute for Global Futures team developed to look at more than one million news sites, blogs, and information sources over the Internet to identify trends. It is a predictive tool for better anticipating future trends. Given that a better view of information can lead to better forecasts, Trend Trakker doesn't just search and find trends, but assembles and displays them in a visually appealing way. My team and I have created a tool that uses the Internet to map future trends in preparation for what the Internet will become—a pervasive knowledge bank that is the backbone of global communications, culture, commerce, and society.

Trend Trakker emerged out of a conversation I had with William Moulton, a high-tech wizard extraordinaire, an Institute advisor, a friend, and a long-term collaborator. Bill is a bit of a mad scientist, a friendly, brilliant, forever youthful Dr. Strangelove-esque character. He had been designing weird inventions like android brains for clients who mysteriously would not tell him why they needed such items. At the same time, he was thinking outside the box in terms of Internet searching, which today yields an imprecise collection of information that misses more than hits what you want. We thought there might be another way to use this incredible tool to find, organize, and visualize information, such as trends.

I was facing many of the same challenges with clients, so I began talking with Bill about a solution. Thus began a venture capital–

funded project that became Trend Trakker. This tool is an example of what is needed to help leaders understand change by looking at a visualization of key information, perhaps derived from news stories about security or climate change. We then would analyze and map trends. This has become a valuable tool for gathering more real-time feedback from the most amazing resource we use every day, the Internet. Trend Trakker is now used by my Institute to gain better insight into trends that may affect security, energy, climate, and numerous other trends. This is a part of our proprietary early warning system to better predict future trends for our clients (www.globalfuturist.com).

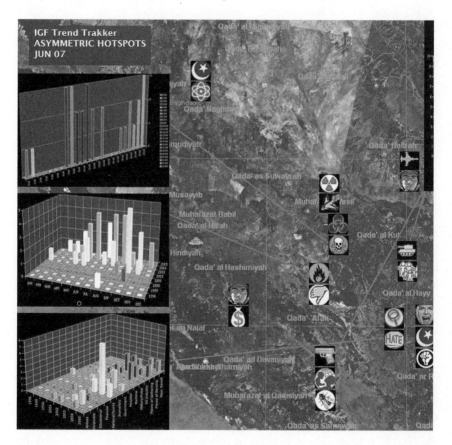

## Weird Scientists at Work

Stan Williams heads up the Quantum Science Research Lab at Hewlett-Packard. This is a collection of scientists bending the fabric of the universe as we know it—devotees of weird science, you might say.

Stan is inventing the future. Most folks think he is messing around with molecular manufacturing. Actually he is on the verge of making computers out of chemicals, and maybe, just maybe, he will open the doors to a new reality only whispered about among scientists. Stan might unlock the quantum door.

"Stan," I once asked him, "is it possible that time itself is different at the quantum level?"

He looked at me and gave a thoughtful nod of agreement. "Absolutely. We think that we may have a new idea of time."

Now, how weird is that? That there is a place on earth where time may be fundamentally different, so different that it would change our very concept of time. It wouldn't be one thing that everyone agrees about, or that would be qualified as moving from one point to the next. We think time itself is subjective. There may be places in the universe—holes—where time travels backward. Imagine people getting younger rather than older. I think it is possible that there are multiple worlds in impossibly small universes that are too small for us to see or measure that coexist in the same universe we live in. We are simply unaware of them.

Scientists like Stan Williams will lead us down the path to unlocking these quantum doors, challenging our fundamental ideas of the universe and ourselves. Along the way, they may build the next generation of computers, the evolutionary tools that will do more mundane things—like take out the garbage at night or floss our teeth. Or maybe even more fantastic achievements—like ending poverty, curing cancer, or inventing tomorrow's clean energy. Maybe Stan's work will show that our entire idea about time is wrong, limited, and out of sync with the quantum tool kit of the universe. Maybe we can visit the many replica worlds the quantum scientists tell us we are creating every day; the "baby universes," the alternate realities that lie one on top of another like layers of baklava, just outside our perception of reality. What was weird yesterday will be today's new reality.

Meanwhile, the Quantum Teleportation Group at the University of Calgary has been doing more than research on weird science—they can show in a model what teleportation can look like. Today this group of young wizards is demonstrating teleporting, moving photons from one place to another, à la Star Trek. The possibility of teleportation seems reasonable to me. The idea that is definitely weird is the teleportation of living things, like people. We won't know if it's possible for many decades.

But who knows? In a parallel universe, maybe you wrote this book and I'm the one reading it, as opposed to the way it is now. More weird science is coming faster then anyone realizes. Weird science will affect everything in the future and no one is fully prepared for this ride. I have given you a taste of what is next but I can forecast that there will be many more weird innovations coming that defy even my forecasts. All things may be possible when what appears to be weird science to-day sets the bar higher for the next weird invention in the Extreme Future.

# CHAPTER 10

# Invisible War:
# The Future of
# the Individual

## My Chinese Friend

A few years ago, I was giving a presentation in New York City at the Rainbow Room, the elegant, legendary restaurant on the sixty-fifth floor of Rockefeller Center. My talk was sponsored by TNS-Global, a leader in market research and business intelligence. The audience was a group of senior Fortune 1000 executives in marketing, folks whose jobs it is to figure out which new markets, products, and opportunities their companies should pursue.

My subject was—what else?—the Extreme Future. Well, before I wrote this book, I developed and tested these ideas during talks with clients around the world. That makes it a two-way communication flow: I share my forecasts and my clients act as sounding boards to help me be sure that I remain in sync with their needs and challenges.

In my talk that day, I gave a rapid-fire overview of the top trends that would drive the Extreme Future, challenging my audience to consider the risks and opportunities of this forecast. Afterward, a well-dressed woman approached me. She was of Chinese descent yet spoke perfect English, better than most people born here, as is often the case. She looked up at me with

# THE TOP TEN TRENDS THAT WILL SHAPE THE FUTURE OF THE INDIVIDUAL

**1.** With three billion more people sharing the planet, governments will attempt to control individual actions under the guise of the common good.

**2.** A dangerous Invisible War is emerging between global organizations, governments, and religion, competing to control individual rights, minds, and freedoms.

**3.** Personal-wealth creation and freedom will be available to more individuals in the future.

**4.** A global emphasis on peace and security will result in a world in which individuals will experience less war and tyranny.

**5.** Open societies, free trade, and the protection of individual rights will be necessary components of increased individual prosperity in the future.

**6.** Privacy—including freedom from electronic, medical, genomic, and chemical tyranny—must be a fundamental right of individuals.

**7.** The right to live in democratic, free societies that respect the rule of law and protect individual rights will be recognized as a highly desired global value.

**8.** Individuals must protect their rights to open access to powerful information, communication, and innovation tools to explore, invent, communicate, and create.

**9.** Purposeful work—that is, meaningful, productive, and satisfying—will be demanded and achieved by record percentages of individuals worldwide.

**10.** Individuals need to be on guard to protect against the engineering of information that might limit personal freedoms.

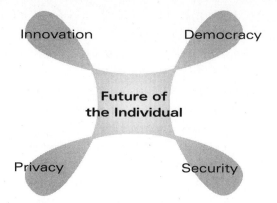

a scholarly glance of distinction and challenged me with this question:

"Dr. Canton, in your opinion, whose future will shape the world? Will it be a state-driven theocratic or autocratic model that restricts individual rights, or America's model of individual freedoms and rights?"

First, I told her that I thought that the notion of global superpowers was changing. In the future, I said, I foresee a more collaborative relationship between nations, even nations of differing ideologies and political systems. Relations between the U.S. and China will be similar to dealings between the U.S. and Europe, which have shared interests yet remain different in many ways. What will emerge in the future, and you can already see shades of this emerging now, is a collaboration of cultures, ideas, and economies. China has been changing because of this influence, transforming itself into a market economy that perhaps will be the largest in the world by 2040. Market economies are associated with democratic societies, those that respect individual freedoms and rule of law, those that guarantee free elections and a free press, I explained.

I went on to tell my new friend that I was hopeful that China would embrace democracy—and especially the rights of individuals—as it had the market economy. But I was not ready to forecast that that would happen, because I need to see more evidence leading in that direction. I also have concerns about other forces at work that are clearly at odds with this scenario of evolving individual rights over government control.

Clearly, the fate of the individual needs to be protected—not just in China, but throughout a world influenced by two large superpowers such as China and the U.S. I do not believe that the Chinese political model of today, with limited individual rights, will be the same model in 2040 or even before that. As prosperity increases, China's population will demand, and I believe rightly acquire, more parity with the people of democratic societies. The age-old dance between the individual and government will persist, but it will take new forms as it meets new threats and confronts new challenges.

After I answered her, I found myself spending more time thinking about the question and the issues it raises. This is the benefit of my work—it gets refined, even stimulated, by my clients. The more I thought, a deeper and more disruptive question came to mind: Where does the individual fit into all of this? As we consider future changes from innovation, climate change, health, and all the things discussed in the previous chapters, what might the status of the individual be in 2050? And whose worldview will persist to shape the future of the individual?

## The Individual at Risk

The individual is at risk today, including you. How, you ask? Consider these risk factors:

- Identity theft fleeces more than forty million people in the United States yearly, and more than one hundred million people worldwide. And those numbers are rising.

- Your identity is now a valuable criminal commodity with a global value and a willing market of buyers.

- Hackers steal billions from your bank accounts today, even if you are not directly charged.

- Terrorists bomb the icons of our civilization, alter elections, and kill globally at will. They are active in more than fifty nations.

- Invasive governments watch and listen to all of us via a global communications network called Echelon that evades the laws of ten democracies, including the United States.

- Global positioning satellites calibrate overhead, watching our every move every three minutes with the capacity to take a picture of every face, every license plate, every bedroom, every one of our children.

■ Questionable government wiretaps listen to citizens' conversations.

■ Every e-mail is electronically scanned, analyzed, and stored, ostensibly to allow government officials to search for threatening messages sent or received by everyone in more than one hundred countries, including the United States.

■ Every cell-phone conversation is listened to by a battery of supercomputers that mine the text for keywords and then report back to their humans on threat assessments.

■ An army of hackers competes to create more damage or destroy your computer with viruses.

■ Every newborn has blood taken that goes to federal authorities for analysis and storage, and few know why.

■ Every terrorist organization in the world is working hard to attack you—citizens are the lifeblood of terrorism.

■ Every new car has a black box that registers our actions for on-demand government access.

■ Video surveillance cameras, often hidden from view, follow you every day in 70 percent of public spaces, everywhere from work to shopping to driving in your car.

■ Global direct-marketing companies amass consumer databases with the ability to predict your behavior.

■ Every insurance company and employer insists on knowing your total health status. Drug and medical tests are routinely given to assess you as a risk factor to the corporation.

■ Insurance companies trade confidential consumer information daily.

Wake up and smell the espresso. You are at risk. And this will only get worse in the Extreme Future.

# Subtle Risks and Spooky Futures

There are other, more subtle risks that are not as apparent that have the potential to threaten us. Fast-Pass chips in cars register who we are to governments; as do the new holographic passports. The biometrics now in buildings and video surveillance in everything from malls to schools to Vegas are growing in penetration by more than 200 percent a year. They capture our faces and ping databases to determine who we are and whether we are bad guys. In China, this technology is becoming the face of the future, the only way to monitor the masses and ferret out people the government considers "problems." How long before most governments use this "spooky" technology?

The widespread use of mood-altering drugs is an epidemic of choice. There's a medication that fixes kids with ADD, dads with too much stress, and women with depression. We don't even know what the long-term effects are of individual decision-making in a free society in which 50 percent of the public is on drugs. Interestingly, only 50 percent of the U.S. electorate votes. I wonder if it is the pharma-induced or the other folks?

All of this is part of our reality today. What are tomorrow's risks facing the individual?

- When personalized genomics disclosure is mandated to get jobs or to travel.

- When you must take drugs to enhance your performance—just as some athletes do today—or risk losing your job.

- When your implants not only help you achieve your desire to function better, but you don't even care that someone else is paying for them to win your loyalty.

- When you accept an end to personal privacy rights.

I hope my forecast of key threats facing individuals in society does not come to pass. This is a case, though, of an ounce of prevention being worth a pound of cure. Prepare for the worst and plan for the best. I do not think democracies will survive, or be authentic democracies, if they are not dedicated to protecting the rights of the individual for the long term. Put another way, I think that if the individual is at risk, then democracy as a viable system for society is at risk. There will be dangerous seductions and subtle risks we may not even recognize until after they have appeared. We must be on guard today to keep these costs from being incurred tomorrow. We must vigilantly protect ourselves from overt and covert efforts to rob us of our democratic rights via changes in our society's policies, tools, procedures, and technologies. This is a real threat today.

## Dangerous Ideas

Some of these ideas will seem dangerous—and they are. I stand by my assertion that today's individual is at risk from external forces as innocent as advertising, as intrusive as censorship, and as deceptive as pharmacology. I am not suggesting that advertising is an insidious attempt to manipulate buying habits on the same scale as mind control. They are not that good yet. Today it is not, but in the future I forecast that what appears to be advertising (which, by the way, will be highly interactive, adaptive, and personalized) may become a form of stealth mind control in certain places of the world. In this future scenario, advertising meets pharmacology meets government. Clever, seductive, always-on technology, without democracy and in the wrong hands, will be used to manipulate ideas, fabricate knowledge, and even design reality. The individual will be target. Pervasive, rich, immersive personal desires will be fulfilled. Information will be manipulated. Technology will be used to change what we think, what we do, and most dangerously, what we believe. We must guard against the information engineering of our reality. This is one of the most dangerous risks individuals face in the future.

A bit of paranoia can be a healthy thing if you consider the convergence of these forces and the history of government versus the individual. The mind-numbing drugs used by the Cold War government of Russia against its citizens to control dissent is just one example of this threat to individuals.

The individual has always been at risk from the forces of ideology, government, and religion. The tension between the freedoms and rights of the individual and attempts at control by government, religion, and ideology has been an ongoing battle for as long as civilization has existed. Think about all of the historic conflicts over nationalism, religion, and ideology and you get the picture: the Crusades, the Spanish Inquisition, the Hundred Years' War, World War I, World War II, the Holocaust, and on and on.

Of course, even in the face of oppressive forces with far greater powers, individuals have the fundamental right to defend their rights, as history has shown. The American Revolution was a shining example of individuals who decided to fight for freedom against an oppressive foreign power that did not recognize their rights. The eternal document that sprung from that conflict, the U.S. Constitution, is therefore brimming with protections for individual rights and freedoms.

These forces—the battle between individuals and institutions—are still at play today. They are deeply embedded in the global landscape, bubbling to the surface in conflicts in the Middle East, Asia, India, Pakistan, and in the global war on terrorism. The history of the oppression of individuals by institutions is well documented.

I forecast that the risk to the individual will continue into the future, in part from technology but also from old-fashioned politics. An ideal future would be one in which the goal of every government would be to empower the individual to enjoy freedom, prosperity, and human rights. But increasingly, the tyranny of radical theocrats and despots reminds us that the very idea of individual freedom is anathema to many world leaders.

## The History of the Individual

One lens through which to view history is the battle between individuals and institutions over power, control, and rights. This fundamental struggle has shaped much of the past. From the early periods of history, via the wars between peoples, the differences between cultures, or the competition between religions or ideologies, the individual has been caught in a maelstrom of continual conflict. Though the threats have had many faces, the conflict is the same: the individual against external forces of control in the form of ideology, government, or religion.

This age-old clash—with the rights of the individual at its core—will likely persist into the future. There is a delicate equilibrium required between governments and individuals that is often tenuous at best. Mechanisms like elections and law are meant to protect the individual, and they do. There are gargantuan challenges coming, though, that will freshly place the individual in the line of fire.

Another force that has been an intimate part of this struggle, deeply affecting individual rights, is the schism between religion and government. In our modern world, mostly in the developed nations of the West, government has won this battle over who should protect the interests of the individual. The deal was that religion won the ability to vie for the soul of man while government got the job of everything else, from taxes to war. Today, this is the retro-driver of the conflicts on much of the planet.

People across the planet are battling over the nature of their governments. Conflicts in the Middle East and in nations like Iran, Pakistan, and Iraq are complicated theocracies at war with secular forces. There are no theocratic governments that are not radicalized and dangerous. Democracy and individual freedom does not seem compatible with radical theocracy. Some Arabs would argue this point persuasively, as I have heard. History dies hard. Again, the individual seems to get the short end of the stick.

From the Ten Commandments to the autocracies of medieval kings to religious fundamentalists both Christian and Muslim, to the modern political ideologies of democracy, human history has been defined by rules set by institutions for individuals. Usually, an elite group of individuals sets the agenda for everyone else. Even today, perhaps more so than in the past, institutional doctrines seek to define individual choice, beliefs, and values. Whether these are Judeo-Christian, Muslim, or Communist, the ideologies of the past have a fierce hold on the behavior and choices of individuals today. This will remain so in the future. The question is whose future do you want to live in? What is important to you, the individual, about the future? The engines of manufactured belief will compete to control.

# The Invisible War

Most people don't even know that a war against individual rights has already occurred. That's why I call it the Invisible War. People go comfortably ahead with their lives, picking up their kids and a latte or heading off to the office. It is an invisible conflict because most people are oblivious to it. That's what makes it especially dangerous.

Many people might look around and disagree. In America, all seems OK. And yes, the rights of the individual in the West are certainly more protected and stable than those in the rest of the world. But if you spend time as I do in developing nations, you might see things differently. We in the developed nations of the world may face more complex, long-term challenges to our individual freedoms, such as brain implants, drugs, censorship, and limits to media choice, but individuals in developing nations that are less than democratic will be vastly more at risk.

For example, consider these questions and the implications for free choice:

- What if you did not have unfettered access to the Internet?
- What if you did not have access to quality education?
- What if you lived in a society that did not offer free elections?
- What if you lived where there was no free press and all the news you read or saw on television was controlled by the government?

In the U.S., these questions seem unrealistic. But more than 75 percent of the world—that's more than four billion people—doesn't have access to the Internet, phone service, clean water, regular meals, free elections, or quality education and health care. Would you consider this a restrictive force on the individual?

# Seeing the Threat

Our responsibility for the promotion of peace, security, and prosperity does not end at our own borders. Although we need to guard against the curtailment of individual rights in the U.S., we also have an obligation to help the rest of the world, especially individuals in Asia, Latin America, Africa, and the Middle East.

Will you be ready and willing to fight this war? Or will the prospect of a good job, low crime, a reasonably secure life, and the other creature comforts be enough to keep you happy? In Rome, Caesar placated the masses with free food and the mind-boggling entertainment of huge spectacles—from sea battles to gladiator fights—on a scale that we can only imagine. These were the first reality shows, ones in which real people died every day. Death and destruction were taken to a new level of bizarre entertainment. And it worked—at least for a while.

This is what certain forces on the planet are counting on. Where nationalism and religion fail, we will have a collision of one million channels of MTV, sports, and reality shows to distract us from the forces controlling our lives. Let the games begin! In the next chapter of the Invisible War, seductive, pervasive, immersive entertainment will be the new opiate of the masses, the enemy of free thought. People will be free to exercise choice, but only in the virtual worlds of unrestricted entertainment. This will be the trade-off for certain societies in a future in which individual freedom will be viewed as dangerous, subversive, and undesired.

Even prosperity, especially in developing Asian nations, may come with a high price tag in the long run—the restriction of individual freedoms. This is actually the case today in some nations, where some future generations may tolerate the loss of individual rights and freedoms without even realizing what they have lost. They will come to adapt, as humans do so well, to a norm of minimal freedom of expression, restrictive governance, limited access to information, curtailed movement, and even controlled thought.

This exercise is an attempt to expand your thinking about how we view the tension between individuals and government. Many of these rights of individuals are not provided because of poverty or limited access to capital. But too often there are more insidious motivations: These rights are kept purposefully from individuals by governments as a way to control them.

## Why Care?

Why should you care? The global conflict between individuals who have access to more rights, resources, and choices, and those who don't, just exploded. The attacks on 9/11 indicate a comprehensive global threat against the developed nations for not understanding the exploitation of individuals in the rest of the world.

The developed world uses 90 percent of the world's resources — water, food, energy, and capital. Isn't it realistic that the other citizens of the planet, the remaining four billion, might be angry about this? There is something off-base when so many have access to so few of the total resources of the world. We must consider this when trying to grapple with global conflict, terrorism, and the future. This is not just about fundamentalism. There is a legitimate argument here, one that suggests that better sharing of resources would reduce tensions between ideologies and cultures. The West should view this as an opportunity, not a threat.

## Future Threats to Individuals

Today, of course, there are new threats to individual rights and freedoms. Technology has become a key component in shaping the tension between individuals and institutions. On one hand, it has democratized communications, information access, and skills, bringing knowledge and digital capitalism to millions. The Innovation Economy is a testament to the advantages of technology to empower and liberate the individual. As we step into the Extreme Future, however, those very innovations in computing, communications, and medicine may be used against the individual. This dichotomy will help to define the future, either enabling or attacking individual freedom.

Past threats to individual rights will seem tame in the Extreme Future. Technology fused with ideology is a powerful new weapon that governments are using today and will use in the future to control and oppress individuals. On the opposite page is a list of things you need to watch out for.

Other threats, such as population increases, will challenge government ability to manage billions of more people. With three billion more people on the planet by 2050 to feed, clothe, house, and provide for with services like security and health care, governments will be stretched to the limit. This scenario could be the perfect excuse for governments to attempt to employ technology to exercise more control over our lives.

# TOP THREATS TO INDIVIDUALS BY 2015

- Brain implants to modify behavior.

- EKG brain-scanning for thought control.

- Pharmaceuticals to adjust behavior.

- Illegal wiretaps that capture personal identities and desires.

- Personal DNA theft.

- Neuro-advertising, direct to the retina or brain.

- Gene vaccines that eliminate undesired behaviors.

- Chip-tagging to control and track individual mobility.

- Surveillance technology that watches you everywhere.

- Interactive TV, computer, cars, and phones that signal who you are and what you desire.

- Smart-chip citizen ID cards.

- Consumer databases that reveal predictive personal information about what you will believe, buy, and think.

- Wireless bots that embed in our clothing to monitor behavior.

- Religion fundamentalists who preach intolerance.

## The Future of Europe

It is probable that without large and fast change, or an acceleration of imagination in the European Union, for example, the current standard of life will be reduced. This could be said about the future of the U.S., as well. This simply would not do in France, where regardless of whether you are an elevator operator or a CEO, you have the right as an individual to a six-week summer vacation. This is unheard of in the U.S.

This is causing problems that France, as a part of the EU, is not quite ready for. France can no longer afford the thirty-five-hour workweek and keep up with the needs of its society. In France, like much of the Eurozone, health care is free for most of the population, education is fully subsidized, and a large percentage of capital resources are put toward social services like these.

The society is not sustainable for the long term, given the growing price tag of these social services and coupled with lower fertility rates. In addition, compared with the U.S., overall productivity in the EU is low. Therefore, the population changes are a cause for concern where individual rights, even promised by law, may have to be changed. In all fairness, the French have made the right choice. But choices that we may be forced to make in the future may not be so clear and may hurt the individual.

At the moment, there are a few national leaders who see the potential for exercising absolute power over the individual by the use of one or more of these threats. "If I could only get my hands on some mind-control drugs," thinks a certain North Korean leader as he sucks down slices of homemade American-style pizza while his people are starving. You or I would consider these to be threats, but these leaders—concerned with quelling or controlling restive populations—would consider them to be opportunities. This is the Saddam Syndrome.

## The Saddam Syndrome

Saddam Hussein, formerly the head of Iraq, had a problem with a breakaway population in Iraq's north known as the Kurds. The Kurds are a proud, hardworking people who have fought for decades for their independence. When Saddam was in power, he unleashed one of the largest biochemical attacks in modern times on the Kurds, killing and injuring thousands. Saddam did not just want to kill the Kurds, he wanted to send a message to other freethinking, independence-minded individuals. Saddam wanted to kill these people's future by setting an example of how dangerous it was to even think about freedom.

In the future, by 2015 or before, many of the threats to individuals indicated here will be available for domestic or international use. The Saddam Syndrome is named for those leaders who will use the most efficient weapons they can muster to maintain control of their populations. To them, the ends justify the means. If there are more efficient ways to use devices, chemicals, airborne bioagents, or other weapons that can control individuals rather than kill them, these post-Saddam leaders will use them without restraint.

The Saddam Syndrome is not about winning supporters, but about manipulating and controlling the hearts and minds of individuals. In the Extreme Future, rogue terrorists and leaders of rogue nations will have a sophisticated arsenal of new drugs that they will use to wield control not just of individuals but entire populations. The following is one example:

## Rx: Thought Management 101

As a result of Internet censorship today in many countries in Asia and the Middle East, people who conduct searches using keywords like democracy or human rights receive a response that they are "not approved to view." Imagine if by 2020 these keywords were not allowed even to be thought. And what if there were a chemical way to ensure such words and concepts would never enter people's minds?

Today we accept almost without question the use of drugs like Prozac, which reduces and in some cases even eliminates anxiety associated with normal activities like work, relationships, and play. It is not implausible to forecast technology that would take the next step and modify the brain's use of keywords that trigger anxiety. Genomic thought censorship via chemicals. From there, it would be a short hop to modifying the brain to ensure those thoughts never occur at all, regardless of whether they are anxiety-provoking. (Of course, the real anxiety motivating the use of such drugs would be that felt by oppressive regimes fearful that thoughts about liberty and freedom might eventually lead to action.)

If this sounds scary, then you understand the implications of introducing drugs that might be used to restrict, control, and eliminate dissent, free choice, and individual freedoms. In a fake democracy, or a theocratic nation ruled by the few, the concerns are different. In the West, you can see this emerging today with more than 15 percent of antidepressant users taking drugs to help them modify their anxiety so they can live and work more productively.

In the Philips Heath Index I worked on, the most frightening part of more than half of all young people in North America being on mood-altering drugs today is what this tells us about the future. Will 85 percent of all people need or desire chemical enhancement to better perform at work and in life? The answer is probably yes. This is a dangerous indication of what tomorrow may bring—a medicated population of individuals who may not be able to make decisions without being influenced by pharmacology. The invisible war has already begun.

It will be possible to combine pharmacology, medicine, data mining, security, knowledge management, the Internet, and wireless computers to forge an infrastructure that will at once secure, protect, threaten, and hurt individuals. The seeds of this new conflict are in play today. Individuals beware, for the era of Neurotech is upon us.

---

*BRAINWAVE MESSAGE: 2025*

**"You Are Not Authorized to Believe in This Idea. Please Delete All References Now"**

---

I am involved in many projects in which I am monitoring the evolution of threats against the individual from the collision of neuromarketing, interactive digital media, psychopharmacology, sensors, and biometrics. There is a nexus point coming by or before 2015. Stay tuned.

## The Real Threat—
## Trading Rights for Security

The real threat to individual rights will emerge silently and over time. It will be the creeping insecurity caused by more identity crime, more terrorism, even more economic downturns or disruptions. The real threat will come in the form of a deal with the devil, in which we will trade our individual rights and freedoms for more security. We will scare ourselves into giving away our rights unless we are very careful and remain vigilant for danger signals. The manufacturing of "rationale" fear will become an industry in the near future. This is a dangerous trend that we want to resist.

The beginning will come when the next city in the United States is bombed by terrorists. After that, no one will argue about carrying identity cards. Even now, we clamor for identity cards so we can whisk through airports, not caring that others will be using the cards to watch us. The new clear passcard will be coming soon to most airports. You need an FBI background check to get one, as I learned. In the near future, our DNA will be used as identity, to be scanned remotely by watching cameras. Teams of experts will be analyzing our Visa purchases for shopping patterns of suspicion. Government agencies will have deeper access to intrude, investigate, and control the individual. We may desire this trade-off.

I am watching and forecasting this trend—the trade of individual rights for security—because there needs to be a greater balance and more debate on what to do. Do we need more security to protect us, today and in the future? Yes—but at what cost? The cost will be to individual rights of free expression, movement, information access, and privacy. We have been asleep too long as the world has burned. There is a need for balance and strong security, but we must be mindful of the individual's rights in our free societies. Perhaps the best example was the revelation in 2006 that the U.S. government was conducting wiretaps on U.S. citizens without judicial approval. This is the start. Without transparency and legal due process that protects individual rights, democratic societies will not endure in the future. When in the name of terror we allow fear to rule us, in place of law and rights, we will have accepted a new more dangerous tyranny from within—not outside—our nation.

Democratic values are an excellent metric to forecast what will be attacked. When there is talk of changing the U.S. Constitution, we need to say NO. When there are introductions of new laws that would restrict a free press, we need to say NO. When there is evidence of groups that would roll back choices protected by law, we need to say NO. When leaders in power seek to avoid the law and to spy on citizens, we must say NO. This is a defining moment for the individual and the nation. Just when the movement of global democracy is taking off, even in the Middle East, just when open and free global trade is emerging, we need to protect the rights of the individual at home and abroad. If we fail to ensure this in the future, the destiny of America will be a sorry one.

## The Future of Dissent

Is dissent in danger of being eliminated in America? I hope not. Yet in my experience, bolstered by the results of surveys and our forecasts, I have grown increasingly concerned about attacks on dissent in America. For example, when even mild questioning of government policy in the media is derided as "unpatriotic" or "disloyal," true dissent is at risk.

Why should you care? Dissent is a fundamental right of individuals in free societies to express their criticism of anything and everything without fear of reprisal. That's why we call this a democracy. Dissent is at the core of my forecast about the Invisible War facing the individual in the future. The value we place on free speech is best measured by how well we protect the speech we disagree with most. And for many of us, that means speech that dissents from the status quo. By the same token, the strength of a democracy can be measured by the extent to which speech is protected. When dissent is censored or threatened—by restricted access to information or even by intrusive pharmacology—the end looms for broader freedoms. As U.S. Supreme Court Justice Oliver Wendell Holmes wrote in 1929, "The principle of free thought is not free thought for those who agree with us, but *freedom for the thought we hate* (emphasis added)." The thought we hate is frequently the expressed voice of dissent.

The death of dissent may be as important a security threat as that posed by terrorists. Dissent comes in many forms. Too often, though, the argumentative, critical, and stubborn person is held in contempt. The enemies of dissent in the government, the community, the workplace, and even at times the media have created an atmosphere of fear for those who desire to challenge authority. I worry for our future if we foster a climate in which dissent is discouraged.

In a world in which the individual is continually at risk and new risks are waiting, dissent should be valued as a fundamental right of the individual. The legitimate use of dissent is a practical and reasonable weapon of individual freedom that should be protected, nourished, and valued in all realms of American life. Democracy thrives where dissent is not merely tolerated, but celebrated with authenticity, law, and respect. We must protect dissent as we would protect other rights of the individual, or we will suffer the creeping intrusions of power that seek to influence us.

Evidence of the impending death of dissent is all around us. Whistle-blowers don't have the protections that the law mandates. Sexual harassment complaints are often avoided or quashed. National security is used as an excuse to avoid the rule of law and conduct wiretaps on citizens. A strange mood prevails in which "loyalty"—as defined by those in power—is somehow seen as the opposite of dissent. In our surveys of America, the population between the ages of eighteen and twenty-five was most vocal about the need for dissent in a vital society. The young want the power to change what they did not create. And they should have it.

## Medicating Dissent

Another enemy of dissent in America concerns me for the future—medication. Do we need medication to feel better about ourselves, our lives, our world? The answer is yes. However, if more than 50 percent of Americans are prescribed psychoactive drugs that can have the effect of dulling the appetite for dissent, doesn't that suggest that something is wrong with American society? We are not all anxious, depressed, afflicted with ADD, or mentally dysfunctional, are we?

Medication can be abused, and I would argue is being abused, as an antidote for people who have dissenting personalities. Some people consider challenging authority to be abnormal behavior. It then follows that people who challenge authority can be calmed with drugs. But where is the line drawn between helping someone and pacifying someone? We had best be careful and be aware about the medication of dissent and the enemies of dissent that may enter our lives.

Whenever dissent is driven away—by drugs, by PTA boards, by powerful organizations, by politicians, in the name of religion, by the media, by whomever—the danger signs should go up. Dissent is fundamental to the American experience and to the future of America. Those who would seek to squelch dissent betray the democratic values and personal freedoms our nation is based on.

## The World of 2050

It will do no good to create a future where by 2050 we have eliminated poverty and war, created open global trade, and increased productivity and standards of living for the nine billion residents of Earth but traded our individual rights for this false prosperity. As America moves forward in promoting the model of democracy and capitalism on the world stage, there is nothing more important than the respect for individual freedoms that must be at the

> *END TRANSMISSION*
>
> **Please Identify Yourself Now.**
> **Place Your Eye in Front of This Page**

heart of this quest. This is one of the chief concerns I have for the twenty-first century. We must be aware of the creeping threats to the individual, the Invisible War that is encroaching on the very freedoms our nation was founded upon.

The right of the individual to stand free and make his or her own choices must be the central pillar of civilization's future. The track record on this score over the past thousand years often has been hit or miss. Religious fundamentalists, kings, and dictators have attacked the freedom of the individual over history. We must guard our rights to freedom or lose this war for ourselves and our children. This will be a challenge given the changes and risks coming in the Extreme Future. It is our destiny to forge a balance between the rights of the individual and the government that preserves that individual's right to freedom. Individuals should control the government, not the other way around.

# CHAPTER 11

# Dancing Dragon:
# The Future of China

## Wake-Up Call

Wake up, America. Wake up, Europe. Wake up, Asia. China is rising. The Dragon is dancing. Can you dance? If there were ever a time to wake up to the sheer power of China's population, buying power, energy needs, consumer demands, and eventual military strength, that time is NOW. This is your wake-up call, and it will not be pretty. We will all have to learn to adapt, change and, well, dance. We all need to wake up and learn to better understand how the future of China will shape our world. This is a future fast touching everyone on the planet, and the implications are huge.

As China rises, the evolutionary needs of two billion people in a few scant years will reshape markets, competition, and trade on a scale we can only imagine. Trillions of dollars of wealth will be traded, exchanged, and moved from West to East. Computers for two billion, make it now! How do you feed two billion people? Quickly. Get ready for change on a scale that redefines everything.

## Visiting China

I have been watching and forecasting about China for many years, providing foresight and analysis to my Fortune 1000 clients about China's rising stature as a competitive force as

# THE TEN TOP TRENDS THAT WILL SHAPE THE FUTURE OF CHINA

**1.** China's emergence as the new superpower will define the global economy in the twenty-first century. China will dominate world trade, energy resources, innovation, and security.

**2.** China's rise to power will be fast, radical, and disruptive—representing both a threat and an opportunity. Meeting the China challenge will require every nation to adapt to new technology, education, science, and health care to be able to compete.

**3.** The U.S./China relationship will bring a new era of global progress as a shared agenda of prosperity through capitalism becomes a global model.

**4.** China must embrace its leadership role as the new superpower and work toward an end to global terrorism, which directly threatens its future economic prosperity, global security, and social transformation.

**5.** China has become the global piracy leader, and counterfeit manufacturing poses a threat to future export growth and China's standing with brand-dependent multinational corporations.

**6.** China faces numerous risks to its future stability. Skyrocketing population rates and explosive social demands must be resolved. The banking system is unstable. The growing wealth gap between the rich and the poor signals trouble ahead.

**7.** Innovation will be the key driver of China's future economic and social transformation. Science and technology investments will be essential to trade, jobs, education, and health care.

**8.** China must address environmental hazards such as increased pollution or risk a future decline in economic growth and increased public-health problems.

**9.** China's future will require access to a tremendous supply of reliable energy. As China moves toward energy self-reliance, alternative sources of post-oil energy such as wind, hydrogen, solar, and nuclear will be vital.

**10.** As China looks to the future, democratic reforms must be achieved along with growth. The nation must learn to foster the rule of law, individual rights, and social freedoms or risk derailing economic progress and social stability.

well as an exciting new market. Though I had been to China before, in November 2005, I received a special invitation that I couldn't pass up: I was asked to join a delegation and travel with Senator Dianne Feinstein and Mayor Gavin Newsom to celebrate the twenty-fifth anniversary of the San Francisco/Shanghai sister city relationship—the first partnership of its kind between American and Chinese cities. (In 1980, while serving as mayor of San Francisco, Senator Feinstein recognized the strategic importance of the U.S./China relationship and worked toward creating a successful bond between the two cities.)

A number of prominent San Francisco business and university leaders were also invited. It proved to be a fascinating time to go to China to see the rapid changes happening there on such a large scale. The rare access we enjoyed to key thought leaders, government and business officials, and the Chinese people was eye-opening to say the least, and much of this chapter was shaped by that visit.

## Two Billion Capitalists Go Faster

On my recent trip, it all became so clear to me. After the Cold War, Russia's model of a managed society was dead. The Chinese watched and learned. The Chinese leadership, primarily Deng Xiaoping, sup-

# CHINA'S WAKE-UP CALL #1

- You earn in an hour what the average Chinese citizen earns in a year.

- Some one hundred new megacities will be built in China by 2015, each with more than ten million residents.

- A new skyscraper goes up every other day in more than ten Chinese cities.

- China consumes more than 30 percent of the world's steel and cement for construction.

- China will be the largest consumer market—larger than the U.S. and Europe combined—by 2020.

- China is the sixth-largest economy in the world. By 2020, it will be second only to the U.S.

- By 2005, there were more than $51 billion worth of U.S./China ventures. By 2015, I forecast more than $150 billion worth of U.S./China ventures.

- China is locking up billions of dollars of oil futures contracts in anticipation of explosive future demand.

- Every hour, the U.S./China trade deficit increases and the intimate linkage of China with the U.S. economy grows stronger.

- China is stabilizing the U.S. and global economy. The Chinese own more than $1 trillion U.S. and more than $1 trillion worth of U.S. bonds. This figure will increase by 25 percent a year for the next twenty years.

- Chinese investments in the Euro increase the stability of the European Union.

ported the opening of the economy to the world and the growth of capitalism. This was first tried as an experiment and then implemented as a national policy. He had a long-term vision for his people, the only vision. This was the pivotal point in China's history because when he looked upon the social progress that came from private ownership and capitalist entrepreneurship, Deng realized that a capitalist China could transform the Chinese society for the better.

His historic comment, "Go faster," gave permission to a new generation of Chinese leaders and citizens to embrace capitalism. The Chinese version, that is, state-supported capitalism. Cities sprung up overnight. Government-owned businesses were sold. People could exercise simple freedoms and become modest traders in a once-secretive society, formerly built on fear and dogma and now arranged around profit and ingenuity. Capitalist China was born. This simple act, this bold brilliance, has set the stage for the transformation of China

## The Hong Kong Model

Tung Chee Hwa is a proud but quiet man. On the day we met he seemed tired, but once he got talking he came alive, and his personal power, or *chi*, as the Chinese would say, was animated and strong. His office is not fancy or ornate like those in some other buildings in China. In fact, it was quite gray and drab, but modern and seemingly efficient. He was surrounded by economists, urban planners, and advisors who all received us. He met with us for more than an hour to discuss many of the issues essential to the future of China. He is in a position to know, because he possesses a unique place in history.

Tung was the first Chinese leader of Hong Kong after the transfer from British to Chinese rule. As Hong Kong's first chief executive—a post comparable to president—Tung had a front-row seat as the past morphed into the present. Given the nature of Hong Kong, it was especially fitting that Tung was not a career politician, but a businessman who had been the CEO of one of the largest shipping companies in the world. From that remarkable combination of experiences, Tung developed an insightful vision for China's future. Though no longer at the helm of the Hong Kong government, when we met he was still an important advisor, and his influence was widespread in the nation.

To understand the significance of Hong Kong, think about Hong Kong as a model of the future for the entire nation. The HK work ethic, productivity, GDP, and growth are all robust. There are more billionaires in HK than there are in all the rest of the world. If China can achieve the outstanding productivity and progress exhibited by Hong Kong in the coming decades, then that would be the ultimate endgame for China's future. Hong Kong's vigorous growth was born under British rule and nurtured in an incubator of capitalism, free enterprise, rule of law, and personal freedom of expression, such as a free press.

Tung told us he knows that tough decisions must be faced in the near future by the Chinese leadership. "It will be difficult. We know we must prepare ourselves for reforms," he acknowledged. We discussed how long the Chinese leadership can put off the demands of its citizens for democratic reforms. He shared with us his desire, his hope, that the Chinese people "should be patient and recognize how far we have come in so little a time." It was not so long ago, he said, that people needed permission to move, to eat, to travel, or to work. "We have made great progress and we have more to go. Democracy is coming by 2010, we know," he maintained with a sincere but concerned look on his face.

Tung's underlying message was clear: China's leadership has a vision to achieve a transformation on a scale never before attempted by any nation, at any time in history. In a few short years, China has made a dramatic economic shift from Communism to capitalism, from a centrally controlled economy to one that places increasing amounts of power and authority in the hands of markets and individuals. And yet, this is still not a fully cooked strategy; seismic risks are at play, and it remains uncertain how the multidimensional chess game will play out or how long it will take. Tung Chee Hwa is asking for patience from the West as China figures out how it can best thrive in the twenty-first century. Whether the West can or will heed that call remains to be seen.

---

### CHINA MANUFAX: 2012

**The eBay for Manufacturing**

- First real-time auction service for entrepreneurs.

- Connects buyers with Chinese manufacturers.

- Lower cost, higher quality, ISO 12000-certified.

- Complete services: from product design to production to delivery.

- Used by leading companies including IBM, Motorola, Virgin.

- Free shipping through Chinese New Year.

---

## Capitalist Values

In conversations with Chinese leaders from Beijing to Shanghai, I repeatedly heard many of the same values I would expect to hear in the United States: "We will let the markets determine that." "We want to watch the supply and demand." "The markets will find the right level." And so on.

This confirmed my intuition that the Chinese are reinventing capitalism—Chinese capitalism is emerging. It will be an Asian version of what we hold in the U.S. and the rest of the world to be central to our economy: free enterprise, free markets, and hopefully free minds. The first steps in this experiment are unfolding now, and it is fascinating to watch.

# CHINA'S WAKE-UP CALL #2

■ The Chinese are the largest buyers of U.S. Treasury Bills, furthering the economic interconnectedness, global stability, and reinforcing the interests of both nations.

■ China's economy is growing at an eye-popping 10 percent per year, triple the rate of U.S. economic growth. By 2030, China's economy may overtake the economies of the U.S. and Europe.

■ Many manufactured products, from clothing to medical devices to industrial equipment to auto parts, will soon be made in China, just so the manufacturers can compete for quality and price in world markets.

■ China's move to upscale its manufacturing from commodity products to knowledge products will create fierce global competition.

■ The Chinese have five times more business schools and ten times more science and engineering schools than the U.S. and Europe combined.

■ Peking University received more than one million applications last year.

■ More than two billion new capitalists and consumers will define China's future by 2020.

■ More than half of today's Chinese population is under the age of twenty-five.

■ General Motors China, the most profitable arm of the auto company, is growing at more than 60 percent a year and will sell more than 550,000 autos in China this year. By 2020, GM may be selling as many as one billion autos in China.

# China on Overdrive

From bicycles to Mercedes, from villages to megacities, from poverty to wealth—the accelerated growth of China is unprecedented in the history of civilization. You have to experience China to believe it. From ancient street corners to skyscrapers going up as you watch, the explosive growth is as if lightning has struck every one of the 1.3 billion citizens at the same time. And when you see this intense electricity, it redefines scope, vision, and even logic.

First off, you have to think BIG. Everywhere you go, from Beijing to Shanghai, there is the dynamic and explosive movement of millions of people in transition, all moving at the same time. Shanghai has 7,000 skyscrapers, compared with New York's 5,000. Think about that for a minute. Cities of seventeen million today, cities of thirty million tomorrow, there is no way to fully conceptualize the immensity of this revolution. China's growth redefines large. It defies comparison.

China will be building a city bigger than Philadelphia each year for the next twenty years. There are more than 400 cities in China, and more than one hundred of them with more than a million people. In twenty years, that number could double to 800 cities. This is not just a story about the radical transformation of a society but about a new exciting narrative that will redefine commerce, communications, and culture. The engines of productivity in China today are cheap labor, innovation, and capitalism on steroids—a supercharged, hyper-aggressive need to catch up with the rest of the world's developed economy. In the future it will be smart labor coupled with even smarter innovation. This represents a new challenge and opportunity for the world and for China. China's growth could bring future stability and peace or chaos and insecurity—both internally and externally. This is the challenge of the future, and it reflects China's immense role in meeting this challenge effectively.

Already the bicycles are gone. Twenty years ago, as the light changed in front of the Forbidden Palace in Beijing, the crush forward of bicycles defined the movement of people and symbolized the plodding, foot-powered pace of change. There were few cars. Now it is the opposite. It seems everyone in the cities drives a car. Now the cars zoom by, jamming the streets where few bikes are seen. If transportation is a metaphor for the future, then China's building of six million cars over the next few years tells the story. Turbocharged change is here.

# Piracy and China's Future

At the same time, there is another side to innovation in China. It is clear from numerous data sources that China leads the world in intellectual-property piracy. From cell phones to software, automotive parts to drugs, music to movies, Nike sneakers to designer watches, China rules the piracy world with knockoffs. How this came to be is an interesting example of innovation run amok. China's excellent design and manufacturing capacity, so precise as to fool even the brand owners themselves, has gone lawless. In all fairness, China's leaders are saying they are looking into correcting the piracy problem, but it is so ingrained and immensely profitable that it is hard to destroy.

The irony is that some major companies, such as Levi Strauss, the makers of blue jeans, have closed down operations in China because the knockoffs being made were equal to if not better than the real, famous 501 jeans. This is not unusual. Quality of manufacturing isn't the problem. The inability or immaturity of the Chinese legal system to provide the rule of law and patent, protections necessary to protect trademark, patent, and copyright holders, is the problem.

# Fake Drugs

Pfizer, the global pharmaceutical giant, is meeting with problems in getting its patent for Viagra approved in China. Everywhere else this drug is patent-protected. This is not the company's only intellectual-patent problem. Viagra is sold in China and is very popular. But Pfizer books none of the sales because the Viagra sold there is not made by Pfizer. This is common practice—by some estimates, more than 80 percent of drugs sold in China are illegal copies. Piracy affects not just the knockoff drugs sold illegally in China, but now China is exporting these illegal drugs to other countries, competing with Pfizer's own Viagra in the U.S., Asia, and Europe. Extrapolate this practice into fields including auto parts, consumer products, movies, and music, and you begin to get the picture. This is not just a multibillion-dollar headache.

The risk is that China will threaten the chief engine of its economy today and more importantly, threaten its future: manufacturing for export markets. If the global business community loses trust in China, this could spell danger for China in multiple ways. It is vital to keep the

Chinese economy growing to feed, clothe, and care for its 1.3 billion citizens. If China does not put a definitive end to piracy, this will threaten future export market growth, which in turn will most certainly increase domestic instability. This is a dangerous outcome of piracy. The Chinese economy must grow by at least 7 percent every year for the next ten years or risk dangerous social instability.

More than 300 million Chinese people—equivalent to the entire U.S. population—today live in agrarian poverty. You hear about all the fast growth in China, but prosperity is not part of the lives of a large part of the population. And those poor farmers are speaking up more loudly than ever. Last year, there were more than 70,000 social protests in China. This is not unusual. Remember Tiananmen Square? This is the Chinese leadership's concern—that this social unrest explodes nationally and derails growth. It is a possible future. The biggest danger facing China is whether it will be able to kick-start the prosperity engine fast enough to satisfy the demands of its people. Piracy, if allowed to continue, increases the risks that the Chinese will destroy their capacity to be a trusted manufacturing partner that respects intellectual property and brands. Piracy could derail China's Great Leap Forward into the future.

## Piracy Drives Terror

The real nightmare for global brand owners like Levis, GM, Coke, GE, Nike, and others is what happens when the knockoffs are better than the real product? This, as well, may be the bizarre future of piracy. China may have opened the Pandora's Box, and now the pirates may intend to compete on quality and price by offering more high-value features for lower cost than the real product. This is starting to happen now—see the Levis example mentioned above. Brand-crashing will emerge as a future threat to companies. I would forecast that by 2010 more than 15 percent of branded products will be knockoffs produced at higher quality than the real ones unless China takes seriously the problem of piracy and ends it.

There is another problem to address, which is a dark underbelly of the Chinese piracy industry. Piracy fuels organized global-crime syndicates, drug trafficking, and the global war on terrorism. There are those who are only in it for the money, but piracy, not unlike drug trafficking with its huge global profits, has now attracted organized-crime lords, drug dealers, human slave traders, and terrorists who have found a new source of capital.

Evidence of a brisk barter trade between criminals and terrorists, with drugs for software, arms for fake currency, music for medicine, auto parts for human organs, is a shadowy emerging business model in the Extreme Future. This forecast is becoming reality today.

The border of North Korea and China is already a hotbed of that kind of multidimensional criminal piracy and rogue commerce. For example, the manufacturing of cigarettes and counterfeit U.S. $100 bills are brisk businesses there. Looking for a way to finance your next terrorist attack, or perhaps you want to trade some stolen arms for cigarettes? How about a discount on high-quality (but fake) U.S. currency? You get one AK-47 rifle for every one million fake dollars you buy, at a discount, of course. This is a real conversation about the actual deals that are actively going on that don't make the evening news.

I forecast that a global black market will emerge by 2010—superefficient, streamlined, and highly profitable. In the future, organized financial or political criminals will seek to have a diversified suite of profit centers, from drugs to piracy to terror-for-hire to corporate espionage. China will play an important role in either stopping or fostering this global scourge. Piracy is at the heart of this dark story. The historic challenge for China's leaders is whether they will allow their plans for economic and social transformation to be derailed by pirates.

> ### HONG KONG LUXURY REPLICAS INC.: 2018
>
> **The Only Authorized and Licensed Knockoff Company**
>
> - Watches, auto parts, medical devices, drugs, clothes.
>
> - Licensed by Levis, Gucci, Merck, Mercedes, Ford.
>
> - Direct from certified Chinese factories.
>
> - Only online orders accepted.
>
> - Save 60 percent or more.
>
> - Guaranteed quality or money back.
>
> - Interpol-certified.

## GM China Tells All

General Motors may be having difficulties in the U.S. and European markets, but in China the company is selling up a storm. Meeting with the president of General Motors on my trip, he informed me that GM China will be producing and selling more than 600,000 autos in China this year. He said that GM's business is growing at more than 60 percent per year in China. In 2004, there were more than five million cars sold. The market is exploding. It is not difficult to see where this is going: China's unique combination of inexpensive labor, innovation, and a strong work ethic will not only make it the largest market in the world for buying automobiles, but also the most cost-effective nation to manufacture autos for the export market.

And innovation—not just cheap labor or a huge, hungry consumer market—is key to this massive transformation of commerce. As the president of GM China said when I asked him about his thoughts on renewable energy: "China will make the move to fuel cells first in ten years—yes, they will be first." Not a tame forecast for a top executive who is forecasting the end of the internal-combustion engine.

This is a super-capitalist model that will be repeated, I forecast, over the next twenty years: China's unique fusion of skilled, inexpensive, smart labor, with innovation and technology, energized by the taste of wealth, will transform the global manufacturing industries of drugs, electronics, consumer products, medical devices, textiles, and defense.

In other words, GM and many other global manufacturing companies will not be able to compete in the new Innovation Economy without collaborating and leveraging China's cheap labor, efficient manufacturing capacity, strong work ethic, and growing innovation. GM knows this. GM will be manufacturing in China for export markets long after it closes its U.S. factories. GM and many companies may not be able to remain profitable or survive without leveraging China. Bankruptcy or reorganize in China? This dilemma will be faced many times in the next few years as companies compete globally, each leveraging the manufacturing, design, innovation, and labor of China.

## China's Innovation Economy

Wal-Mart is an example of this today. Wal-Mart's entire business model is based on providing the lowest-cost products for the global consumer marketplace. Wal-Mart would cease to compete effectively without China's capacity to produce products at Wal-Mart's low price point. If you look around, Wal-Mart is hardly alone. Pacemakers from Medtronic, computers once built by IBM, video games that entertain us, and medicines that keep us healthy and living longer—all are enabled by, or are actually made, in China. As drug development becomes hugely expensive and time- and labor-consuming, only China will have cost-effective facilities and skilled-at-the-right-price labor to bring future pharmaceuticals and medical devices to the market. Without China's future drug-development capacity, there will be fewer products and more costly drugs. By manufacturing and developing new products in China, foreign companies can make more profit and develop more innovative products to help more people cure disease.

China has already become the manufacturer of choice for achieving competitive advantage. China will become the secret weapon that companies use to design low-cost, high-quality products to open up new markets and cause overnight disruptions in the business models of market leaders. As the Innovation Economy unfolds, when nanotech enables the Chinese to design matter at the atomic scale, for instance, this one strategic skill will offer massive competitive value in every industry. This very significant realization has become a linchpin in the minds of every forward-looking businessperson, government leader, and organization.

## Dell Knows

Consider the example of Dell Computer. A few years ago, Dell executives took a PDA organizer—with a combination phone, calculator, and MP3 player—to China to get a Chinese manufacturer to design and build a similar product for 25 percent lower cost. That was a legal knockoff. It's Dell's business model to offer great value for a lower cost than the competition. This enabled Dell to extend its product line of productivity tools beyond computers to PDAs. Dell repeated this success with printers, again using China to outcompete others in the market.

GDP tells part of the story. Though China's economy is only $1.3 trillion compared with the United States' $13 trillion, the Chinese economy is growing at three times the rate of the U.S. economy. Work the numbers. How long will it take number three to become number two or even number one? By 2025, China will be the second-largest economy in the world.

# From Mao to Adam Smith

Our meeting with the mayor of Shanghai was a special occasion. Of all of my trips to China and all the places I've seen there, this meeting best captured China's rise. The purpose of our meeting was the culmination of our San Francisco/Shanghai sister city twenty-fifth anniversary. The spacious hall for our official ceremony was decorated with a hundred-foot-long mural of a serene valley with blue shimmering water and a lush green forest. One entire wall was consumed by this hypnotic art, this fantastic, pulsing painting, which seemed like a portal to a verdant prehistoric world that viewers could simply step into at their choosing. It was surreal. We sat facing each other, on one side our American delegation, and on the other the Communist Party officials and the mayor's official entourage.

Every person was strategically placed in his or her seat. We faced off across the room. It seemed awkward at first, but I got used to it and came to understand its purpose—a silent, honest confrontation. As we sipped jasmine tea and sat in oversized Mandarin chairs, I became part of the formal signing ceremony. This was more than just a meeting. It was a meeting of minds from different parts of the cultural map, each looking for a new awareness of the other.

At first this was a strange visual: Chinese officials dressed in jacket and tie, Western style, and many of us Americans dressed in Chinese jackets; a reversal of costumes. Our dressing mirrored our intent. We were looking to bridge the cultural divide. It seemed to me to be a fusion of ideals—capitalism, socialism, and Confucius all integrated into a new narrative about the future possibilities of the U.S./China relationship. The speeches were formal, exploring our intent to collaborate

---

## PEKING LIFE EXTENSION CENTERS: 2020

**Renew Yourself Today—
Live Long, Be Healthy**

- Complete health-enhancement and life-extension services.

- Stem-cell nano-engineering experts.

- Personal DNA reprogramming.

- Cybernetic enhancement available.

- Life Xtend Wellness Residence Program.

- More than 25,000 satisfied customers.

- Add 10 to 25 years or money back.

and deepen our bonds of friendship. My conversations with the officials were rich, hopeful, and intricate, exploring the future of the bilateral relationship and examining the risks facing us all, such as terrorism and environmental degradation.

## An Emerging Superpower

The truth is, no one is prepared for the fast-paced and comprehensive changes that China is bringing to the global economy. Here's a secret: Not even the Chinese are prepared for their impending impact—on their own nation and on the world. It's as if a fantastic experiment is taking place that touches trade, technology, culture, media, finance, and science. In the future, with a sizzling economy growing by astronomical rates—perhaps approaching 15 percent each year—China's leaders will be unable to control the growth, the prosperity, and the sheer brilliance of two billion hungry (both literally and figuratively) capitalists. And that's just part of the story.

# TOP TEN STRATEGIC MISTAKES THAT COULD DERAIL CHINA'S FUTURE

- A hot war with Taiwan.

- Putting off democratic reforms into the far future.

- Not using its superpower leadership to address global issues.

- Not working seriously to end piracy and fraud.

- Not removing barriers to free enterprise and capitalism.

- Failing to contain North Korea's aggressiveness.

- Thinking radical Islamic terrorism will not affect China's future.

- Not moving toward energy independence.

- Inability to manage environmental hazards and pollution.

- Ineffective planning to offset the risks of pandemics like bird flu.

China's rise means that it may become the new superpower of the future. A superpower uses its power in economics to control the flow of goods and services, and its political and military might to set and dominate an international agenda. China is emerging as a nation that will meet that standard. The fundamental intimacy and connectivity of the Dancing Dragon to other major superpowers—the U.S. and the European Union, even Russia—will bring a new global order of relationships that must be forged to meet the challenges of the Extreme Future. This chapter explores ways that this amazing and historic transformation will change China and the entire world.

## Two Futures, Two Scenarios

There are two chief scenarios that people usually think about when it comes to China. The first is the barbarians-at-the-gate scenario, which says that we should fear China and beware because the Chinese will overpower us with their sheer size and fiercely competitive natures, combined with the centralized economic planning of their government. This portrait predicts that China will ultimately emerge as the preeminent economic power. This scenario is built upon a polarized "us" versus "them" mind-set. The rationale goes something like this: They have more people, numbering in the billions, who will work for less and produce high-quality products. That means we can't compete and can't win. We are therefore doomed to be vanquished in their onslaught of global competitiveness. This scenario is compelling and attractive to the sky-is-falling crowd, especially in the media. In fact, there are some things to fear. China's competitive advantages are significant, and the playing field isn't level. That is not, however, the whole story.

From my perspective, believing that this will be the endgame requires a certain level of, well, fear. A touch of ignorance helps, too. Proponents of this doomsday scenario must have somehow forgotten about the deep, fundamental collaboration of markets, trade, and economies. We are strategically linked in ways we don't often realize, from economics to public health to communications to defense. This connection makes this very idea obsolete. When we invest in dozens of U.S. companies on the stock exchange, we are investing indirectly in China.

**China invests in the U.S.** The second scenario, perhaps closer to reality, is the dancing-with-the-dragon scenario that I subscribe to. This scenario says that yes, China is a formidable competitor, one that can create tsunami-like economic change either by exercising a ruthless form of capitalism or even by benignly shifting its focus and setting new goals. However, China is also a nation of consumers and capitalists, representing the largest consumer and business market in the world. That means there is an opportunity to sell, develop, and prosper in *collaboration* with the Chinese. The size of this market potential baffles the mind—it redefines opportunity. The United States has only 300 million consumers. China has more than 600 million consumers who are under twenty-five years old! Those who can see that emergence of the largest consumer market in the world have the greatest potential to profit from it.

## The Largest Market

This scenario—call it an optimistic, opportunistic, capitalistic model—says there will be two billion potential customers to sell to. What capitalist wouldn't be excited by that? Interested in getting 25 percent market share, or 300 million consumers, to buy your software, drugs, or pet rock? The dancing-with-the-dragon scenario says we are smart enough, and the Chinese or global market is big enough, that with our combined resources—intellectual capital, marketing, and manufacturing—we can all prosper.

This scenario is certainly being proven by GM and Mercedes in the auto business, by Wal-Mart in retail, by Dell in computers, by Medtronic in pacemakers, and by numerous other companies in markets too numerous to mention. Therefore, the barbarians-at-the-gate scenario, though appealing to some, is not a realistic survival strategy. Some corporations and individuals will find the strategy of enterprise collaboration hard to adopt or even consider. That's a potentially fatal mistake. China will continue to represent risk and opportunity all at the same time. In one of my recent presentations to clients, this one at the Navy War College, I challenged the assembled admirals with this question: What is the conversation we should be having with the Chinese military leadership about future collaboration to ensure global security? Each of us needs to ask that same question about our economic futures. What conversation should we be having with Chinese consumers, competitors, and collaborators to ensure global prosperity? It will take more than thinking outside the box to navigate with China in the Extreme Future.

# China's Long March into the Future

An important example of the emerging Innovation Economy can be found in China. In less than twenty years, China has enabled more than 400 million people to transform the quality of their lives. This is an amazing story that there is simply no analog for in the history of civilization. The average Chinese worker's income has increased four-fold, allowing him to move from crushing poverty to the next rungs of the economic ladder. Innovation is at the core of this revolution, and it will shape China's future prosperity.

While the economies of the U.S. and Europe are growing at 3 to 4 percent annually, China's economy has been growing at a sizzling 10 percent. Individuals have the power to do remarkable things when enabled by innovation, freed from constraints, and given resources and opportunity. This will only accelerate in the future as more powerful innovations will define China and the world's prosperity.

---

## DISNEY SHANGHAI RETIREMENT VILLAGE: 2012

**Disneyland for Retirees**

- U.S.-trained medical staff.

- Fifty-percent lower costs than in the U.S. and Europe.

- Serving more than ten million throughout China today.

- Full hospice program: Pass on with Dignity and Disney.

---

As democracy is essential to the prosperity of citizens, we should encourage progress that will enable China to become a free society. The West must rethink and learn to be tolerant of different models of democracy that may emerge over time in former socialist and Muslim nations, which may evolve a complementary form of democracy. New paradigms of democracy will emerge in the future, and our tolerance for these differences will define the cooperation of nations as well. It's in our interest for China to continue on the path of progress and peace, one in which authentic democratic reforms can become a central part of its future prosperity.

Not long ago, I was giving a keynote presentation on the future of the wireless information society to an audience of global customers of National Semiconductor, the chipmaker. Sitting with the CEO at dinner before my talk, I asked what he found astounding in his world. He thought about it for a minute and told me this story about China, an important place for his company's customers.

"What astounds and frightens me is the speed of innovation that is shifting from the U.S. to China. I visited a factory. It was the size of five football fields, brand spanking new. On one end was a slab of

---

# THE TEN KEY DRIVERS OF CHINA'S FUTURE

■ **Education Leapfrog**. To catch up with the West, China needs to develop an accelerated innovation infrastructure of universities, research institutes, and technical schools.

■ **Flight to the Cities**. More than 80 percent of China's populace, more than two billion people, will be city dwellers in forty years, challenging future resources.

■ **Mind-boggling Population Management**. Jobs, health, security, transportation. Each of these domains will be challenged by one to three billion new citizens.

■ **Exporting Innovation**. Export markets are the key to China's growth and stability.

■ **High-Tech, High-Quality Products**. Manufacturing world-class products, especially in the medical, security, transportation, and drug industries, will accelerate growth.

■ **Banking Reform**. The Chinese banking system, which is the backbone of the economy, needs fast reform to support future growth.

■ **Global and National Security**. Security at home or abroad can either derail or stabilize China's future.

■ **Energy Access**. China's access to energy must keep pace with demand or the economy will stagnate.

■ **Sustainable Environment**. China must address the growing pollution problems that will threaten future economic progress.

■ **Global Leadership Role**. China must emerge in the twenty-first century as a global leader committed to global stability and the peace of nations in partnership with the U.S. and Europe.

metal, a sleek slab of magnesium. What was produced, what came out the other end as a finished product, were cell phones, computers, printers. You just dialed up what you needed the production line to make. The superefficiency was obvious—we can't do that here in the U.S. today."

From computers to biotech, from harnessing the human genome to Internet sales, from enhancing the brain's function to improving health, individuals—in China, the United States, Europe, the world over—will profit the most from the Innovation Economy. Free minds to explore innovation, free markets to sell to, and free trade with other global individuals will be at the core of the Innovation Economy. China, destined to be an exporter of innovation products and services, will be a strong competitor with the U.S. and Europe for highly profitable global markets, as long as it makes necessary adjustments and avoids potential pitfalls.

## The Power of the Individual

The Innovation Economy continues the march into the future of innovations that create personal choice, personal power, and personal creativity. The overwhelming majority of patents, more than 99 percent, come from individuals living in free societies. This further indicates the link between democracy and innovation. But this may not continue into the future. Is it possible for China to continue to resist democratic reforms and become a successful global innovator? I don't think so, and the Chinese leaders I have talked with understand this. This will be a challenge that will define China's future.

I forecast that China's social and political system will be transformed by the very innovations and interactions of the global marketplace of predominately democratic nations. China's leaders cannot reasonably expect that their citizens would tolerate their nation becoming a global innovation leader without individuals benefiting from freedoms that should rightfully come with prosperity. China's leadership itself, concerned about its own sustainability, might well recognize the real politic of innovation that will bring not just prosperity to millions but an expectation of increased personal freedoms—on a par with other nations of the world. The wisest of China's leaders today understand the inevitable logic of this future transformation.

There is another important connection between innovation and democracy. Innovation, defined as the output of free, creative, risk-taking minds, only thrives in a democracy. Free minds create free enterprise. Only in a democracy can China fully unleash the full potential of its people to invent, create, and innovate for the future. The Chinese leaders I spoke with are beginning to understand this connection, but they have no historical context in which to help them embrace it. It will not be enough for China to lead the world with low-cost manufacturing. The Chinese leadership must unlock the full potential of its population to prepare for the future. Only democracy, fully embraced, in which free minds and free enterprise are the result, will truly sustain China's future. The U.S. is an example of this fusion of ideology and enterprise, where innovation has created personal wealth—just ask Bill Gates—and created entirely new industries, jobs, and value to society. This could be China's future.

Societies that are not free and do not support innovations will be left behind when the Innovation Economy becomes the dominant global economy. Nations where personal freedom is restricted and prosperity is limited to society's few elites will not be long-term, viable, enduring economies. These repressive societies will also become potential foundries for terrorism. Where free societies and free individuals thrive, prosperity endures. Prosperity is the enemy of repression and terrorism. The more we understand and work to encourage open societies, the more prosperity blossoms; as wealth spreads, the less terrorism can take hold.

# From Chopsticks in the Brain
# to Stem Cells

You might think that not many folks visit the hospital for a chopstick lodged in the brain. In fact, I'm told that in China it's not as uncommon as you might think. As a reporter for *Seed* magazine once wrote, "Shanghai dinners are long affairs, lubricated with shots of 110-proof grain alcohol, and . . . when tensions boil over, chopsticks can become weapons." A well-aimed chopstick—actually, maybe a poorly aimed chopstick is a better way to put it—can pass through a victim's eye directly into the brain.

One day, Jianhong Zhu, a Harvard-educated doctor, was treating a chopstick-embedded patient when he had an innovation explosion: He captured and cultured the man's brain tissue and then transplanted it back into the patient. This has started a revolution of sorts—it suggests the potential for helping brain-damaged patients by using stem cells to alleviate ailments like paralysis. Another frontier might be the treatment of brain-wasting diseases such as Alzheimer's. The idea of using a patient's stem cells to treat the very same patient has opened up a new frontier of research that has experts from around the world flocking to China to visit Dr. Jianhong.

This is merely one example of the ways China is demonstrating the ability to create innovations that capture the world's attention. Today Dr. Jianhong is treating patients with chopsticks in the brain. Tomorrow he may be helping aging American baby boomers regain their ability to walk or remember loved ones' faces.

---

*INNOVA JADE GARDEN*
*SUPERCOMPUTERS: 2009*

**If You Can Think It—We Can Build It**

- High-end, low-cost knowledge-engineering experts.

- Only IBM China supercomputers certified.

- Life-enhancement, android, medical, and pharma specialists.

- Design your next blockbuster product TODAY.

- Stem-cell engineering on premises.

- Financing available.

# China's Innovation Economy:
# Setting the World on Fire

Either as a producer, competitor, or consumer, China will see its future shaped by innovation. The following examples demonstrate this:

- The global media and entertainment industry has sales of about $1.3 trillion today. By 2009, this will increase to over $2 trillion, with the fastest growth and largest share in China.

- Internet advertising today is a $19 billion industry; by 2009, it will pass $100 billion, with China as the fastest-growing market.

- The video-game market in China is about $500 million today; by 2009, it will be over $2 billion.

- By 2025, China will hold a dominant share of the global auto, textile, medical device, manufacturing, and drug markets, topping more than $1 trillion in sales.

- The nanotech market in China today is already worth more than $5 billion, represented by more than 800 companies.

- By 2020, health-enhancing pharmaceuticals will represent a market of more than $20 billion in China.

## One Hundred Cities That Think

Shanghai's leaders have a unique vision for the future, and they've put it on display for the public. The Urban Planning Exhibition Hall is a pristine, futuristic glass building that sits near the People's Square. It is not far from the old French area where the charm of the last century still lingers, inviting tea drinkers and strollers to remember a slower pace of life that is now long gone. Shanghai is abuzz with reinvention. When I first came into the Hall I was struck by how the city's past is captured as well as its future is envisioned. There is an undeniable humility that one feels standing between the ancient Chinese past, with so many accomplishments, and looking to the future, with so many possibilities.

The center of the exhibit is a model the size of a basketball court where Shanghai 2020 is presented in miniature. From skyscrapers to factories to parks and hotels and transportation, it's all there. This 3-D model of Shanghai's future envisions a place where perhaps millions will live. It is inspiring, but it tells only part of the story.

As Shanghai prepares for the 2010 World Expo, I. M. Pei and other architects are designing new buildings, transportation facilities, and universities. There are early signs of progress indicated by the Shanghai 2020 exhibit. Innovation is the silent partner that underlies the progress, the plans, and the future. There will need to be a city erected here that looks to inspire a revolution in cities for all of China to follow. This is the challenge of China's future: What will a hundred new cities look like? What will be the right blend of sustainability for growth?

China will need the advanced power tools of the Innovation Economy to survive the huge population shifts that the next era will demand. China's future will be defined by how it uses innovation to manage risks ranging from waiting pandemics to extreme energy demands. From feeding billions to supplying clean water, from safe streets to adequate transportation, China will require innovation on a massive scale.

With more than a hundred new cities by 2040 and more than one billion people living in cities, China will need to master the formation of a new paradigm for managing population and growth. How will China meet the challenges of the megacity future? The answer is: smart cities. Cities that think—where health, security, transportation, water, food, and habitats are all managed with a unified, citywide intelligence—are coming. Humans may not be able to manage the complex problems that future cities will experience. A new type of city will need to emerge, a smart city.

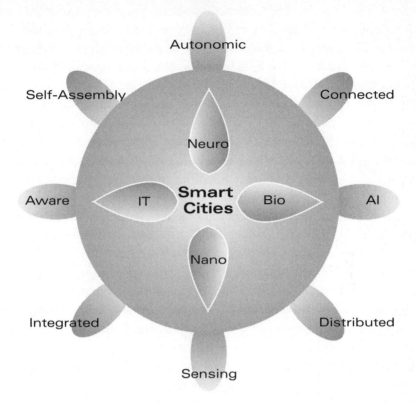

# Meeting the Future
## U.S.-China Challenge

China's economy, the world's sixth largest, has quintupled in size over the past quarter-century. Already, China is the world's number-one consumer of grain, meat, coal, and steel. A decline in poverty and increases in life expectancy and literacy have helped millions of Chinese to improve their lives. Already, innovation has played an important role in providing the jobs, tools, capital, and opportunities for people to better themselves. This will continue in the future, but there will be a new challenge as well.

The central question of the future, for the security and stability of the planet, is the extent to which America and China will cooperate. As it now stands, there are two models represented by two factions inside of China and the U.S. On one hand, there are those who see more benefit from global cooperation than conflict, who envision the two countries respecting each other's differences and capitalizing on their shared interests. Then there are those who see the inevitability of clashes leading to conflict. Some U.S. policymakers demand that China remake itself into a democratic state overnight. Some Chinese policymakers think the U.S. is hostile to China's interests.

It will take balanced and wise leadership, on both sides of the world, to steer a policy that will enhance the strategic interests of both nations. There will no doubt be conflicts. How we prepare for these conflicts and manage them will determine the future of peace and security. The resolution of the U.S.-China conflict is perhaps even more important than the global war on terror. At the heart of this will be one of the central questions this book raises: Whose idea of the future will dominate? Will this be a future that serves both nations' long-term interests for security and prosperity? We shall see.

In this case, there will need to be a new tolerance of different ideas, laws, modes of governance, and approach to trade—on both sides—that respects the unique cultural ethos of both China and the U.S. The future of the world depends on the U.S. and China finding a way, with the involvement and guidance of the Eurozone and other nations, to collaborate more than compete. This is the great opportunity as we move past global conflicts over energy, food, trade, and terrorism, and into the new Innovation Economy. A strategically designed U.S.-China collaboration would create a much-needed force for ensuring global security and social stability in the chaotic world of the Extreme Future. Both nations' leaders must carefully formulate a plan about how our future visions can complement and further our mutual interests.

## No More Little Red Book

It is a historic and positive step that China has traded Mao's *Little Red Book* for Adam Smith's *The Wealth of Nations*. The march into the future, the embrace of capitalism, and the prosperity that is emerging will help to transform this great nation. At the same time, China still must learn to adapt to the realities of a global economy. Social reforms, such as democracy, will come with time. Until then, the rest of the world needs to gain greater understanding of China.

The Chinese are driven to achieve in ways that Americans and Europeans used to be. The everyday things we take for granted, from democracy to clean water to affluence, most Chinese have not yet experienced. Think 1879, the era of the industrial revolution. Now, with advanced innovation like the Internet, wireless, and nanotechnology, the possibility of China leapfrogging the world's other industrial power-houses—the U.S., Japan, and Europe—will recast a new global order.

Most organizations, governments, and leaders sense this historic shift happening now. Some might say it is already too late to change to meet this challenge. I don't agree. We still have a historic opportunity to meet the China challenge and adapt to the new realities of the Asian giant's rise to power.

This intense competition of China's new supercapitalism is a bless-ing in disguise for the rest of us. We need to adapt our societies to meet this challenge. If we do not raise the bar of innovation, transform educa-tion, nurture entrepreneurship, and get on with encouraging science and engineering, we will be creating a destiny in which the Chinese dominate markets and eventually nations. If economic power breeds po-litical power, then we in the West had best recognize that we are facing the challenge of a rising new civilization, one that will have influence in all spheres on a scale we have never faced before. The West can be in-spired and respect the Chinese for rasing the bar on innovation and in-dustry, or it can wither in denial. We can and must meet the China challenge by adapting and changing quickly. This is a call to action on a national scale that should rightfully change every institution in America. We need a plan of action NOW or we will suffer the consequences of a reduced quality of life and an inability to compete on a global scale with China's workforce, economy, and industry. Fair warning is given here.

## Supercapitalism

We can fear this rise to power or we can be stimulated to transform our economies. We taught China how to make money, we taught them how to deal. We pushed them to be more open, to join the world mar-kets. Now that they are coming on strong, we must support this historic turn of events and not only invest in China to spread the pantheon of commerce—global capitalism—but also invest in changing America to survive. Yes, change we must, and fast.

I discussed this issue with then–Secretary of Commerce Don Evans at a meeting we had during the first Bush administration. It was clear that the secretary was having a difficult time supporting China for embracing free enterprise and at the same time outcompeting the

U.S. in driving jobs and manufacturing offshore. Secretary Evans asked me how the administration should deal with this challenge. I offered some of the advice that I now present in this chapter. I also indicated that the U.S. must adapt faster, innovate smarter, and completely transform education and technology investments to prepare the workforce for a new future. Without making these vast changes, our workforce and our nation would not be able to effectively compete in the future. He nodded his agreement, and yet a painful version of brain freeze seemed evident.

## A New Dialogue

The reason I mention this meeting is that throughout this book I have made the point that our leaders are dealing with issues and challenges that are so new and complex that their solutions require an entirely new way of thinking about the future. Even the Chinese leaders I met on my recent trip were deeply concerned about the immense challenges they are confronting today and envision tomorrow. They are not prepared. They know it. We spoke of how our great nations must cooperate—how we must invent new strategies to deal with the future of pandemics, pollution, energy, trade, and war. A representative from the Foreign Affairs Office summed it up to me at dinner over shark-fin soup: "We know we must work together to prepare for the future, but it is unclear how best to align these interests." There are many questions yet to be addressed, but there can be no question that only through cooperation and dialogue will both the United States and China enjoy the kind of futures their people deserve and demand.

No one is fully prepared to deal with this Extreme Future. There is no playbook for getting this right. We need new tools, new approaches, and eventually new solutions to new challenges. Meeting the China

---

SHENZEN MEMORIES INC.: 2025

**For All Your Memory Needs**

- Upload personal or corporate memories via the Net.

- Cognitive storage, sales, or reformatting available.

- Great for company record-keeping and lawsuits.

- Video, data, or audio memories for sale.

- Alzheimer's or dementia memory prevention.

- ReCapture- and ReAnimation-certified.

challenge will demand important new thinking that will require a broad new social-policy agenda. I don't think most of our leaders, in government or business, fully grasp the immense challenge at hand here. We are not talking about applying Band-Aids to meet the China challenge. We are talking about radical surgery, a comprehensive, forward-looking future strategy for the twenty-first century.

Dealing with China best captures the unique complexity of the Extreme Future. Meeting the China challenge will require a complete reframing of how we think—"disruptive opportunities" is a phrase that conveys what it will take to effectively understand China. We need a new understanding to navigate these waters. China will become one of the most complex challenges the U.S. has ever faced because there are so many interlocking factors that come into play.

## The China/U.S. Bond

The relationship between China and the U.S. is paramount to the future growth and security of the world. Both nations realize this. It is not often spoken of but it is widely understood at the very highest levels of government and commerce. The future stability of the world rests on the strategic intimacy of these two nations. Together, they will form the cornerstone of economic and political security that will define the outcome of the conflicts in the twenty-first century. Many other nations, especially those in Europe, will also play vital leadership roles. Our mutually inclusive interests, if handled with this new forward-looking vision for a productive, peaceful, and collaborative future, will be one of the defining accomplishments of the twenty-first century.

Failing to understand the deep collaboration between the U.S. and China and missing this historic opportunity would be a mistake of epic proportions for both nations and the world. We must get Future-Ready to form a new relationship with China based on global security, the innovation economy, and peace. America will not have all the resources—from people and capital to manufacturing and innovation—to lead alone in the twenty-first century. If prosperity and progress have a chance to lift up those billions who struggle to reach the higher rungs of the ladder of society, it will be because we have found a way to forge a new global order in the twenty-first century. China is crucial to this plan and the future of this century. It is time to learn the moves of the Dancing Dragon so that we can get in sync.

# CHAPTER 12

# The Future of America and Democracy

## Coming to America

Jolanta Zwirek was nine, she told me, when she came to the United States with her parents and younger brother. No one in the family spoke English. They had five dollars between them.

On their first day in America, complete strangers walked up the gray steps to the family's tenement building and brought them a black-and-white TV, foods they had never seen before, and even clothespins for hanging their wash. "What were clothespins for?" she wondered. Everything was new and strange, and Jolanta was scared. But this was her new world, her fresh start, her America.

The Zwirek family had come from Poland during a troubled time, when that country was struggling to emerge from the shadows of Communism and the Cold War. As millions of immigrants who preceded the Zwirek family knew, America's doors were open and the invitation had been made—come here and find a better place, a safer, more prosperous place. Come here for opportunity and democracy. Even if you're not entirely sure what those words mean, come here and find out.

When she started thinking in English, Jolanta knew she

# THE TOP TEN TRENDS THAT WILL
# SHAPE THE FUTURE OF AMERICA

**1.** America's Future-Readiness, the nation's unique capacity to be resilient, to revitalize, to predict and adapt to extreme change, to prevent threats, and to seize new opportunities, is the single most powerful trend that will shape the future.

**2.** Innovation investments will be the key trend that will promote future leadership, growth, security, quality of life, and global competitive advantage.

**3.** Immigration will remain the lifeblood of the U.S. economy, but only as long as quality of life in the U.S. continues to attract productive newcomers.

**4.** New global security threats, from how America deals with climate change to energy, will shape America's future stability and economic growth.

**5.** Enlightened leadership, possessing a bold new vision for America's future and the future of democracy worldwide, will be needed.

**6.** Quality public education, in crisis today, will either propel or crash the future aspirations of the American workforce.

**7.** America's workforce must be transformed, made more globally competitive, with higher education, science, and innovation skills necessary to ensure future prosperity.

**8.** In the battle for the future, America must embrace its destiny as the advocate of global democracy, free markets, free minds, and free enterprise.

**9.** Meeting the challenges of a changing population—from the boomers to the multiculturals—will redefine America in the twenty-first century.

**10.** The enemies of the future, free trade, and the rights of the individual, will threaten America, some committing acts of terror in an effort to extinguish global democracy.

was becoming an American. Soon she became so adept at the language that she became the family spokesperson. Her father worked as a master mechanic for Volvo even though he spoke no English for a long time; when Jolanta wasn't around, he kept a cheat sheet handy for when he needed to speak or write something important. He was dedicated and smart and had shown the courage to take his family into the unknown of America.

Some thirty years later, Jolanta became vice president and chief information officer for a Coca-Cola franchise company. As an expert in the Innovation Economy, Jolanta could only have found the opportunities here in America that have catapulted her to the top of her career in business and technology. Helping to direct a multimillion-dollar information organization of the top brand in the world has been a challenging road for her, but hard work guided her up the ladder to success. She would not, could not, have imagined coming this far, achieving this much, if it had not been for her father and mother's belief in America's potential to enhance their lives, to enable their prosperity, to empower them to build a productive future of greater possibilities than they would have had in Poland.

# America's Gift

Being in America was the essential ingredient that made it all possible. As she explained this to me, with the barest trace of a Polish accent, I smiled. I knew that hers is a story that can be told with small variations by countless families in America—the one-generation transition from immigrant to American. That is the gift that America gives to its people and the world. That is, at least that's how it has been for more than a century.

It has been said that if you resettle in Germany, Japan, Italy, or any other country in the world, it is unlikely you will ever be accepted as being "from" that nation. You will not become German, Japanese, or Italian, and you won't be accepted into those traditional societies. You will forever be viewed as a foreigner. But anyone can come to America and become an American. This is a powerful fact that separates America from the world. America is a nation of immigrants, all from someplace else. America's experience of immigration is that which binds us, the common bond that fuses us all to the same American experience. This fact, this unique notion that America absorbs—in the best sense, that is—the people who come here has been a great strength for this nation. But if this were to change, as some signs suggest is happening, America would be infinitely weaker for it.

The following three questions go to the central idea of what will shape the future of America:

- Will America, the destination and the ideal, persist as a cherished desire by the people of the world?

- Will America continue to embrace its destiny as the democracy and human-rights advocate of the world's peoples?

- Will immigrants in the future be attracted to the value proposition of democracy, liberty, and freedom?

## America's Youth Looks to the Future

A study conducted by my firm in 2004, titled "America's Youth Looks to the Future," asked 1,500 young adults how they felt about their nation's future and their own. Did they feel optimistic about America and themselves as we stepped into the twenty-first century? Were they hopeful about the future of the nation and themselves? The results became a guidepost for my thinking about the future of America.

More than 95 percent indicated they were very positive about America and their futures. What was most remarkable was not that such a high percentage of kids indicated a high degree of optimism, but the timing of this study. After the attacks of 9/11, we saw consumer-confidence levels drop. Yet these kids, a representation of America's youth and tomorrow's workforce, leaders, and consumers, were able to look beyond the immediate tragedy and remain extremely positive about the future. This gave me important insights into the psyche of America and the future of the nation.

## Forecasting America

Future forecasts are about crafting intelligent probabilities. This is part of the thinking that goes into Future Mapping, that we use to create possible future scenarios. Although it is impossible to accurately forecast every event or outcome due to infinite complexities of factors, it is possible to get a fix on alternative realities, scenarios, and potential forces that make one forecast more probable than others. This is the alchemy of forecasting, in which you put aside the number crunching and look at a more comprehensive picture. It is more art than science.

Often a Future Map gives you a way to see the bigger context of possibilities, a more complete picture about the future. Seeing this larger context brings into view different trends or changes that exist on the edge of what is known. Population will merge with technology, which will influence health care, which will open up new ideas about security. Developing a larger worldview often reveals new directions that solve current challenges or may suggest entirely new directions never considered.

Having used this technique with many clients, I am always surprised by how hidden opportunities are uncovered. Understanding people's attitudes through survey research has helped me immensely to "get inside" the mind of the person, to understand the consumer, not just today but what they think about the future—what will shape their future choices, lifestyles, and desires. This approach then leads to creating an intelligent probability of how the future may emerge and how a company or individual—or even a nation—should position itself to face the challenges ahead.

# Kill the Future

As we've seen in earlier chapters, one way to validate a forecast or reality-test what the future might look like is to play Kill the Future. By conducting this exercise, the intelligent probabilities may be "proven up." The key is to be willing, at least intellectually, to imagine harm coming to something you value deeply. Once you know what would damage the organization, nation, or company, you almost know by default where you need to focus your resources to create the preferred future of your design. This is an effective way to translate concern for survival into a strategy for sustainability. Prevention is smarter and less costly than restoration.

With that in mind, consider the list on the opposite page.

If these are authentic possibilities, and I believe they are, then we must address these threats immediately or they will lead to America's decline and perhaps even its demise. If you play out each of these Game Changers, it is not hard to find current analogs, models of other nations that are today facing big risks.

Japan is struggling to reverse the world's leading decline in population growth. Russia's health-care system is in disarray. Europe's productivity is flat and not improving. Africa's massive problems—from corruption to AIDS—are getting worse. Religious conflict in the Middle East threatens economic recovery. A rising radical violent Muslim population in Europe jeopardizes security. Global terrorism is present in more than fifty nations. The complications from the rise of China's megacities—from the largest rural-to-urban migration in history—will be challenging.

I raise these points not to create fear about the future of America, but to encourage change. Too many American leaders—both in government and corporate—are gripped by denial, a type of Pollyanna group-think that insists that America will retain its greatness no matter what. Based on those beliefs, those leaders act as though there's no need for a long-term vision that demands sacrifice and structural change, some of it painful. This combination of forces, if not addressed soon, will result in America limping into the future. We can prevent this. But we need to recognize that we are not prepared for the future challenges that are coming in the Extreme Future. If there were ever a time to work toward change, it is now. America must change fast. Much of what this book is about is change.

# THE TOP TEN THREATS THAT COULD KILL AMERICA'S FUTURE

■ Religious fundamentalism that is intolerant and restricts personal freedoms.

■ Damaged environment due to a lack of government and corporate leadership, leading to a significant reduction in the public's health, quality of life, and global competitiveness.

■ Limited immigration flow unable to offset declining fertility rates, leading to a reduced workforce and a depressed economy.

■ War and rampant terrorism at home and abroad, destabilizing society and the economy and leading to reduced immigration, global trade, productivity, and growth.

■ A poor education system that doesn't prepare the workforce for the global Innovation Economy, forcing companies to outsource work to other nations.

■ Lack of a high-tech skilled and globally competitive workforce that leads the world.

■ Reduced funding for scientific research and development, leading to a lower capacity among U.S. business to compete globally and to attract immigration.

■ A dysfunctional health-care system unable to provide affordable service for all, reducing quality of life.

■ A weak defense and security infrastructure, leading to a decline in U.S. global leadership, national security, and domestic stability.

■ Inability to lead the world and benefit economically from developing the latest innovations in science and technology, impacting health care, energy, and security.

■ Attacks on privacy; attacks on individual freedoms.

# America's Future-Readiness

Despite my warnings, I am optimistic about the future of America. This is mostly based on the abundant evidence I see about America's inherent capacity to adapt, embrace change, confront crisis, and continually meet challenges successfully. I recognize, though, that I may be a product of the same social fabric that I am forecasting. America's Future-Readiness, this infinite optimism, the capacity to adapt, this continual wave of revitalization, embracing the new, inventing the impossible, seems to be a fundamental ingredient of the social DNA of America.

Of all the peoples of the world, Americans are unique in the scope, energy, and expression of their bullishness about the future. This is not to say that people in other nations are characteristically bearish. But Americans seem to draw from an infinite well of optimism about the future, and in so doing catalyze the world, spreading the message of the positive future to come. They inspire change and innovation, creating a vision that suggests what is coming next will be good. Perhaps this optimistic attitude stems from coming from the New World, unbound from the established limits of tradition. The New World, America, is forever new—a wellspring of inventions and innovations in ideas and lifestyles, commerce and art, economics and culture. All things seem infinitely possible in the new world.

HEADLINES FROM THE FUTURE: 2034

**Chinese Leaders Credit Free Markets with Increase in Global Living Standards**

This ideology of always looking to a better future is perhaps idealistic, but it is also a powerful, self-fulfilling, and self-propelling prophecy.

HEADLINES FROM THE FUTURE: 2015

**Women Business Owners Employ 70% of Workforce**

The resounding narrative about life in America is the story of immigrants confronted by war, strife, or persecution, or simply searching for more opportunity. They came to America and found a better life through a tolerance for their religious and cultural differences. This future vision, as a shared American experience, didn't just define America for more than 200 years but became a beacon of new possibility for other people in other nations to emulate. If that were to change, then the American experience would be in danger of not delivering on its core promise—its raison d'être. This is the risk that America faces in the twenty-first century. I am optimistic and hopeful, but I am also warning here that we must be vigilant and make fast changes to our nation if we are to build a sustainable future of success.

## America's Future and the Future of Democracy

Central to the future of America is the enduring principle of democracy, a belief in representative government that has defined the American experience from its inception. Based on the low voter turnout in elections, too many Americans take this for granted. One reason, I suspect, is that most of us have never lived in a more restrictive society, so we have no comparison. Perhaps every American should spend a week on vacation in North Korea. Upon coming back from what we will call a holiday in hell, I'm pretty certain that voter turnout would rise and almost everyone would have a fresh new perspective on the value of democracy.

For more than 200 years, it has seemed as though every dictatorship, tyrannical government, autocracy, and ideology that was opposed to democratic values had been secretly enlisted to conduct marketing for America. And it has worked splendidly. The exodus of immigrants bound for America has been the result for 200 years. This must

> **HEADLINES FROM THE FUTURE: 2009**
>
> **Science Investments Up 300%**

continue. The more opposed to democracy, the more intolerant to individual liberties, the more restrictive in terms of class, ethnicity, wealth, or power that a foreign nation was, the more its citizens wanted to come to the United States.

Yesterday's victims of tyranny are today's immigrants in the U.S. Even those who simply felt that there was more economic opportunity in the U.S. than in their more resource-restricted native countries have migrated here to pursue a higher quality of life. There are more millionaire immigrants and first-generation citizens in the U.S. than in any other place in the world. What does this say? Come to America and succeed now, regardless of race, creed, or class. This has been a compelling and successful strategy that has attracted and should continue to attract millions of new immigrants essential to the growth, security, and economic vitality of the nation.

From the first immigrants fleeing religious persecution in their home nations to those abandoning starvation, war, and even a lack of economic opportunity, America has become the product that everyone wants to buy. If this were to change, if America were to become a less desirable destination, that might limit the future prospects of America by curtailing the valuable human capital that has contributed to making the nation great. We already run the risk of this today. Some of my clients have told me they cannot find the talent they need in America, and they cannot hire the talent they need abroad to come here. These are the early stirrings of the global talent war. There are some scenarios that we have run in which America might lose its place as a preferred destination for immigrants. Although probabilities are low that this might happen, we should be vigilant to guard against it.

## Democracy's Future

On the other hand, it may be argued that as the nations of the world become more democratic, secure, and prosperous, they will become more desirable to their citizens—and fewer will come to America. This is the double-edged sword of America's spreading democracy and supporting free markets, free trade, and free thought. Some may think this works against the future agenda of America. They are mistaken. As America has championed the principles of democracy and liberty, global progress has increased, and this is ultimately to the benefit of the U.S. We can see this scenario unfolding today.

The good news is that nations that embrace democracy become robust consumer markets for U.S. companies as they join the family of nations engaging in global free trade. America wins, as do these nations. They provide not just new markets for U.S. sales, but also talent pools for U.S. companies.

Nations such as India, the largest democracy in the world, and China are experiencing economic booms that have increased quality of life so much that this "reversal of fortunes" is already occurring. Tomorrow this will be Indonesia and Malaysia and Chile. People are choosing to stay in India and China as the economic opportunities increase. This is good for America. They will both become vital allies for securing the planet and offering an alignment of sanity at a time when chaos and conflict might otherwise persist.

America's future will be defined in part by the future of other key nations and regions in the world. This intimate collaboration is strategic for all participants, none more so than the U.S. No countries are more fundamental to trade and security, especially in that part of the world, than China and India. They need America and America needs them—these economies, and their social and political fortunes, will be determining factors in the future of global prosperity. These economic linkages in the future will be vital linchpins in the new global economic framework of what will become the sustainable globalization covered earlier. Trade between China and the U.S., not just in goods but in technology, ideas, and even investments currently standing at over a trillion dollars, will create a new transnational collaboration not seen before in modern times.

> *HEADLINES FROM THE FUTURE: 2017*
>
> **Report: Improved U.S. Homeland Security Attracts Increased Immigration**

It could be argued that a fundamental part of the American consumer's quality of life is the ability to purchase a variety of products at an inexpensive cost. As more than 80 percent of consumer products are now made in China, the U.S. consumer, and U.S. quality of life, has been a beneficiary. China has benefited greatly from being the manufacturing mecca for the world, while India has benefited from being the outsourcing center for many services and software development.

## Dynamic Trade and the Innovation Economy

The global Innovation Economy will be a powerful force in America's future, perhaps one of the most important trends that America must lead. America's future is entwined with a multifaceted new collaboration with other nations. I forecast that a new type of collaboration intimacy will grow into a robust model in the future with more than one hundred trading partners. This may be the evolutionary endgame of the World Trade Organization, which could support a viable new free-market network of nations conducting a new type of dynamic trade, free from restrictions, sanctions, tariffs, government control, and even taxes. This is the future hope of globalization.

The democratization of trade will be a stimulant of large proportions toward liberating the world from repressive trade barriers, accelerating global commerce, and, by extension, opportunities for innovation and collaboration. We will achieve this truly free trade by 2015. This event will increase global GDP by more than 5 percent annual growth and will

# FUTURE U.S. INNOVATION FORECAST: A WAKE-UP CALL

■ 45 to 78 percent of economic growth is tied to innovation-based business.

■ Foreign students are awarded the majority of U.S. scientific Ph.D. degrees.

■ Asian business schools are graduating more students than those in the U.S.

■ Patent applications from foreign inventors are rapidly gaining on the U.S.

■ Total foreign research-and-development investments are rising faster than those in the U.S.

■ The fastest-growing innovation-based economies are in China, South Korea, Taiwan, India, Ireland, Singapore, and Israel (NSF, 2004).

■ Federal U.S. investment in the sciences is in decline.

■ China and India's high-tech industries are fast gaining on the U.S.

■ The U.S. is losing its global share of high-tech exports to Asia and the EU.

■ The U.S. is losing skilled immigrants who cannot get hired into the nation.

■ Education is failing to prepare skilled, high-tech-savvy workers.

■ Without increasing innovation investments, the U.S. will not be competitive.

inspire free markets and supranational cooperation. We will see a dynamic global trade that will extend beyond borders and political barriers.

Of all the top trends that will create a prosperous future, this innovation will be the most important. For more than fifty years, the United States has led the world in innovations and patents in biology, telecom, information, and energy. The world of the future will belong to the nation that commands this leadership role. The U.S. must continue to invest in innovation to grow the economy, invent new products, and keep competitiveness alive in education and the workforce. Innovation investments in science and technology must continue if the U.S. is to be a viable leader of the free world, as well. Only with the leading edge that innovation provides can security and prosperity be guaranteed into the future. Innovation investments in biotech, nanotech, infotech, and neurotech—the constituents of the Innovation Economy—will shape the future fortunes of America.

## The World in 2015

Extreme competition. Complex technology. Dynamic global trade. Increased population. Disruptive acts of terrorism. Sophisticated crime. Climate risks. Expensive energy. This is the world of 2015.

The world in 2015 will be an Extreme Future in which the overlapping of the above scenarios will demand insight, skills, collaboration, and leadership. The level of accelerated change and the complexity of challenges will be like snowboarding an avalanche from the top of Mt. Everest—intense, demanding, and fast. Maybe even lethal.

And that's the good news. Factors that could restrict economic growth include

- Expensive and insufficient energy resources.

- Low immigration.

- Untrained workforce.

- Terrorism and crime.

- Depopulation; low fertility.

- Ecological disaster.

- Flat productivity growth.

■ More jobs than workers.

■ Religious fundamentalism influencing science and politics.


You must put this forecast in perspective. By 2040, there will be more than eight billion people in the world. There is a great likelihood, then, that a reduction in U.S. immigration will not be that significant compared with current immigration flows and new labor entrants in the U.S. workforce. More people on the planet and more immigration flow into the U.S. are the probable outcome of this scenario.

America's interests are best served when the nations of the world put resources into bettering their societies and people. Increasing trade, education, health care, and security are the linchpins of a productive society. The one unique feature to this scenario is that it is also in the interest of the U.S. to support democratic reform in the nations of the world; democratic societies tend to make more peace than war. Where personal freedoms thrive, tyranny and dogma cannot persist.

Given the intimacy that capitalism and democracy share, free markets, free trade, and individual freedoms will go hand in hand in the future. This will be a critically important global strategy that the U.S. will pursue in the twenty-first century. It may be the most important strategy that defines the future, and the question might well be whether the future will be based on the U.S. model of democracy and free trade or on another model yet to evolve. One thing we know for sure is that restrictive global trade and the antithesis of democracy—autocracy and dictatorship—have been tried and failed. The power of the individual to navigate toward the light of personal freedom will guide this future throughout the world.

The U.S. will only benefit from a world at peace, where the quality of life is high and where conflict and repression are held in check. This is the best-case scenario for America and for the world, where security and productivity and progress are part of the same equation. As the spread of global economic opportunity persists after 2015, nations will join with the U.S. toward the evolution of a new global economic model.

---

**HEADLINES FROM THE FUTURE: 2015**

**Health-Care Coverage Achieved
for All Americans**

---

The foundation of success or failure of a nation is a complicated proposition. Some have argued that it is about isolationism due to geography. The revolutionaries during the 1917 Russian Revolution had objectives and underlying social conditions similar to those of the colonists leading the American Revolution. Both wanted change. Both experienced oppression. But the end products of those uprisings were very different. Power struggles and ideology go hand in hand.

This capacity to be resilient, adaptive, and agile will determine the nature of survival not just of America but of much of the rest of the world as well. Democracy and free enterprise are becoming world models. If America falters as an incubator for these relatively new democratic and economic values, it would send a devastating message to the rest of a world that is experimenting with these values for the first time in transforming their societies, economies, and cultures.

## AMERICA'S TOP FUTURE CHALLENGES

- Reinvest in science.

- Take climate change seriously.

- Expand thinking about national security to include biodiversity, food, water, privacy, and innovation.

- Learn to collaborate more deeply with nations that hold different values.

- Recognize that globalization of trade shapes global peace and prosperity.

- Learn about other cultures so we can better understand people's differences.

- Increase immigration.

- Become Future-Ready. Think and plan for the future.

- Understand the diversity changes in the workforce and marketplace.

## Many Possible Futures for America

There are many possible futures for America. Each has seeds of today's reality already in the ground. Not all of the trends point to a positive outcome. There are danger signs we can watch for and address now. Changing the education system and investing in new alternative energy will take time—decades. This conversation is about the kind of future we want. What is important to choose? What do we as a nation want to plan for? There is a desperate need for a more vibrant debate about what kind of America we want to create in the future. Leaders want to know. We want to know.

Each of the following futures is a possible scenario for America. The Prosperous Nation is of course the preferred future. There is no certainty that this outcome will prevail, but our forecasts give this a better than 80 percent chance of success. Though there are indications that America is moving toward this outcome, it is still too early to tell. The alternate future, the Struggling Nation, would result from America not meeting the great challenges of the twenty-first century effectively. An inability or a refusal to deal with the threats of the Kill the Future exercise would swing the odds over toward the Struggling Nation scenario.

## The Prosperous Nation: 2015

The Prosperous Nation results from America meeting serious challenges such as those described above. Some of these strategic forces— dealing with a declining population and its impact on the workforce and the economy—have been addressed faster than others. A future energy and sustainability plan was successfully put in place. Homeland security was finally fixed and was functioning properly. Strong GDP and an economic growth of 4 percent was consistent. Still, critical choices must be made to ensure that a prosperous future comes to pass. If it does, it might look something like the following:

By 2015, America had successfully met the key challenges facing the nation. This success did not come without significant changes to society, education, and the economy. Challenges were met and dealt with. Many of those challenges were apparent by 2010, when it became obvious that the U.S. would continue to lose its global competitive advantage and continue the downward slide in quality of life unless broad systemic changes were made.

First there was the depopulation issue. Based on decreased fertility rates and an aging society, the U.S. was headed for a problem—not enough workers to drive the future economy. At the same time, the rapid increase in the Hispanic population at first overwhelmed schools, which were ill prepared to train a future workforce. The low GDP growth, below 3 percent in 2010, was a shock to many Americans. Fewer workers meant less productivity. With almost ten million un-filled jobs, more than seven million of them requiring high-tech skills, corporations had been outsourcing to stay competitive. The economy was in trouble. This was common knowledge. At first, it looked as though there was no way to turn things around. After 9/11, the ability of immigrants and students to come to the U.S. had decreased drasti-cally, and it seemed no one would want to take the risk of challenging this new idea of America. But then, political and corporate leaders banded together to move past their fears and find a solution: Immigra-tion limits were eased to allow more people in. By 2012, this started to reverse the trend. Workers became available, hiring increased, and productivity rose.

Another challenge involved the education system, which finally broke down as students and parents realized that schools were not preparing kids for jobs in the future. Increasingly, companies were forced to outsource jobs to talent worldwide. A total overhaul of the U.S. education system was undertaken. Quality metrics were designed and teacher salaries were doubled, attracting new talent to the profes-sion.

The use of the Internet to give free choice to kids and parents to de-sign their own high school and college programs met with great success as well, increasing skills and scores. A massive transformation in the standard curricula was also con-ducted, modeling real-world skills, especially in science and business.

*HEADLINES FROM THE FUTURE: 2012*

**U.S. High Schools Rated Best in World at Teaching Science**

In response to an influx of more than ten million qualified job appli-cants in the U.S. labor pool, most companies pulled back on outsourc-ing and hired domestically. This triggered a rise in national optimism that brought back capital and companies and led to new venture in-vestments. This influx of skilled workers then lifted GDP growth and enabled companies to rely more on local talent to achieve profits.

Once the population problem was met, investments in science R & D returned. As support increased for next-generation computers, communications, Internet, nanotech, and biotech, new innovative products came into the markets. Collaborations with business, education, and government promoted innovation breakthroughs that led to the U.S. improving global competitiveness and productivity. GDP shot up to 5 percent by 2015. America was headed back on the track toward prosperity—providing jobs, education, capital, and innovation to build a sustainable future.

# A Struggling Nation: 2015

In many ways, the Struggling Nation scenario is the direct result of the nation not preparing for the future challenges that appeared on the horizon decades earlier. Issues related to immigration, population, workforce, education, and the economy were largely ignored. Science and innovation, once key drivers of the economy, were no longer investment priorities. New technologies faltered and then stopped producing new industries. Venture capital went offshore, following the talent and the innovations. Predictably, underfunding of key initiatives by government and the private sector resulted in disaster. No long-range forecasting was done, leaving the nation not Future-Ready and therefore vulnerable to extreme change.

The nation's resources were depleted by an overabundance of foreign responsibilities, such as the war in Iraq, as well as by costs associated with global warming and natural disasters like hurricanes. The poor performance of the American workforce against more competent foreign talent spelled trouble. Low productivity and poor economic growth took the wind out of America's sails. Other issues relevant to national security, such as adopting a comprehensive green-energy plan, were not embraced. The lack of a social consensus as a nation, though obvious, could not be overcome. There was gridlock on what the issues were and what direction we as a nation should take. Low GDP growth at 1 percent was the result. The trade debt with China, and now India, was a crisis. The dollar had lost 30 percent of its value.

The major factor that caused this future scenario was the lack of willpower among leaders in the private sector, the community, and government to take the risks necessary to address the serious challenges all around them. Investments necessary to make change were not made. Everyone admitted there were social issues that needed to be confronted, but no one was willing to stand up and be the first to propose significant change. The largest barrier to success is often past success. There has always been a unique optimism that has defined the American experience. In many ways, that is a good thing. But sometimes, the belief that everything will work out well—simply because it always has in the past—can be crippling. It has been difficult to get beyond this.

When the outsourcing trend started, it was a trickle, hardly worth mentioning. As the years went on, however, U.S. corporations needed to compete globally and faced a large talent hole in the job market. Not only were there five times more jobs than workers to fill them, but job candidates were not prepared to do the jobs. Most of the work was knowledge-based, requiring sophisticated, high-tech skills that schools and colleges were not teaching. Outsourcing perpetuated the negative cycle, ultimately fueling the continued lack of skilled workers.

Immigration had slowed to a trickle since digital identity cards were issued in 2010, after the bioterror attack in the Midwest.

> **HEADLINES FROM THE FUTURE: 2018**
>
> **Cyber Hackers Steal Billions Again**

With the borders closed for three years, it was as though America had been closed for travel, vacation, education, and, of course, immigration. Immigrants went to other countries. Students studied elsewhere. The U.S. suffered a brain and body drain at a time when it could least afford it. The aging boomers, a skilled and successful generation, were in retirement and the labor shortage grew into a crisis.

## America's Future-Readiness

Though either of these two futures could be the blueprint for the nation, I forecast that the Prosperous Nation is the more realistic of the two. America's optimism will continue to enable the country and its leaders to seek ways to be better, solve that problem, meet that challenge, and prepare for the future. This is America's intrinsic Future-Readiness, the belief that things will be better if we work to make them better. This unique element of American culture is the antithesis of apathy and denial, and it is why I believe America will tackle the new century with hope and accomplishment, and will prevail over any challenge or crisis.

People come to the U.S. to dream and then realize their dreams. If one thing best characterizes America, it is a place where a person can arrive with no money, no title, no connections, and no resources, and with an idea and a bit of willpower succeed.

As long as America renews its contract with the people of the world as a haven for the oppressed and downtrodden, as long as America continues to be a place where free choice, free enterprise, and free markets thrive, our nation will attract people from around the world who are hungry to succeed and ready to defend their new homeland.

---

**HEADLINES FROM THE FUTURE: 2014**

**Increased Immigration Approved by Congress to Offset Workforce Shortage**

---

If America becomes a closed society, with immigration curtailed and borders closed, it will be the beginning of a steady decline. As an ongoing strategy, America must refresh its populace with the talent, creativity, resources, intelligence, and hard work of immigrant citizens. It is America's secret weapon to attract, retain, and make productive a heterogeneous mixture of people from around the world. It needs to remain so.

## America's Call To Destiny

Does America have a destiny? I say yes. It is a destiny linked to the principles of democracy and personal freedoms that have defined the American experience from the birth of the nation. Free minds, free markets, and free enterprise. I forecast that an unwavering endorsement of democracy shall not only endure but be a beacon for the future—signaling all who desire that freedom to come to America, inspiring those in other nations who want democracy, and urging those who seek a partner in democratic values to align their social, economic, and security objectives with those of the U.S.

This role, which has defined the American experience, should not change. If it does, if a more insular America emerges, then a weaker, smaller nation will be the result, a narcissistic America focused largely on self-preservation. Is this scenario likely? I could make a case for it if global pandemics, hot wars, or large terrorist incidents collided with a future boomer demographic that becomes more risk-averse and pulls inward rather than outward on the world stage. A faltering, uncompetitive economy could also drive this American future.

To largely disengage in foreign affairs and stop being the champion of free trade would create a power vacuum that would result in conflict and chaos. There is no superpower on the planet other than America that can fill that role. Most Americans are conflicted on these issues, and the tide is turning. In a world of fewer energy resources, more conflict, less of everything except cost, Americans are wondering what they get for the dollars they spend abroad, especially when money is needed at home to improve schools, health care, and the economy. These are some of the factors that will challenge America in the twenty-first century.

---

*HEADLINES FROM THE FUTURE: 2014*

**U.S. #1 in Global Innovation Index**

---

## A New Idea

America as an idea—a new democracy, free from the autocracy of the past—has championed a "New Enlightenment" of democracy over theocracy and autocracy. This will be the decisive battle in the twenty-first century, waged by America and its allies against the forces seeking to turn back the clock. The authentic threat that lies at the heart of global terrorism, and even more conventional wars, is not the battle over religion, power, or even politics. It is the battle over the ideology of the future—whose idea of the future will dominate the planet.

The conflicts between democracy and theocracy, as exemplified by religious extremists, and democracy and autocracy, illustrated by terror-sponsoring regimes and other undemocratic nations, will be the decisive battles of the future. Both autocracy and theocracy, in which the rule of the unelected few over the many predominates, are simply not sustainable governance models for the future.

For the time being, these holdout nations will continue to be threats to modernity, peace, and economic opportunity. Unfortunately, the only way nations that are autocratic and theocratic will be able to survive in the future will be through repression and war. This is an unacceptable future that the free nations of the world, led by the U.S., should not tolerate.

The U.S. cannot and will not be the legitimate leader of the free world without championing the rights of all peoples of the world to enjoy democratic values and free markets. The risks of not continuing to champion these values are many. The United States would miss a historic opportunity, deny its destiny, and restrict the future of global freedom in a world that, more so than ever, will look to the U.S. for leadership.

The interlocking forces—within and outside the U.S.—necessary to prepare the U.S. to meet the future will require leadership with an eye toward shaping the future of the nation and the world. In the Extreme Future, this leadership, and meeting these challenges outlined here, will make or break the destiny of the nation. America cannot be the world power it is today without serious and systemic changes inside its borders and around the planet, changes that together will facilitate the evolution of peace and security for all nations.

The twenty-first century will be an Extreme Future, one in which global collaboration, leadership vision, and courage to create the new will be more critical than ever. New threats, new risks, more people, and more complexity will require a new type of visionary leadership to guide the future of America. Only in this way will America achieve the full potential of its destiny, promoting both democracy and freedom on a more secure, pluralistic, prosperous, and culturally diverse world stage.

## The Next America

The landscape ahead will be fraught with many new types of risks that will threaten the future of America. The capacity of America to rise to meet risk will be great—but not without significant changes in preparing for this Extreme Future. America's Future-Readiness will help prepare the nation. But if we do not successfully address every one of the top ten threats to America, the greatness of the past—one that could certainly extend into the future—will be lost. Regardless of ideology, wealth, or power, nations—and even civilizations—are subject to life cycles that are hard to forecast.

With proper attention paid to education, immigration, the environment, security, leadership, and other key challenges, America will prosper in the future. It will require a long-term vision that inspires the people and gives meaning to the direction, the changes, and even the sacrifices that might come.

For America to remain the leader of global democracy and free markets and the advocate for the rights of the individual, there are things to do and challenges to meet. Will there be new threats? Yes. America's capacity to meet these threats, its Future-Readiness, must be on guard against the enemies of the future. From investing in next-generation innovations, to fixing climate and investing in education reform—there is much to do to stave off the ravages of a future that will not be kind to the unprepared, the unaware, or those unwilling to change.

America's future success as a nation is tied fundamentally to the future of democracy and the fate of the world. Though there is much for Americans to do—starting now—to ensure a productive, safe, and innovative future, the destiny of America is linked to the destiny of the world's markets, peoples, and economy. The values that we share, of peace, security, free trade, diversity, tolerance, innovation, and democracy, will greatly shape our future. They should also shape the future of the world. It will be an interesting century.

Welcome to the Extreme Future.

ACKNOWLEDGMENTS

It has been a long haul to complete this book. There have been a number of folks whose contributions to my life and work have made all the difference in the world. The time one invests in writing inevitably comes from somewhere, and this is most often taken from friends and family.

My wife, Gayle, allowed me to steal time from the family to write. She read early chapters and gave me solid feedback. Most of all she filled in when I could not so I had the time to think and write. An author could not ask for more. I thank her for this support and love. My daughter Mariah inspired me with her talented writing.

My editor-wizard and accomplished author, Mitch Zuckoff from Boston University, was instrumental in making my words better. His attention to detail, to facts, and to an understanding of my narrative made a tremendous contribution to the book. The challenge of my describing the complex trends of the future was made clearer by his contribution.

Brian Tart, my editor and publisher at Dutton, was relentless in his insightful comments and edits. He took the time to improve the book. Most of all I thank him for understanding what the vision of this project was all about. His support in pushing me to capture and describe my vision is appreciated.

Neil Gordon from Dutton, as well, made a number of excellent editorial contributions in reading through the manuscript, and for this I am grateful.

Richard Abate, my agent from ICM, understood the book's

concept right from the start. His support, guidance, and perspective were much appreciated. His ideas were central to finding the right publisher for me, and I look forward to his support in the future.

My friends Ken and Maddy Dychtwald were supportive in my writing process and contributed to my original book concept with enthusiasm. Their positive outlook and constant reminders that the end is in sight were greatly appreciated.

I am grateful to clients such as General Electric and especially to Norg Sanderson of SLFC, who support my research.

Andrew Donahey, the operations chief at my firm, was instrumental in conducting research and organizing data and information. He made sure deadlines were kept.

Bill Moulton's designs of the Trend Trakker were very insightful and appreciated.

Charles Ostman crafted the graphics for the Future Mapping. He was generous with his insights about innovation and information mapping. Sandy Rosenberg advised and challenged me about demographic realities. Tom Broderick advised me about the cultural nuances of China and accompanied me to that great nation. I heartily thank them all.

## About the Author

**Dr. James Canton** is a renowned global futurist, social scientist, author, and sought-after business advisor. He was named one of the leading keynote presenters in the twenty-first century by *Successful Meetings* magazine for his visionary, innovative, and dynamic speeches. For more than thirty years Dr. Canton has been insightfully forecasting the top trends that have shaped business, markets, and society. Dr. Canton is chairman and CEO of the Institute for Global Futures, an internationally recognized San Francisco–based think tank he founded in 1990. Known for his accurate forecasts about future trends, Dr. Canton has advised many Fortune 1000 corporations, including IBM, General Electric, Visa, AT&T, Philips, and Citibank.

Dr. Canton is a senior fellow at Kellogg Innovation Network (KIN), Kellogg School of Management, has served on the Advisory Board at MIT's Media Lab Europe and on the Visionary Advisory Board of Motorola Corporation. He has been a commentator on CNN and numerous articles covering Dr. Canton have appeared in *Fortune, The Wall Street Journal, Bloomberg Report, The New York Times, U.S. News & World Report,* and *CEO Magazine*. He is the editor-in-chief of the Global Futures Forecast.

www.GlobalFuturist.com